Getting to the Core of Writing

Essential Lessons for Every Third Grade Student

Richard Gentry, Ph.D.

Jan McNeel, M.A.Ed.

Vickie Wallace-Nesler, M.A.Ed.

SHELL EDUCATION

Publishing Credits

Dona Herweck Rice, *Editor-in-Chief*; Robin Erickson, *Production Director*;
Lee Aucoin, *Creative Director*; Timothy J. Bradley, *Illustration Manager*;
Sara Johnson, M.S.Ed., *Senior Editor*; Jodene Smith, M.A., *Editor*;
Jennifer Kim, M.A.Ed., *Associate Education Editor*; Tracy Edmunds, *Editor*;
Leah Quillian, *Assistant Editor*; Grace Alba, *Designer*;
Corinne Burton, M.A.Ed., *Publisher*

Standards

© 2004 Mid-continent Research for Education and Learning (McREL)
© 2007 Teachers of English to Speakers of Other Languages, Inc. (TESOL)
© 2010 National Governors Association Center for Best Practices and Council of Chief State School Officers (CCSS)

Shell Education

5301 Oceanus Drive
Huntington Beach, CA 92649-1030
http://www.shelleducation.com

ISBN 978-1-4258-0917-1

© 2012 Shell Educational Publishing, Inc.
Reprinted 2013

Table of Contents

Table of Contents *(cont.)*

The Importance of Writing

In recent years, many school districts and teachers referred to writing as the "Neglected R" and viewed reading as the path to literacy success. Today, as research has revealed more information about the fundamental connection between reading success and writing competency, we are realizing that the road to literacy is a two-way street (Graham and Hebert 2010). While working as literacy consultants, we encountered numerous, capable teachers struggling with the complexity of implementing rigorous writing instruction. We wrote this book to enable all teachers to implement a successful writing program with a high degree of teaching competency. The success enjoyed by many of the teachers using the materials in this book has relieved frustrations, rejuvenated careers, and rekindled enthusiasm for teaching.

This book was written to fulfill two major objectives. The first objective involves motivating teachers to value and incorporate writing instruction as an essential element of literacy development. It should help them implement best practices and simplify the planning of writing instruction. New writing standards have been applied by education leaders at every level. Ultimately, the responsibility for implementing these standards is placed on the classroom teacher. Historically, the lack of emphasis on writing instruction in teacher education programs has left teachers feeling woefully unprepared to teach primary students to write, particularly at a level which meets the expectations of the standards for writing. The burden of this responsibility and feelings of inadequacy have left both experienced and novice teachers feeling empty-handed and unprepared.

Since 2010, most states have adopted the Common Core State Standards (CCSS), which are designed to provide teachers and parents with a clear understanding of what students are expected to learn. Since the CCSS are newly adopted, many teachers have not received professional development to become familiar with the standards nor have they received resources for their instruction, particularly in the area of writing. Therefore, the second objective of this book is to assist teachers in becoming familiar with these standards for writing and provide resources to support the implementation of these standards in their classrooms. *Getting to the Core of Writing* provides lessons outlining four key areas of writing: Text Types and Purposes, Production and Distribution of Writing, Research, and Range of Writing. It offers suggestions to meet those standards in instruction during Writer's Workshop. It also addresses how speaking and listening standards are easily practiced by engaging students in an interactive lesson format.

It is no secret that students become better writers by writing every day. This book contains the foundational structure and best practices that will guide teachers as they establish a daily Writer's Workshop that includes consistent, structured instruction to engage students in the writing process. Beyond that, a flexible pacing guide is provided to aid in planning writing instruction.

It is our hope that this book provides teachers with all the tools needed to inspire and equip young writers in today's classrooms.

—Richard, Jan, and Vickie

Traits of Quality Writing

The traits of quality writing continue to gain recognition as the language of successful writers. Educators at the Northwest Regional Educational Laboratory, now Education Northwest, searched for an accurate, reliable method of measuring student writing performance. Six attributes of good writing are identified in *Seeing with New Eyes* (Spandel 2005). These characteristics are used to inform and guide writing instruction:

- **Ideas** are the heart of the message, the content of the piece, and the main theme.

- **Sentence fluency** is the rhythm and flow of the language, the sound of word patterns, and the way in which the writing plays to the ear, not just to the eye.

- **Organization** is the internal structure, the thread of central meaning, and the logical and sometimes intriguing pattern of ideas within a piece of writing.

- **Word choice** is the use of rich, colorful, precise language that moves and enlightens the reader.

- **Voice** is the heart and soul, the magic, and the wit, along with the feeling and conviction of the individual writer that emerge through the words.

- **Conventions** are how the writer uses mechanical correctness in the piece— spelling, paragraphing, grammar and usage, punctuation, and capitalization.

Knowing and understanding the traits of quality writing supports teachers, students, and parents in thinking about writing and understanding what makes for writing success. Even in the early grades, students can communicate and recognize the characteristics of quality writing. The works of Ruth Culham (2008) and Vicki Spandel (2008) emphasize the value and benefits of using these traits to provide a common language—"a writer's vocabulary for thinking, speaking, and working like writers" (Spandel 2008, 7)—to enrich instruction and assessment in primary classrooms.

The value and importance of using this trait language in writing instruction is well supported by research (Gentry 2006). It is particularly important when working with students in the early grades to provide instructional tools to support students' different learning styles. In *Getting to the Core of Writing*, the traits are personified through student-friendly characters. Each of the characters represents a different writing trait, and collectively they are referred to as the Traits Team (traitsteam.pdf). Students are introduced to the individual team members through the mini-lessons. The Traits Team becomes a valuable tool for a Writer's Workshop experience. A more detailed description and poster of each Traits Team member is provided in the introduction to each trait section.

The Reading and Writing Connection

Students' writing abilities often shift in third through sixth grade as student readers make a giant cognitive leap from learning to read to reading to learn. Students have likely advanced through all five phases of beginning reading and writing development, attaining a degree of independence as both readers and writers by the time they enter third grade.

In some ways, reading advances faster than writing, and the complexity of writing is accentuated during third through sixth grade. It becomes apparent that writing is more demanding and, in some ways, harder than reading for third, fourth, fifth, and sixth graders. For example, fourth graders can read fairly complex novels, but they would not be able to write novels at that same level of complexity. In the words of writing expert Ralph Fletcher, "Reading is up here and writing is down there. Probably the smartest fourth grader in the country cannot write a novel" (Fletcher 2000).

One expectation of the reading and writing connection in third through sixth grade is that students gain facility in reading a book like a writer (Yates 1995). During this period, students likely begin viewing writing more from the author's perspective, bringing structure and organization to pieces they create based on the reading they do and the study of literary authors' crafts.

In earlier grades, young writers often have a linear sense of writing; they follow a story map or a simple structure, such as *first*, *then*, *next*, and *last*, or *beginning*, *middle*, and *end*. Younger writers often move purposely straight through their composition in a step-by-step approach, rarely rereading or reflecting as they write. Rereading and reflecting as they move through a text becomes more important in the intermediate grades, helping students make sense of what they have written (Gentry 2002).

Not only do they read like a writer, the Common Core State Standards help them think like a writer.

Moving from Concrete to Abstract Thinking

Third-, fourth-, fifth-, and sixth-grade writing often mirrors how children think. Initially in this period of elementary school, students' writing can reflect thinking "limited to concrete phenomena and their own past experiences: that is, thinking is not abstract" (Bjorklund 1999). A third-grade writer following a clear-cut, step-by-step sequence may reflect thinking "limited to tangible facts and objects and not to hypotheses" (Bjorklund 1999). During third grade through sixth grade, students will learn to shift back and forth during drafting to survey the piece from both the reader's and writer's perspective. This includes responding to varying demands of audience, purpose, task, and genre, often guided by the Common Core State Standards and based on a rich array of appropriate models for writing.

The Reading and Writing Connection *(cont.)*

As third- through sixth-grade writers mature, they begin to reflect on their own thinking, pausing and rereading to see how the piece they have crafted sounds or discovering alternative routes for a story plot or other written presentation. They are more likely to begin to consider the reader before putting words down on paper. They gain greater mastery of paragraphing, revising, and editing.

Towards the end of elementary school, writers are much more likely "to introspect about their own thought processes, and generally, can think abstractly" (Bjorklund 1999). Moving from the constrains of story mapping or events in their immediate experience, they advance in ability to critique, consider the impact of specific details, choose just the right word, cite specific textural evidence to support their views, and make other appropriate choices for their writing. They demonstrate both deductive and inductive reasoning, moving from the general to the specific or moving from specific observations to broad generalizations, respectively. Their understanding of components and conventions of the writing process grows, and with the support of the Common Core State Standards, their writing becomes more sophisticated, moving along the grade-by-grade continuum that will eventually lead to college- and career-readiness.

As students move through third through sixth grade, the reading and writing connection likely changes them as thinkers, helping them develop abilities to assimilate information into abstract schemes, question their own thinking, test their own hypotheses, and develop deeper levels of knowledge and thinking (Mann 2002).

The Reading and Writing Connection (cont.)

Basic Common Core Goals for Writers

Students engage in a rich array of literature as models for writing.
Students continue to develop the ability to write both fiction and nonfiction.
Students' writing ties into a comprehensive, content-rich curriculum.
Students demonstrate independence as writers appropriate for their grade level.
Students demonstrate strong content knowledge through writing.
Student writers respond to the varying demands of audience, task, purpose, and discipline.
Students' writing demonstrates ability to both comprehend and critique.
Student writers cite specific textual evidence in their writing to support their views.
Students consider the impact of specific words and details and make appropriate choices.
Students bring structure and organization to their own writing based on studies of the literary authors' crafts.
Students use technology to enhance their writing.

Adapted from "College and Career Readiness Standards for Reading, Writing, and Speaking and Listening" (Shanahan 2009).

The Purpose of Assessment

Assessment plays an integral role in writing instruction. It may occur at the district or state level to measure the student's ability to meet specific standards. Many classrooms include self-assessment where students use rubrics and checklists to score and reflect on their own work. Writing assessment can also take place informally as we sit and confer with young writers, taking anecdotal notes. Maintaining student writing portfolios comprised of both spontaneous and directed writing provides assessment information of a student's writing development and performance over a specific time. No matter the type or form of assessment, it should enable you to determine students' strengths and weaknesses so you may revise your instruction to meet the needs of your writers.

> *Assessment must promote learning, not just measure it. When learners are well served, assessment becomes a learning experience that supports and improves instruction. The learners are not just the students but also the teachers, who learn something about their students.*
>
> —Regie Routman (1999, 559)

Monitoring students' writing over time provides valuable information about their growth and development. The samples, collected periodically throughout the year into student portfolios, reflect where the Writer's Workshop journey began and the student's ongoing progress and achievement relative to the instructional goals. Portfolios, along with your anecdotal notes, not only inform parents of their child's growth but also show students the variety of concepts and skills learned during Writer's Workshop.

In addition to ongoing classroom assessment, it is valuable to conduct benchmark assessments at the beginning, middle, and end of the year. The beginning of the year benchmark provides you with a baseline of data that represents the foundational skill level of the student writer. The middle and end of the year benchmarks show areas of achievement and needs as well as identify effective instructional strategies. *Getting to the Core of Writing* refers to these benchmarks as Benchmarks 1, 2, and 3 respectively. After each benchmark, it is important to analyze the student's work using the grade-level rubric (pages 263–264; writingrubric.pdf) in order to identify the additional support needed for the student.

Collaborating with other teachers encourages targeted conversations about student work and helps build confidence as you become more knowledgeable in interpreting and evaluating student writing. Although *Getting to the Core of Writing* includes a Suggested Pacing Guide (pages 12–13; pacingguide.pdf) and a Year-at-a-Glance plan of instruction (yearataglance.pdf) that provide benchmark prompt suggestions, it is not a one-size-fits-all classroom writing map. Your assessments and observations provide essential information to guide instructional decisions designed to meet the needs of all of your students. For additional assessment resources, including benchmark support information, a rubric, a scoring guide, a classroom grouping mat, and scored student writing samples, see Appendix B (pages 261– 272).

Planning Writing Instruction

Essential in any literacy development is planning and scheduling. *Getting to the Core of Writing* supports teachers as they learn and grow as writers along with their students while at the same time implementing Writer's Workshop. Growing requires nurturing like writing requires practice. The provided plan of instruction is based on the conviction that Writer's Workshop happens each and every day throughout the school year. Mini-lessons may be retaught, when necessary. Some mini-lessons may require more than one day for students to fully grasp an understanding of the writing concept. Additionally, teachers proficient in writing instruction may select individual mini-lessons and teach them in an order that meets the specific needs of their students.

When writing is shared consistently and enthusiastically, students learn, love, and choose to write. As always, instruction must also be guided by the developmental needs of the students as revealed through their daily writing. The structure provided by Writer's Workshop and the lessons in this book allow both students and teachers to recognize themselves as successful writers. Once the routines of Writer's Workshop are in place, it is much easier for the teacher to focus on a quality daily writing time. Things become so routine that teachers will find themselves feeling motivated and passionate about writing instruction instead of overwhelmed.

The pacing guide found on pages 12–13 provides a suggested sequence for when to teach the lessons in this book. It serves as a guide for consistent practice in the writing process and incorporates the traits of quality writing. It is suggested that some lessons be taught more than once throughout the year. When this occurs, if desired, the content of the student writing pieces can be modified slightly to provide students with opportunities to practice writing opinion-, informative-explanatory-, and narrative-based texts. By doing this, students get to write different genres in formats that are familiar to them. For example, in Ideas Lesson 1, students can change the content about which they brainstorm to create an opinion piece on why dogs are the best pet, a narrative on their summer vacation, and an informative piece on the types of plants around the school.

Planning Writing Instruction (cont.)

Suggested Pacing Guide

Month	Lesson
August/September	• Managing WW Lesson 1 (page 35) • Managing WW Lesson 2 (page 38) • Managing WW Lesson 3 (page 41) • Managing WW Lesson 4 (page 50) • Managing WW Lesson 5 (page 52) • Managing WW Lesson 6 (page 58) • Organization Lesson 1 (page 133) • Managing WW Lesson 7 (page 62) • Managing WW Lesson 8 (page 65) • Ideas Lesson 1 (page 77) • Sentence Fluency Lesson 1 (page 105) • Word Choice Lesson 1 (page 179) • Conventions Lesson 1 (page 227) • Sentence Fluency Lesson 2 (page 108) • Ideas Lesson 2 (page 80) • Organization Lesson 2 (page 136) • **Administer Benchmark 1:** Have you ever met someone famous? Think about what might happen if you ran into a famous person you admire. Create a real or imaginary situation and write a story to tell about your experience.

Month	Lesson
October	• Review Managing WW Lessons 1–8 as needed • Managing WW Lesson 9 (page 68) • Managing WW Lesson 10 (page 71) • Ideas Lesson 3 (page 83) • Sentence Fluency Lesson 3 (page 111) • Organization Lesson 3 (page 139) • Word Choice Lesson 2 (page 182) • Conventions Lesson 2 (page 230) • Ideas Lesson 4 (page 86) • Sentence Fluency Lesson 4 (page 114) • Conventions Lesson 3 (page 233) • Ideas Lesson 2 (page 80)

Month	Lesson
November	• Review Managing WW Lessons 1–10 as needed • Ideas Lesson 5 (page 89) • Organization Lesson 4 (page 142) • Word Choice Lesson 3 (page 185) • Sentence Fluency Lesson 5 (page 117) • Conventions Lesson 1 (page 227) • Conventions Lesson 4 (page 236) • Voice Lesson 1 (page 211) • Ideas Lesson 2 (page 80) • Publish

Month	Lesson
December	• Review Managing WW Lessons 1–10 as needed • Ideas Lesson 1 (page 77) • Ideas Lesson 6 (page 92) • Voice Lesson 2 (page 216) • Ideas Lesson 2 (page 80) • Organization Lesson 5 (page 145) • Organization Lesson 6 (page 152) • Sentence Fluency Lesson 6 (page 120) • Word Choice Lesson 4 (page 188) • Conventions Lesson 5 (page 240) • Conventions Lesson 4 (page 236)

Planning Writing Instruction (cont.)

Suggested Pacing Guide (cont.)

Month	Lesson
January	• Review Managing WW Lessons 1–10 as needed • Ideas Lesson 1 (page 77) • Ideas Lesson 4 (page 86) • Organization Lesson 7 (page 155) • Word Choice Lesson 5 (page 193) • Sentence Fluency Lesson 4 (page 114) • Organization Lesson 6 (page 152) • Organization Lesson 8 (page 159) • Voice Lesson 3 (page 219) • Sentence Fluency Lesson 7 (page 123) • Conventions Lesson 5 (page 240) • Conventions Lesson 6 (page 243) • Ideas Lesson 2 (page 80) • **Administer Benchmark 2:** Which of the four seasons if your favorite? Tell about a perfect day in your favorite season. In your opinion, what makes it perfect?

Month	Lesson
February	• Review Managing WW Lessons 1–10 as needed • Ideas Lesson 7 (page 96) • Sentence Fluency Lesson 1 (page 105) • Voice Lesson 4 (page 222) • Organization Lesson 9 (page 162) • Conventions Lesson 4 (page 236) • Word Choice Lesson 6 (page 198) • Sentence Fluency Lesson 6 (page 120) • Word Choice Lesson 5 (page 193) • Organization Lesson 10 (page 166) • Conventions Lesson 7 (page 246) • Ideas Lesson 2 (page 80)

Month	Lesson
March	• Review Managing WW Lessons 1–10 as needed • Ideas Lesson 8 (page 99) • Word Choice Lesson 2 (page 182) • Sentence Fluency Lesson 4 (page 114) • Voice Lesson 2 (page 216) • Organization Lesson 11 (page 170) • Organization Lesson 8 (page 159) • Word Choice Lesson 7 (page 201) • Sentence Fluency Lesson 8 (page 127) • Conventions Lesson 7 (page 246) • Conventions Lesson 8 (page 250) • Ideas Lesson 2 (page 80)

Month	Lesson
April	• Review Managing WW Lessons 1–10 as needed • Review genre studies based on students' needs • Ideas Lesson 3 (page 83) • Sentence Fluency Lesson 3 (page 111) • Sentence Fluency Lesson 5 (page 117) • Word Choice Lesson 3 (page 185) • Organization Lesson 1 (page 133) • Conventions Lesson 6 (page 243) • Organization Lesson 12 (page 174) • Word Choice Lesson 8 (page 206) • Publish • Ideas Lesson 2 (page 80)

Month	Lesson
May	By this time of the year, students will have mastery of many concepts. Although you may have completed your state writing assessment, it is important to continue writing workshop. Revisit mini-lessons based on students' needs and interests. **Administer Benchmark 3:** Have you ever thought of building and designing your own home? Explain how you might plan it on the inside, outside, and why it would be special to you.

Components of Writer's Workshop

Writer's Workshop entails common characteristics that are essential to developing enthusiastic and successful student writers (Graves 1994, 2003; Fletcher 2001; Calkins 1994; Calkins, Hartman and Zoe 2005; Ray 2001; Ray and Cleaveland 2004; Gentry 2000, 2004, 2010). The guidelines that follow have been time-tested by years of classroom practice and collaboration with master writing teachers. The framework of this structure includes the following: the mini-lesson, writing practice time, and sharing time.

The Mini-Lesson

The mini-lesson is 5–15 minutes in length and begins the workshop. It is an opportunity to review past learning, introduce new writing strategies through modeling, and engage students in practicing those strategies through oral rehearsal. Each mini-lesson is focused on one specific topic that both addresses the needs of writers and reflects these skills as practiced by real authors. The mini-lesson is always energetic and challenges students to participate while building their confidence as writers. Students gather in a common area and become part of a comfortable, safe environment that provides guidance and encouragement.

In the appropriate mini-lessons, introduce the Traits Team poster as a visual reminder for students of the writing traits. The Traits Team includes *Ida, Idea Creator* (page 76); *Simon, Sentence Builder* (page 104); *Owen, Organization Conductor* (page 132); *Wally, Word Choice Dectective* (page 178); *Val and Van, Voice* (page 210); and *Callie, Super Conventions Checker* (page 226). These characters work as a team to show students that good writing is not built one skill at a time but with a team of strategies.

Writing Practice Time

During the 15–30 minute writing practice, students apply the skill, strategy, or craft taught in the mini-lesson. This part of the lesson gives students practice necessary in becoming proficient writers as they compose a message to share with a reader. Simultaneously, the teacher helps individual students or small groups of students compose through conferencing. These conferences provide teachers the opportunity to praise students for applying a strategy, followed by a short teaching point. Teachers document observations in a Conferring Notebook to be used for evaluating students' progress, planning new instruction, and meeting with parents. An important part of the writing practice time is the *Spotlight Strategy*. It calls attention to one or two students briefly each day by spotlighting their work, especially when attempting the focus skill presented in the mini-lesson.

Sharing Time

The 5–15 minutes of sharing echoes the mini-lesson across Writer's Workshop and provides an additional opportunity for student talk time. At the end of the writing practice time, students are invited to spend several minutes sharing with partners, in small groups, or individually in the Author's Chair. Teachers select students to share based on their observations during writing time. A variety of sharing methods is used to promote motivation and excitement. At the end of Writer's Workshop, homework suggestions are made to help students follow up on the mini-lesson ideas. Homework can be shared on the next workshop day.

#50917—Getting to the Core of Writing—Level 3 © Shell Education

Implementing the Lessons

Each lesson supports teachers in their writing instruction and encourages students to write like published authors. Consistent language builds a commonality between students as well as across grade levels. Talking about writers, studying other writers, and practicing the craft of writing give students the gift of being authors. While the focus of the lesson may change each day, the lesson routine remains constant. Building routines in any instruction yields smooth transitions between activities and fewer opportunities for distractions. Some mini-lessons may be taught daily while others might be explored across several days. Several mini-lessons can easily be adapted to multiple themes and various pieces of literature, including those listed in the Common Core State Standards Suggested Works. It is important to consider the specific developmental levels and needs of the students. The lesson format provides structure, support, and a framework for instruction for the busy classroom teacher.

Using consistent language during each section of Writer's Workshop is one structure that students will recognize and that will be helpful for smooth transitions. Suggested language for each section of Writer's Workshop is provided in the lessons. Each Writer's Workshop lesson includes the following sections:

- Think About Writing
- Teach
- Engage
- Apply
- Write/Conference
- Spotlight Strategy
- Share
- Homework

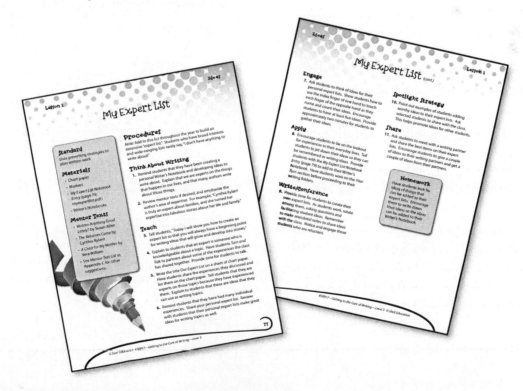

Implementing the Lessons *(cont.)*

Think About Writing—Students reconnect to past mini-lessons and teachers make authentic connections between reading and writing.

Procedures and **Notes**—Special information and teaching tips, followed by the explicit directions for teaching the lesson.

Standards and **Materials**—Indicates the areas of focus for the lesson and all materials needed.

Mentor Texts—Published writing that contains explicit and strong examples of the concepts addressed in the lesson. Use the recommended mentor text as a read-aloud during your reading block or quickly review it during Writer's Workshop. During the writing block, focus on small samples of text that match the mini-lesson skill. Recommended mentor texts are suggested as part of each lesson. Alternative suggestions can be found in Appendix C or on the Teacher Resource CD (mentortextlist.pdf).

Teach—Supports students through demonstration and modeling to help elevate their level of writing.

Implementing the Lessons (cont.)

Engage—Students will talk to each other about what they will apply in their writing. Talk time is short, intense, and focused. The teacher monitors, observes, and offers supportive comments.

Spotlight Strategy—The teacher points out students' efforts and successes, emphasizing a skill or specific task to further student understanding.

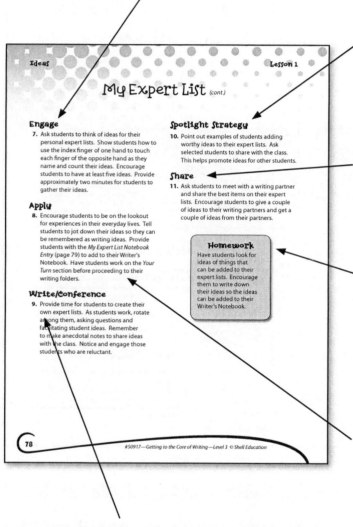

Share—Students converse, explain, question, and give feedback to their groups or partners and share portions of their writing relating to the day's mini-lesson focus.

Homework—Students observe, notice, discuss, and collect important information at home and with their families that can then be used in their writings.

Apply—Students will practice what was taught in the mini-lesson, develop independence, and take ownership of their writing. The teacher restates the mini-lesson concept to solidify it for students.

Write/Conference—Students have essential, independent practice time. The teacher confers with students in one-on-one or small-group settings.

Implementing Writer's Workshop

Writer's Workshop-at-a-Glance

This chart provides an at-a-glance overview of the Writer's Workshop format provided in *Getting to the Core of Writing*. It can be a helpful tool to use when planning instruction.

Component	Time	Description
Mini Lesson	5–15 minutes	Lesson plan subsections include: • Think About Writing • Teach • Engage • Apply

Writing Practice	15–30 minutes	Lesson plan subsections include:
		 • Write/Conference
		   • Praise accomplishments
		   • Make a teaching point
		   • Use Conference Log
		 • Spotlight Strategies

Sharing	5–15 minutes	Lesson plan subsections include:
		 • Share
		   • Whole/small group
		   • Partners
		   • Compliment and comment
		 • Homework

The Writing Conference

Writing conferences are most successful when they occur as a conversation between two writers who are simply talking about writing. It is a time to value students as writers, to differentiate instruction, to teach new strategies, and to gather information for forming instructional decisions. Anderson (2000) notes that a conference conversation basically includes two parts: conversation based upon the student's current writing and conversation based on what will help him or her become a better writer. Katie Wood Ray (2001) and Lucy Calkins, Amanda Hartman, and Zoe White (2003) tell us conferring is hard! It is one part of the day that is a bit unknown. When conferring one-on-one with young writers, there is no script—no specific plan developed prior to the meeting. That is a strong deterrent that can keep many teachers from stepping into the conferring role during Writer's Workshop.

Following Calkins, Hartman, and Zoe's dictum: "Conferring is the heart of Writer's Workshop" (2003, VIII), the sharing of information in conference conversation over the development of a specific writing piece is the very heart of teaching writing. Although difficult at times, especially at first, even the smallest conversation lets your students know you are interested in them as writers and helps nudge them forward in their writing development. Just as students become better writers by writing, you will only become better at conferring by conferring. The sincerity with which you approach this task will not only affect your students' writing future but also your sense of accomplishment as a teacher.

Although the content of the conference conversation is unknown, the conference structure is predictable. The four phases of a conference structure are:

1. Observe
2. Praise
3. Guide
4. Connect

First, study to determine what the writer knows, what the writer is trying to do, and what the writer needs to learn. Next, provide praise. Then, develop a teaching point and guide and encourage the writer to practice that teaching point. Lastly, stress the importance of using what was learned in future writing. For a more detailed explanation of each phase, see pages 258–260 in Appendix A.

The Writing Conference (cont.)

Included in Appendix A and on the Teacher Resource CD are additional resources dedicated to the subject of conferring with students.

- **Essential Materials**—Use this list to assemble a "toolkit" of items you can carry with you as you conference with students (page 253).

- **Mini-Lesson Log**—Keep a record of the mini-lessons taught to serve as a reminder of writing strategies and crafts students have been exposed to during whole-group instruction (page 255).

- **Conference Log**—This conference form serves as a good starting point and makes it easy to view your entire class at one glance. It is a simple summary of the conference listing the name, date, praise, and teaching point. See pages 258–260 in Appendix A for more information on conferring steps. Some teachers prefer a separate conference page for each student as they become more familiar with the conferring process (page 256).

- **Conference Countdown**—This page lists simple reminders of salient points to consider during writing conferences (page 257).

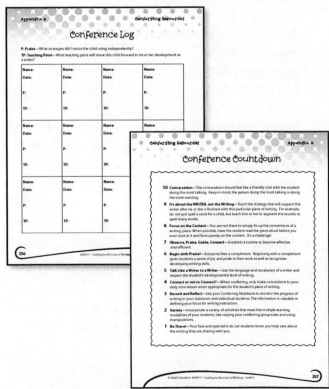

When you take the time to have a conversation, you are sending a message that you care enough to listen and communicate. With so much emphasis on testing achievement, it is important to stay committed to teaching the writer and not just the work of the writer. Carl Anderson (2000) tells us that student efforts and achievements are most likely not due to the questions we ask, the feedback we give, or our teaching. He states, "In the end, the success of a conference often rests on the extent to which students sense we are genuinely interested in them as writers—and as individuals."

The Writer's Notebook

The Writer's Notebook can be a young writer's best friend, always at his or her side to help out. It is personalized, customized, and interactive. Students can refer back to any mini-lesson taught during the year in Writer's Workshop to refresh their memories or find a tip for moving forward. The Writer's Notebook is like a friend, giving student writers a helping hand when they need guidance or are struggling with a writing skill. Consider this scenario:

> *The student's pencil taps incessantly on his desk. He's stuck. He can't think of how to begin an informational piece following a jumpstart mini-lesson in Writer's Workshop. The teacher observes the problem, stops by his desk and asks, "How's your writing going?" The student's response is quick and to the point. "Not so good! I don't have anything to write about." Writer's Notebook to the rescue! The teacher invites the student to return to lessons presented months ago, with notebook entries to gather ideas for writing. As the student moves his finger down his customized expert list, his facial expression completely changes from confusion to a brilliant smile. "I've got it," he exclaims with relief. "It's in my list. I know a lot about model volcanoes." "Then off you go!" the teacher replies with a smile.*

The notebook is intended as a resource that student writers revisit to dig deeper, gather old ideas, or return to an anthology of mini-lessons taught throughout the year. Previous lessons are readily available and students can return to any lesson at a moment's notice for support. The left side of the notebook holds a glued-in notebook entry sheet designed to help the student with a skill or strategy connected to the writing traits and coordinated to a daily mini lesson. The right side of the notebook is used for individual or partner practice of the specific skill or strategy that was taught. Students move from their Writer's Notebook to writing pieces in their writing folders and apply the notebook entry skills or strategies on their essays, stories, and compositions.

Here are some tips for creating Writer's Notebooks and using them with your students:

- Use inexpensive, well-constructed composition notebooks if possible; however, you may also use spiral-bound notebooks or three-ring binders. Aimee Buckner (2005) tells us to select notebooks that match our style of teaching, the space and time available, and the management of the notebooks. There are a variety of brands available that are often on sale during back-to-school season.

- Encourage students to decorate and personalize their notebooks. This activity can be done in class or you may provide directions and make this a student-and-parent activity for a home connection. Personalizing the notebook with pictures, words, and phrases develops ideas for writing projects. (See page 280 of Appendix D for a sample home connection letter.)

- Store notebooks in a location accessible to students, such as small baskets on desks or shelves. If the Writer's Notebooks are easily available, students are more apt to use them as a writing resource.

The Writer's Notebook *(cont.)*

- Copy and cut notebook entry sheets in advance. Notebook entries are easily cut with a paper cutter and are then readily available for students to glue into their notebooks.

- Deliver specific instructions on adding notebook entries. Have materials available so students can add a few dots of glue and have the sheet in the notebook quickly. Develop expectations and routines to save valuable writing time.

- Set up a Table of Contents and create chapter sections:

  1. Managing Writer's Workshop: 10 pages

  2. Ideas: 15 pages

  3. Sentence Fluency: 15 pages

  4. Organization: 15 pages

  5. Word Choice: 15 pages

  6. Voice: 5 Pages

  7. Conventions: 15 pages

  8. Miscellaneous: 5 pages

- Have students number the chapters using flags for ease of management. When teaching a lesson, your prompt should be simple, such as, "Turn to Chapter 4—Organization." Extra pages may be included in each chapter to give teachers the prerogative to add additional lesson ideas for any chapter.

Students react positively to the use of the Writer's Notebook. Ralph Fletcher (1996), author and educational consultant, states, "…the most important tool I use: my writer's notebook. Keeping a writer's notebook is one of the best ways I know of living a writing kind of life." That is exactly the desired response from students as well.

Top 10 Tips for Creating Successful Writers

1. **Schedule Writer's Workshop Daily.** Scheduling Writer's Workshop daily grants valuable, necessary time for students to practice and grow as writers.

2. **Establish and Commit to Routines.** Life is good when everyone knows what to do and when to do it. Take the time to establish foundational routines that will impact your Writer's Workshop throughout the year. Revisit Managing Writer's Workshop lessons as the need arises.

3. **Model, Model, Model!** Modeling gives direct instruction while scaffolding for young writers. Use these steps to model specific skills and behaviors with students (*I* is the teacher and *you* is the student) (Pearson and Gallager 1983):

   - I do, you watch
   - I do, you help
   - You do, I help
   - You do, I watch

4. **Read, Read, Read!** Reading a variety of texts through the eyes of a writer exposes students to the craft of the author and encourages students to explore new avenues of writing.

5. **Display and Celebrate!** Walking down the hallway in a school setting, you can usually get a good idea of the writing that is going on in each classroom. The more students write, the more comfortable they become, and they will want to show off their work. Celebrate student writing and recognize students as writers.

6. **Confer Weekly.** This is your opportunity to learn about each student's writing development. Encourage, guide, and listen.

7. **Share, Share, Share!** Young children love to share everything. Sharing during Writer's Workshop enhances their sense of importance as writers.

8. **Involve and Inform Parents.** Writing is an automatic means of connecting with parents. Wall displays of writing samples show parents how you value their child's writing effort. Hold an Author's Tea and invite parents so they can see first-hand the important writing of their child.

9. **Be Flexible and Reflect.** A well-planned lesson may fall flat. So, go back to the drawing board and ask yourself, "Why?" "What happened?" How can you reteach to make the right connections for students? Take time to reflect on your teaching and student learning.

10. **Set High Expectations.** Be specific with your expectations and articulate clearly what you would like the students to accomplish. Believe in your students' abilities and challenge them to succeed. Every child can be an author.

Correlation to Standards

Shell Education is committed to producing educational materials that are research- and standards-based. In this effort, we have correlated all of our products to the academic standards of all 50 United States, the District of Columbia, the Department of Defense Dependent Schools, and all Canadian provinces. We have also correlated to the **Common Core State Standards**.

How To Find Standards Correlations

To print a customized correlation report of this product for your state, visit our website at **http://www.shelleducation.com** and follow the on-screen directions. If you require assistance in printing correlation reports, please contact Customer Service at 1-877-777-3450.

Purpose and Intent of Standards

Legislation mandates that all states adopt academic standards that identify the skills students will learn in kindergarten through grade twelve. Many states also have standards for Pre-K. This same legislation sets requirements to ensure the standards are detailed and comprehensive.

Standards are designed to focus instruction and guide adoption of curricula. Standards are statements that describe the criteria necessary for students to meet specific academic goals. They define the knowledge, skills, and content students should acquire at each level. Standards are also used to develop standardized tests to evaluate students' academic progress. Teachers are required to demonstrate how their lessons meet state standards. State standards are used in the development of all of our products, so educators can be assured they meet the academic requirements of each state.

McREL Compendium

We use the Mid-continent Research for Education and Learning (McREL) Compendium to create standards correlations. Each year, McREL analyzes state standards and revises the compendium. By following this procedure, McREL is able to produce a general compilation of national standards. Each lesson in this product is based on one or more McREL standard. The chart on pages 25–27 and on the Teacher Resource CD (standards.pdf) lists each standard taught in this product and the page number(s) for the corresponding lesson(s).

TESOL Standards

The lessons in this book promote English language development for English language learners. The standards listed on the Teacher Resource CD (standards.pdf) support the language objectives presented throughout the lessons.

Common Core State Standards

The lessons in this book are aligned to the Common Core State Standards (CCSS). The standards on pages 28–30 and on the Teacher Resource CD (standards.pdf) support the objectives presented throughout the lessons.

Correlation to Standards (cont.)

McREL Standards

Standard	Lesson
Understands the structure of Writer's Workshop	Components of Writer's Workshop (page 35); Our Group Meeting (page 38); The Writing Folder (page 41); The Writer's Notebook (page 50); Organizing the Writer's Notebook (page 52); Sharing (page 58); Turn and Talk (page 62); Guidelines for Writer's Workshop (page 65); Teacher and Peer Conferences (page 68); The Five-Step Writing Process (page 71)
Prewriting: Uses prewriting strategies to plan written work	My Expert List (page 77); I Can Write Like That! (page 80); Collecting Ideas (page 83); People We Love (page 86); Fabulous Faunae (page 89); Story Seeds (page 92); Famous People I Admire (page 96); What Should I Write? (page 99)
Drafting and Revising: Uses strategies to draft and revise written work	Popcorn Sentences (page 105); A Simple Sentence (page 108); The Compound Subject (page 111); Types of Sentences (page 114); The Compound Verb (page 117); The Compound Sentence (page 120); Rubber Band Sentences (page 123); A Complex Sentence (page 127); Name Poetry (page 133); 123 Paragraphs: Opinion (page 136); 123 Paragraphs: Story (page 139); 123 Paragraphs: Informing (page 142); Building a Story Mountain (page 145); Telling a Story (page 152); More Than "Once Upon a Time" (page 155); Circular Endings (page 159); Writing a Letter (page 162); Just Stating the Facts (page 170); Poetry Fun (page 174)
Editing and Publishing: Uses strategies to edit and publish written work	The Capital Rap (page 227); Punctuation Takes a Holiday (page 230); See It! Say It! Spell It! Write It! Check It! (page 233); Editing with CUPS (page 236); Quotation Marks: "Who Said That?" (page 240); Caution Comma Chant (page 243); Using Editing Marks (page 246); Writing Traits Checklist (page 250)
Evaluates own and others' writing	All lessons
Uses strategies to write for a variety of purposes	What Should I Write? (page 99)
Writes expository compositions	I Can Write Like That! (page 80); 123 Paragraphs: Informing (page 142); Just Stating the Facts (page 170)
Writes narrative accounts, such as poems and stories	Name Poetry (page 133); 123 Paragraphs: Story (page 139); Building a Story Mountain (page 145); Telling a Story (page 152); More Than "Once Upon a Time" (page 155); Circular Endings (page 159); Poetry Fun (page 174)

Correlation to Standards (cont.)

McREL Standards (cont.)

Standard	Lesson
Writes expressive compositions	How Do You Feel? (page 211); Looking and Listening for Voice (page 216); Informing Interjections (page 219); Know Your Audience (page 222)
Writes personal letters	Writing a Letter (page 162)
Writes opinion compositions	123 Paragraphs: Opinion (page 136); It's My Opinion! (page 166)
Uses descriptive and precise language that clarifies and enhances ideas	Be Specific! (page 179); Vivid Verbs (page 182); Amazing Adjectives (page 185); Banished, Boring Words (page 188); Transition Words (page 193); Super Similes (page 198); Awesome Adverbs (page 201); Interesting Idioms (page 206)
Uses a variety of sentence structures in writing	Popcorn Sentences (page 105); A Simple Sentence (page 108); The Compound Subject (page 111); Types of Sentences (page 114); The Compound Verb (page 117); The Compound Sentence (page 120); Rubber Band Sentences (page 123); A Complex Sentence (page 127)
Uses nouns in written compositions	Be Specific! (page 179)
Uses verbs in written compositions	Vivid Verbs (page 182)
Uses adjectives in written compositions	Amazing Adjectives (page 185)
Uses adverbs in written compositions	Awesome Adverbs (page 201)
Links ideas using connecting words	Transition Words (page 193)
Uses conventions of spelling in written compositions	See It! Say It! Spell It! Write It! Check It! (page 233); Editing with CUPS (page 236); Using Editing Marks (page 246)
Uses conventions of capitalization in written compositions	The Capital Rap (page 227); Editing with CUPS (page 236); Using Editing Marks (page 246)
Uses conventions of punctuation in written compositions	Punctuation Takes a Holiday (page 230); Editing with CUPS (page 236); Quotation Marks: "Who Said That?" (page 240); Caution Comma Chant (page 243); Using Editing Marks (page 246)

Correlation to Standards (cont.)

McREL Standards (cont.)

Standard	Lesson
Uses a variety of strategies to plan research	Fabulous Faunae (page 89)
Contributes to group discussions	All lessons
Responds to questions and comments	All lessons
Listens to classmates and adults	All lessons
Uses level-appropriate vocabulary in speech	All lessons
Listens for specific information in spoken texts	All lessons

Correlation to Standards (cont.)

Common Core State Standards

The purpose of the Common Core State Standards is to guarantee that all students are prepared for college and career literacy as they leave high school. These standards indicate that all students need the ability to write logical opinions and informational texts with sound reasoning to support their findings. *Getting to the Core of Writing* provides the fundamental writing skills to support students in their continued growth as writers, thus enabling them to enjoy continued success as the challenges presented by the curriculum become increasingly complex.

The structure of Writer's Workshop and the lessons in this book address the Common Core State Standards for **writing**. They also address **speaking and listening** standards, which are the building blocks of written language, through the Engage and Share components of the lesson. Due to the reciprocal nature of reading and writing, *Getting to the Core of Writing* naturally meets many of the Common Core State Standards for **reading** and for **language** as well. The standards below can also be found on the Teacher Resource CD (standards.pdf).

Standard	Lesson
Writing: Text Types and Purposes, W.3.1.	123 Paragraphs: Opinion (page 136); It's My Opinion (page 166)
Writing: Text Types and Purposes, W.3.2.	Fabulous Faunae (page 89); Famous People I Admire (page 96); 123 Paragraphs: Informing (page 142); Just Stating the Facts (page 170)
Writing: Text Types and Purposes, W.3.3.	Story Seeds (page 92); 123 Paragraphs: Story (page 139); Building a Story Mountain (page 145); Telling a Story (page 152); More Than "Once Upon a Time" (page 155); Circular Endings (page 159)
Writing: Production and Distribution of Writing, W.3.4.	All lessons in Ideas (pages 77–101); All lessons in Sentence Fluency (pages 105–129); All lessons in Organization (pages 133–176); All lessons in Word Choice (pages 179–208); All lessons in Voice (pages 211–224); All lessons in Conventions (pages 227–252)

Correlation to Standards (cont.)

Common Core State Standards (cont.)

Standard	Lesson
Writing: Production and Distribution of Writing, W.3.5.	All lessons in Ideas (pages 77–101); All lessons in Sentence Fluency (pages 105–129); All lessons in Organization (pages 133–176); All lessons in Word Choice (pages 179–208); All lessons in Voice (pages 211–224); All lessons in Conventions (pages 227–252)
Writing: Research to Build and Present Knowledge, W.3.7.	Fabulous Faunae (page 89); 123 Paragraphs: Informing (page 142)
Writing: Research to Build and Present Knowledge, W.3.8.	Fabulous Faunae (page 109); 123 Paragraphs: Informing (page 142); Just Stating the Facts (page 170)
Writing: Range of Writing, W.3.10.	All lessons in Ideas (pages 77–101); All lessons in Sentence Fluency (pages 105–129); All lessons in Organization (pages 133–176); All lessons in Word Choice (pages 179–208); All lessons in Voice (pages 211–224); All lessons in Conventions (pages 227–252)
Speaking and Listening: Comprehension and Collaboration, SL.3.1.	All lessons
Speaking and Listening: Comprehension and Collaboration, SL.3.2.	I Can Write Like That! (page 80); 123 Paragraphs: Opinion (page 136); 123 Paragraphs: Story (page 139); 123 Paragraphs: Informing (page 142); It's My Opinion! (page 166); Just Stating the Facts (page 170)
Speaking and Listening: Comprehension and Collaboration, SL.3.3.	All lessons
Speaking and Listening: Presentation of Knowledge and Ideas, SL.3.6.	All lessons

Correlation to Standards (cont.)

Common Core State Standards (cont.)

Standard	Lesson
Language: Conventions of Standard English, L.3.1.	Popcorn Sentences (page 105); A Simple Sentence (page 108); The Compound Subject (page 111); Types of Sentences (page 114); The Compound Verb (page 117); The Compound Sentence (page 120); Rubber Band Sentences (page 123); A Complex Sentence (page 127); Poetry Fun (page 174); Be Specific! (page 179); Vivid Verbs (page 182); Amazing Adjectives (page 185); Awesome Adverbs (page 201)
Language: Conventions of Standard English, L.3.2.	The Capital Rap (page 227); Punctuation Takes a Holiday (page 230); See It! Say It! Spell It! Write It! Check It! (page 233); Editing with CUPS (page 236); Quotation Marks: "Who Said That?" (page 240); Caution Comma Chant (page 243); Using Editing Marks (page 246); Writing Traits Checklist (page 250)
Language: Knowledge of Language, L3.3.	All lessons
Language: Vocabulary Acquisition and Use, L.3.5.	Super Similes (page 198); Interesting Idioms (page 206); How Do You Feel? (page 211); Looking and Listening for Voice (page 216); Informing Interjections (page 219)
Language: Vocabulary Acquisition and Use, L.3.6.	All lessons

Acknowledgments

We stand on the shoulders of national and world-renowned teachers of teachers-of-writing, such as our friend the late Donald Graves, Lucy Calkins, Ralph Fletcher, Donald Murry, Vicki Spandel, Ruth Culham, Katie Wood Ray, Carl Anderson, Charles Temple, Jean Gillet, Stephanie Harvey, Debbie Miller, Regie Routman, Marissa Moss, Steve Graham, and Connie Hebert to name a few, as well as educators at Northwest Regional Educational Laboratory. Thank you. We are also truly grateful to the faculty at Auckland University, workshop leaders, and experiences with the teachers in New Zealand some 20 years ago who got us started.

While writing this series and in the past, there were frequent chats about writing and words of wisdom from Dona Rice, Sara Johnson, Jean Mann, Lois Bridges, and Tim Rasinski. Scores of teachers who read our manuscripts, praised our work, gave us confidence, and adjusted our missteps. We could not have succeeded without two super editors, Dona and Sara, and the great staff at Teacher Created Materials/Shell Education.

We attribute much of what's good about our series to teachers who invited us into their classrooms. Over all the years that went into this project, there are too many people to list separately, but here's a sampling: Thank you to all the teachers and districts who allowed us to visit and model in your classrooms, try our materials, and listen to your insights as we refined our writing instruction. A special thank you to the teachers at Fayette, Logan, Mingo, Pocahontas, Upshur, Wood, Wirt, and Harrison County Schools. We owe special gratitude to French Creek Elementary, Mt. Hope Elementary, and Nutter Fort Elementary teachers. We can't forget the "Writing Teachers Club": Debbie Gaston, Tammy Musil, Judy McGinnis, Jenna Williams, Cheryl Bramble, Karen Vandergrift, Barb Compton, Whitney Fowler, and Jennifer Rome, who spent countless hours learning, questioning, and sharing ideas. "You really need to write a book," you said, and your words have made that happen. You and many others inspired us, including the WC Department of Teaching and Learning (especially Angel, Karen, Lesley, Marcia, Matt, M. C., and Wendy). We can't forget Jean Pearcy, Miles 744, the talented teachers of the West Clermont Schools, the 4 Bs (Bailey, Bergen, Blythe, and Brynne), Candy, Mrs. Hendel, the lab rats (Becky, Mary, Mike, Sally, Sharon, and Vera), and the littlest singers at CHPC. Last but not least, a special thank you to Rick and Ro Jensen, Bill McIntyre, and Carolyn Meigs for years of support, and to Dawna Vecchio, Loria Reid, Terry Morrison, Laura Trent, Jeanie Bennett, Millie Shelton, Therese E., and Kathy Snyder for listening, cheering, and celebrating!

Many thanks to administrators who provided opportunities, leadership, and support for teachers as they explored the implementation of writing workshop and applied new teaching strategies: superintendents Beverly Kingery, Susan Collins, director Kay Devono, principals Allen Gorrell, Frank Marino, Joann Gilbert, Pattae Kinney, Jody Decker, Vickie Luchuck, Jody Johnson, and Wilma Dale. We owe many thanks to WVDE Cadre for continuous professional development—you brought us together.

We owe immense gratitude for having been blessed with the company of children who have graced us with their writing, creativity, and wisdom. Thank you to hundreds of children who have shared marvelous writing and insight.

Finally, for never-ending patience, love and support we thank our families: Clint, Luke, and Lindsay; Lanty, Jamey, John, Charlie, Jacki, Jeffrey; and Bill. You all are the best!

About the Authors

Richard Gentry, Ph.D., is nationally recognized for his work in spelling, phase theory, beginning reading and writing, and teaching literacy in elementary school. A former university professor and elementary school teacher, his most recent book is *Raising Confident Readers: How to Teach Your Child to Read and Write—From Baby to Age 7*. Other books include topics such as beginning reading and writing, assessment, and spelling. He also blogs for *Psychology Today* magazine. Richard has spoken at state and national conferences and has provided teachers with inspiring strategies to use in their classroom.

Jan McNeel, M.A.Ed., is a forty-year veteran of education and leader of staff development throughout West Virginia and Maryland. Formerly a Reading First Cadre Member for the West Virginia Department of Education and Title I classroom and Reading Recovery teacher, Jan consults with schools and districts across the state. Jan's studies of literacy acquisition at the Auckland University in New Zealand serve as the foundation of her expertise in reading and writing. Her practical strategies and useful ideas are designed to make reading and writing connections that are teacher-friendly and easy to implement. She has won awards for her excellent work as a master teacher and has presented her work in early literacy at state, regional, and national conferences.

Vickie Wallace-Nesler, M.A.Ed., has been in education for 30 years as an itinerant, Title 1, and regular classroom teacher. Through her current work as a Literacy Coach for grades K–5, conference presenter, and literacy consultant, Vickie brings true insight into the "real world" of educators and their challenges. That experience, along with Master's degrees in both Elementary Education and Reading, National Board certification in Early and Middle Literacy for Reading and Language Arts, and studies at The Teachers College Reading and Writing Project at Columbia University, drive her passion for helping all teachers and students develop a love for learning.

Managing Writer's Workshop

Writer's Workshop begins on the first day of school and is taught every day thereafter. Establishing routines is critical to developing a successful, productive writing time. Therefore, Managing Writer's Workshop lessons should be focused on early in the year and revisited when necessary. The mini-lessons require time and repetition to develop automaticity during Writer's Workshop. A wide range of topics can be addressed during management mini-lessons. Repeat mini-lessons as needed, especially on the topics of guidelines for Writer's Workshop and having students share their writing with partners. These two particular lessons will be crucial to having Writer's Workshop run smoothly and successfully for the rest of the year. Ensure students are responding to those lessons in the ways you want them to, or spend additional time teaching and modeling. Observe your class to find the needs of your particular students. Lessons in this section include:

- Lesson 1: Components of Writer's Workshop (page 35)

- Lesson 2: Our Group Meeting (page 38)

- Lesson 3: The Writing Folder (page 41)

- Lesson 4: The Writer's Notebook (page 50)

- Lesson 5: Organizing the Writer's Notebook (page 52)

- Lesson 6: Sharing (page 58)

- Lesson 7: Turn and Talk (page 62)

- Lesson 8: Guidelines for Writer's Workshop (page 65)

- Lesson 9: Teacher and Peer Conferences (page 68)

- Lesson 10: The Five-Step Writing Process (page 71)

Components of Writer's Workshop

Standard

Understands the structure of Writer's Workshop

Materials

- Model writing folder
- Model Writer's Notebook
- *Components of Writer's Workshop Anchor Chart* (page 37; writersworkshop.pdf)

Mentor Texts

- *A Writer's Notebook* by Ralph Fletcher
- *Amelia's Notebook* by Marissa Moss
- See *Mentor Text List* in Appendix C for other suggestions.

Procedures

Note: Create a model writing folder and Writer's Notebook to share with students. After students create their own notebooks (Managing Writer's Workshop Lesson 4), review the Components of Writer's Workshop and have students add the notebook entry to the Organization section of their Writer's Notebook.

Think About Writing

1. Introduce the concept of Writer's Workshop to students. For example, "During this time, we will explore and practice becoming writers. We will meet together, practice writing, and share our writing with each other. This time will be called Writer's Workshop. We will follow procedures so everyone knows what is expected at each point during our Writer's Workshop time."

2. Read quotes from the mentor texts by Ralph Fletcher and Marissa Moss, if desired.

Teach

3. Tell students, "Today I will show you the schedule we will use during Writer's Workshop so you can use your writing time wisely."

4. Explain that there will always be three components to the writing schedule.

   - "We will have a daily group meeting where we pull together as a community of writers to get information. This is called a mini-lesson."

   - "You will have time to write quietly about an idea or an experience in your life. While you write, I will meet with you to talk about your writing projects."

   - "We will come back together to share our thoughts, ideas, successes, or concerns."

Components of Writer's Workshop *(cont.)*

5. Tell students that they will have a short homework assignment each night that requires them to think about writing, talk to their families about writing, or make observations.

Engage

6. Review the three components of Writer's Workshop by naming each part: mini-lesson, student writing time, and sharing. Then have students repeat each part in turn.

Apply

7. Display the *Components of Writer's Workshop Anchor Chart* (page 37). Remind students that the three components of Writer's Workshop will help them become accomplished writers. Practice making transitions by moving students to where they will be located for each component of Writer's Workshop. For example, students may be sitting on the rug during the mini-lesson, at their desks for writing, and meeting with a partner, triad, or quad for sharing.

8. Tell students that today will be a free-write day where the writing topic is their choice; however, they must be writing for the entire time.

Write/Conference

9. Provide time for students to write. Do not conference today. Practice moving students through the schedule to help them internalize your management system; then practice sustained writing time.

Spotlight Strategy

10. Spotlight students who know exactly how to move to each designated area without the loss of one moment of writing time. A suggestion is to use a small flashlight, which can be shined on students to spotlight them. Remember to provide lots of praise during these introductory days of Writer's Workshop.

Share

11. Ask students to meet with partners to name and explain the focus of the three components of Writer's Workshop. Provide approximately two minutes for students to share. Choose one or two students who clearly understood the idea and have them share with the whole group.

Homework

Ask students to write the three components of Writer's Workshop on a sheet of paper and share it with their parents.

Components of Writer's Workshop Anchor Chart

Writer's Workshop
Easy as 1-2-3

1 Mini-Lesson

We will learn the writing process and study the writing of other authors.

2 Writing Time

We will practice new ideas, tools, and strategies in our writing.

3 Sharing

We will talk about our writing with our peers.

Our Group Meeting

Procedures

Note: Decide on an area in your room that will serve as a meeting place. You will need to repeat this lesson until the procedure is in place. Build solid routines. To build excitement, share your Writer's Notebook and folder in preparation for future lessons.

Think About Writing

1. Explain to students that today they will begin building an understanding of what a community of writers looks like, sounds like, and feels like.

2. Share from mentor texts, if desired.

Teach

3. Tell students, "Today I will show you how to work in Writer's Workshop with minimal noise and no confusion."

4. Model where and how to sit during the mini-lesson component of Writer's Workshop. You may wish to begin at a student's desk to show students exactly what they will do when they get ready for a mini-lesson. Then have students emulate what you modeled. Practice moving students several times. Throughout modeling and practicing, provide plenty of praise to students. It is important to draw attention to expected behaviors through praise and recognition. Repeat this same procedure for the other components of Writer's Workshop on subsequent days.

5. Begin an anchor chart to record students' observations of what Writer's Workshop will look like, sound like, and feel like. Add to the anchor chart over the next several days as students become familiar with the routines. Use the *Sample Looks Like, Sounds Like, Feels Like Anchor Chart* (page 40) to help guide students as they add information to the chart your class creates.

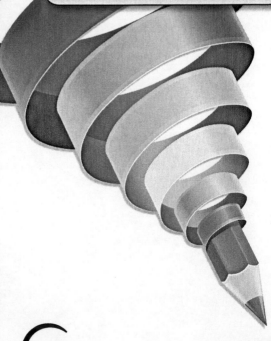

Our Group Meeting (cont.)

Engage

6. Have students tell partners how to move to the community meeting area for mini-lessons.

Apply

7. Remind students that it is important to move quickly to the meeting area so that precious instructional time is not lost. Tell students that today will be a free-write day.

Write/Conference

8. Provide students with paper and have them write for seven minutes. As students work, observe and rotate among them to solve problems. Procedures must be solidly in place to get students moving toward independence in Writer's Workshop.

Spotlight Strategy

9. Spotlight students who move quickly and quietly to and from the meeting area and began to transition into free-writing. Remember to provide lots of praise during these early days of Writer's Workshop.

Share

10. Have students meet with partners and share what they wrote today. Provide approximately two minutes for students to share. Choose one or two students who clearly understand the idea and have them share with the whole group.

Homework

Ask students to think about how important it is to move quickly and quietly during Writer's Workshop. Have students write two reasons why having this routine in place will help them as they work.

Sample Looks Like, Sounds Like, Feels Like Anchor Chart

Our Writer's Workshop...

Looks Like	Sounds Like	Feels Like
		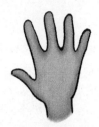
• Pencils, all supplies ready • Journals/folders/notebooks • Crayons/art paper • Word walls • Mentor texts available • Phonics charts/alphabet charts • Labeled items in the room • Author's chair • Partners/small groups • Smiling faces • Writing tool kits • Student engagement • Vocabulary list • Writing prompts • Turn and talk • Productive • Organized • Writing • Busy	• Buzz, hum, beehive • Two-inch voices • Conversation/oral language • Quiet during thinking and teaching phase • "Hum" when sharing w/ partners, triads, quads • Busy • Children making decisions • Learning is happening • Questioning	• Comfortable, natural, happy • Nonthreatening, risk taking • Purposeful • Successful • Confident • Excited • Relaxed • Proud • Comfortable sharing thoughts • "I can" attitude

#50917—Getting to the Core of Writing—Level 3 © Shell Education

The Writing Folder

Standard

Understands the structure of Writer's Workshop

Materials

- Two-pocket folders with fasteners
- Red and green dot stickers
- *Student Mini-Lesson Log* (page 43; minilessonlog2.pdf)
- Reference inserts:

    Dolch Sight Word List (page 44; dolchwordlist.pdf)

    Fry Sight Word List (page 45; frywordlist.pdf)

    Short and Long Vowel Charts (pages 46–47; shortlongvowelcharts.pdf)

    Vowel Teams Chart (pages 48–49; vowelteamschart.pdf)

- Model writing folder
- Protective sleeves

Mentor Texts

- *A Writer's Notebook* by Ralph Fletcher
- *Amelia's Notebook* by Marissa Moss
- See *Mentor Text List* in Appendix C for other suggestions.

Procedures

Note: Implement this lesson over several days. It is important to model and explain how each reference insert can serve as a helpful tool for student writing projects. If not explicitly taught, students will not recognize the value and usefulness of these resources.

Think About Writing

1. Explain to students that they will organize a folder to hold their writing projects for this school year. Tell students that they will keep records of mini-lessons, and at the end of each month, they will clean their folders. Writing projects they want to save will go into their Showcase Writing Folder, and drafts not wanted will be stapled with the *Student Mini-Lesson Log* (page 43) and taken home for their personal records.

2. Review mentor texts, if desired.

Teach

3. Tell students, "Today I will show you how to organize your writing folder."

4. Distribute folders, red and green dot stickers, the *Student Mini-Lesson Log* (page 43), and the reference inserts (pages 44–49) to students. Use the following steps to help students set up their writing folders.

    - Have students place a green dot sticker on the inside, left pocket. Explain that this will hold writing projects that are still in progress. It will also hold the *Student Mini-Lesson Log* for keeping records of what they are learning. Have students record a short note about each mini-lesson on the mini-lesson log on all subsequent days.

    - Have students place a red dot sticker on the inside, right pocket. Explain that this pocket will hold all the writing pieces that are finished. These will be taken home or stored at school to show students' growth as writers.

The Writing Folder (cont.)

- Tell students that the reference inserts you have given them are important tools to help them in their writing. Show students how to put the reference inserts into protective sleeves and fasten them in the writing folders.

- Share what a completed writing folder looks like.

Engage

5. Have students explain to partners the different parts of the writing folder and what each is for. Provide approximately two minutes for students to share.

Apply

6. Review with students the importance of having a personalized and organized writing folder. Provide students time to decorate their writing folders. Tell students that when they are finished, they should take out a sheet of paper and free-write.

Write/Conference

7. Allow time for students to work on their writing folders, depending on the developmental levels of your students.

Spotlight Strategy

8. Spotlight students that are following directions, sustaining themselves, and practicing organizational strategies.

Share

9. No sharing time today.

Homework

Ask students to think about all of the things that happen in their lives that would make good stories. Have students make a list of three things they would like to write about. Tell students to be ready to start writing tomorrow.

Name:_____

Student Mini-Lesson Log

Date	I am learning to . . .	I can use this strategy in my writing.

Dolch Sight Word List

Aa	Cc (cont.)	Hh	Mm (cont.)	Ss	Uu
a	could	had	may	said	under
about	cut	has	me	saw	up
after	**Dd**	have	much	say	upon
again	did	he	must	see	us
all	do	help	my	seven	use
always	does	her	myself	shall	**Vv**
am	don't	here	**Nn**	she	very
an	done	him	never	sing	**Ww**
and	down	his	new	sit	walk
any	draw	hold	no	six	want
are	drink	hot	not	sleep	warm
around	**Ee**	how	now	slow	was
as	eat	hurt	**Oo**	small	wash
ask	eight	**Ii**	of	so	we
at	every	I	off	some	well
ate	**Ff**	if	old	soon	went
away	fall	in	on	start	were
Bb	far	into	once	stop	what
be	fast	is	one	**Tt**	when
because	find	it	only	take	where
been	first	its	open	tell	which
before	five	**Jj**	or	ten	white
best	fly	jump	our	thank	who
better	for	just	out	that	why
big	found	**Kk**	over	the	will
black	four	keep	own	their	wish
blue	from	kind	**Pp**	them	with
both	full	know	pick	then	work
bring	funny	**Ll**	play	there	would
brown	**Gg**	laugh	please	these	write
but	gave	let	pretty	they	**Yy**
buy	get	light	pull	think	yellow
by	give	like	put	this	yes
Cc	go	little	**Rr**	those	you
call	goes	live	ran	three	yours
came	going	long	read	to	
can	good	look	red	today	
carry	got	**Mm**	ride	together	
clean	green	made	right	too	
cold	grow	make	round	try	
come		many	run	two	

#50917—Getting to the Core of Writing—Level 3 © Shell Education

Fry Sight Word List

First 100

a	before	get	I	me	out	there	when
about	boy	give	if	much	put	they	which
after	but	go	in	my	said	this	who
again	by	good	is	new	see	three	will
all	can	had	it	no	she	to	with
an	come	has	just	not	so	two	work
and	day	have	know	of	some	up	would
any	did	he	like	old	take	us	you
are	do	her	little	on	that	very	your
as	down	here	long	one	the	was	
at	eat	him	make	or	there	we	
be	four	his	man	other	them	were	
been	from	how	many	our	then	what	

Second 100

also	box	five	leave	name	pretty	stand	use
am	bring	found	left	near	ran	such	want
another	call	four	let	never	read	sure	way
away	came	friend	live	next	red	tell	where
back	color	girl	look	night	right	than	while
ball	could	got	made	only	run	these	white
because	dear	hand	may	open	saw	thing	wish
best	each	high	men	over	say	think	why
better	ear	home	more	own	school	too	year
big	end	house	morning	people	seem	tree	
black	far	into	most	play	shall	under	
book	find	kind	mother	please	should	until	
both	first	last	must	present	soon	upon	

Third 100

along	clothes	eyes	green	letter	ride	small	walk
always	coat	face	grow	longer	round	start	warm
anything	cold	fall	hat	light	same	stop	wash
around	cut	fast	happy	love	sat	ten	water
ask	didn't	fat	hard	money	second	thank	woman
ate	does	fine	head	myself	set	third	write
bed	dog	fire	hear	now	seven	those	yellow
brown	don't	fly	help	o'clock	show	though	yes
buy	door	food	hold	off	sing	today	yesterday
car	dress	full	hope	once	sister	took	
carry	early	funny	hot	order	sit	town	
clean	eight	gave	jump	pair	six	try	
close	every	goes	keep	part	sleep	turn	

Short and Long Vowel Charts

Short Vowels				
a	e	i	o	u
ant	exercise	igloo	octagon	umbrella
map	leg	fish	mop	duck

Short and Long Vowel Charts (cont.)

Long Vowels				
a	**e**	**i**	**o**	**u**
<u>a</u>corn	<u>e</u>asel	<u>i</u>cicle	<u>o</u>val	<u>u</u>niform
t<u>a</u>ble	g<u>e</u>nie	b<u>i</u>ke	gl<u>o</u>be	c<u>u</u>be

Vowel Teams Chart

CVCe	CVCe	CVCe	CVCe	ai
c**a**v**e**	k**i**t**e**	n**o**s**e**	m**u**l**e**	r**ai**n

ay	ea	ee	oa	oe
h**ay**	**ea**gle	ch**ee**se	b**oa**t	t**oe**

ie	ue	au	aw	ew
t**ie**	gl**ue**	s**au**ce	h**aw**k	n**ew**s

Vowel Teams Chart (cont.)

oi	oy	ou	ow	oo
oil	t**oy**s	h**ou**se	c**ow**	m**oo**n
ar	**ur**	**ir**	**or**	**er**
guit**ar**	t**ur**tle	sk**ir**t	h**or**n	flow**er**

The Writer's Notebook

Standard

Understands the structure of Writer's Workshop

Materials

- Model Writer's Notebook
- Composition, spiral, or 3-ring notebooks
- Scissors
- Glue
- Materials and photos for decorating

Mentor Texts

- *A Writer's Notebook* by Ralph Fletcher
- *Amelia's Notebook* by Marissa Moss
- See *Mentor Text List* in Appendix C for other suggestions.

Procedures

Note: The notebook will be the foundation of the lessons that will follow. Give students the opportunity to decorate, love, and personalize their notebooks. Create a feeling of excitement and allow the time needed to send them on this exciting journey. Allow students the time to collect mementos from home or have magazines available for them to cut and paste to decorate their notebooks. Cover the notebooks with contact paper to help preserve them.

Think About Writing

1. Explain to students that today, they will be thinking and talking about how writers use a special Writer's Notebook. Tell them that just like Fletcher or Moss, the contents of their Writer's Notebooks is going to be unique.

2. Review mentor texts, if desired, and emphasize the use of a notebook. For example, in *Amelia's Notebook*, Amelia writes and draws her feelings about a number of her life experiences.

Teach

3. Tell students, "Today I will show you how to create your own Writer's Notebook." Share your model Writer's Notebook with students. Tell students why you selected the items on your cover, emphasizing how the items generate ideas for writing.

4. Explain to students that a Writer's Notebook is filled with special ideas and thoughts about an author's observations and experiences. Tell students that you will give them information to add to their notebooks that will help them as they write.

The Writer's Notebook (cont.)

Engage

5. Have students tell partners how they plan to personalize their Writer's Notebook. Listen in on conversations, making anecdotal notes. Select several students to share their thoughts and point out brilliant comments.

Apply

6. Distribute blank notebooks and materials to students. Review with students that their notebooks will be the place to keep ideas and strategies for writing. Explain that each notebook will be unique as they work to personalize them.

Write/Conference

7. Provide materials and time for students to personalize their Writer's Notebook. Be available to assist, problem solve, and observe.

Spotlight Strategy

8. Spotlight students who have begun personalizing their notebooks.

Share

9. Have students meet with someone new and share how their special Writer's Notebook is progressing. Through observations, select one or two students to share with the whole group.

Homework

Ask students to tell their parents about how they are personalizing their Writer's Notebook. Ask students to bring a few mementos or pictures to add to the covers of their notebooks.

Organizing the Writer's Notebook

Standard

Understands the structure of Writer's Workshop

Materials

- *Traits of Writing Notebook Entry* (page 54; traitswriting.pdf)
- Chart paper
- Markers
- Writer's Notebooks
- Glue
- *Traits Team Mini Posters* (pages 55–57; traitsteamposters.pdf)

Mentor Texts

- *A Writer's Notebook* by Ralph Fletcher
- *Amelia's Notebook* by Marissa Moss
- Books by favorite authors, such as Eve Bunting, Patricia Polacco, Cynthia Rylant, etc.
- See *Mentor Text List* in Appendix C for other suggestions.

Procedures

Note: Notebook entries are always glued on the left side of the notebook and skills are practiced on the right. The notebook is arranged into sections as described in Step 4 below.

Think About Writing

1. Remind students that the class has been establishing Writer's Workshop routines and creating personal Writer's Notebooks.

2. Review mentor texts, if desired. Authors often integrate all the writing traits in their stories.

Teach

3. Tell students, "Today I will show you each of the writing traits and how we will use them to organize our Writer's Notebooks." Explain that there are six very important keys to writing success, called the *traits of writing*. Display the *Traits of Writing Notebook Entry* (page 54). Briefly explain each trait to students: Ideas, Sentence Fluency, Organization, Word Choice, Voice, and Conventions.

4. Share how to organize the Writer's Notebook as you develop a classroom anchor chart on a sheet of chart paper with the following information:

    Table of Contents

    Chapter 1: Managing Writer's Workshop (10 pages)

    Chapter 2: Ideas (15 pages)

    Chapter 3: Sentence Fluency (15 pages)

    Chapter 4: Organization (15 pages)

    Chapter 5: Word Choice (15 pages)

    Chapter 6: Voice (5 pages)

    Chapter 7: Conventions (15 pages)

    Chapter 8: Assessment (5 pages)

Organizing the Writer's Notebook (cont.)

5. Have students copy the Table of Contents into the front of their notebooks.

6. Model how to glue the *Traits of Writing Notebook Entry* on the first page of the Managing Writer's Workshop section of the notebook. Show students how to count the appropriate number of blank pages in each section and glue the *Traits Team Mini Posters* (pages 55–57) on the first page of each section of the Writer's Notebook.

Engage

7. Have students talk with partners about the traits of writing and how they are essential in developing quality writing. Listen to conversations, making anecdotal notes. Have a few groups share out their thoughts. Point out brilliant comments and notice positive behaviors and knowledge.

Apply

8. Remind students that the traits of writing will help them be successful as they begin to develop their own stories. Tell students that today they will divide their Writer's Notebook into sections for each writing trait.

Write/Conference

9. Provide time for students to divide their Writer's Notebook into sections by gluing the *Traits Team Mini Posters* into the notebook. Remind students to use the anchor chart as a guide so they will have the appropriate number of blank pages in each section.

Spotlight Strategy

10. Spotlight the students who have organized their notebooks neatly and carefully.

Share

11. Have students meet with partners to share their Writer's Notebook. Choose one or two students who clearly understand the idea and have them share with the whole group.

Homework
Ask students to share what they learned about the traits of writing with their families. Challenge students to remember all six traits and to make a list.

Traits of Writing Notebook Entry

Traits of Writing

Ideas are the main topic and details that tell the writer's message. They are the heart ♥ of the story.

Sentence Fluency is the rhythm and flow of our words.

Organization includes the structure of the writing—beginning, middle, end, and more.

Word Choice is using just the right word in your writing.

Voice allows the reader to know the writer—it creates personality.

Conventions are needed to make our writing readable—CUPS!

Traits Team Mini Posters

Ida
Idea Creator

What is my writing about?

✔ Did I choose an interesting topic?

✔ Did I focus on my idea?

✔ Did I include supporting details?

✔ Did I stick to my topic?

© Shell Education

#50917—Core of Writing—Level 3

76

Simon
Sentence Builder

What kinds of sentences will I use?

✔ Did I use long, medium, and short sentences?

✔ Did I use statements and questions?

✔ Did I use different sentence beginnings?

✔ Do my sentences flow smoothly when I read them aloud?

© Shell Education

#50917—Core of Writing—Level 3

104

Traits Team Mini Posters *(cont.)*

Owen Organization Conductor

How do I plan my writing?

✔ Did I sequence my thoughts?

✔ Did I have a beginning, middle, and end?

✔ Did I hook my reader?

✔ Did I include transition words?

© Shell Education

#50917—Core of Writing—Level 3

132

Wally Word Choice Detective

What words will paint a picture for my reader?

✔ Did I use some amazing words?

✔ Did I use sensory words?

✔ Did I use action words?

✔ Did I use a variety of words?

© Shell Education

#50917—Core of Writing—Level 3

178

Traits Team Mini Posters (cont.)

Val and Van
Voice

What is the purpose of my writing?

✔ Did I write to an audience?

✔ Did I share my feelings?

✔ Did I make my reader smile, cry, or think?

✔ Does my writing sound like me?

Callie
Super Conventions
Checker

How do I edit my paper?

✔ Did I check my capitalization?

✔ Did I check my punctuation?

✔ Did I check my spelling?

✔ Did I use good spacing?

✔ Did I read over my story?

Sharing

Procedures

Note: You may need to repeat this lesson until procedures are consistent and automatic. Sharing can take place in the meeting area or at student desks, depending on the personalities in your class.

Think About Writing

1. Review with students that they have been learning the expected behaviors to manage themselves during Writer's Workshop.

2. Explain that another component of Writer's Workshop is sharing. Remind students that sharing is the last part of Writer's Workshop and will take place after students have had an opportunity to write.

Teach

3. Say, "Today I will show you how to meet with classmates to share." Tell students that sharing can take place in several different group situations. Remind them that they will need to use this time productively.

4. Explain to students that when you say, "Meet with a partner," they should each find a partner by the time you count to five on your fingers. Model this group formation. Then, ask students to practice. Use this procedure to practice forming other groups of three called *triads* and groups of four called *quads*.

5. Remind students that sharing time will be short and is not an opportunity to read an entire writing piece. Reinforce that students should share their best example on the topic of the mini-lesson that day.

Sharing (cont.)

6. Share the *Compliment and Comment Cards* (page 61) with students. Explicitly model how to use these cards to compliment and comment on students' work.

7. Revisit the anchor chart created in Managing Writer's Workshop Lesson 2 and add student insights about what Writer's Workshop looks like, sounds like, and feels like.

Engage

8. Have students meet with partners and share what they learned about sharing today. Then, ask students to move into quads and share in a larger group. Provide lots of praise as students work to form the various groups.

Apply

9. Remind students that sharing gives them opportunities to have conversations with others about their writing work. Provide students with copies of the *Sharing Notebook Entry* (page 60) and have them paste the entry into their Writer's Notebook. Distribute the *Compliment and Comment Cards* and have students store them in their writing folders.

10. Tell students that today they should either work on a piece of writing from their folders or begin a new piece.

Write/Conference

11. Provide time for students to write. All students write every day, even when mini-lessons are on managing Writer's Workshop. As students work, rotate among them to assist those who are having a difficult time getting started.

Spotlight Strategy

12. It will not be necessary to spotlight students until the end of Writer's Workshop, during the sharing component.

Share

13. Tell students that they will practice the procedures for sharing. Remind them to use the *Compliment and Comment Cards*. First, have students meet with partners. Allow students to share their writing for one minute.

14. Repeat Step 13, this time having students meet in quads. Finally, have students meet in triads. Provide praise for students who are moving to form groups and share quickly.

Homework

Ask students to think about how to meet with partners, triads, and quads. Have students tell their parents the kind of compliments they might give to a friend about his or her writing.

Sharing Notebook Entry

Compliments and Comments

Compliments

A **compliment** is something you like about your partner's writing.

- I like the way you…
- Your details made me feel…
- The order of your writing really…
- Your sentences have…
- You used words that…

Comments

A **comment** is a positive statement that will improve your partner's writing.

- Can you say more about…?
- I am confused about the order because…
- Your sentences are…
- You might use a variety of words, such as…

Compliment and Comment Cards

Directions: Cut out the cards to distribute to students. Have them use the sentence stems to compliment and make suggestions about their partner's writing.

Compliment

Tell your partner what you like about his or her writing.

"I like the way you…"

"Your details make me…"

"Your sentences have…"

Compliment

Tell your partner what you like about his or her writing.

"I like the way you…"

"Your details make me…"

"Your sentences have…"

Comment

Make a suggestion that will help your partner improve his or her writing.

"Can you say more about…?"

"I am confused about the order because…"

"You might use a variety of words, such as…"

Comment

Make a suggestion that will help your partner improve his or her writing.

"Can you say more about…?"

"I am confused about the order because…"

"You might use a variety of words, such as…"

Turn and Talk

Standard

Understands the structure of Writer's Workshop

Materials

- *Turn and Talk Notebook Entry* (page 64; turntalk.pdf)
- Writer's Notebooks

Mentor Texts

- *Swimmy* by Leo Lionni
- *Nothing Ever Happens on 90th Street* by Roni Schotter
- See *Mentor Text List* in Appendix C for other suggestions.

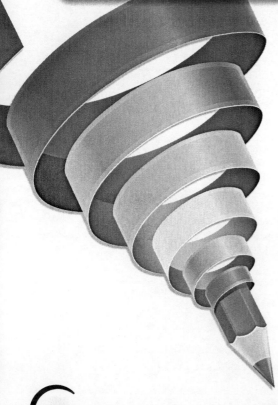

Procedures

Note: Teachers may assign writing partners that have been carefully selected based on language acquisition, or have students select their own partners. The collective personality of your class should guide your decision. You will need to repeat this lesson until the procedure is in place. Glue the notebook entry on the left side of the notebook. Students can reflect and write their thoughts on the right side.

Think About Writing

1. Tell students that they are getting the routines and procedures of Writer's Workshop in place. Remind students that it is important that they have a way to talk to others about mini-lessons and the writing that they do.

2. Review the mentor texts, if desired.

Teach

3. Tell students, "Today I will show you how to have conversations with partners." Explain to students that when you say, "Turn and Talk," that is a signal for them to immediately turn to the person who is nearby and quickly follow directions on the discussion topic. Tell students to use a "two-inch voice"—a quiet voice that can only be heard two inches away. Explicitly model for students what this will look like, then have students practice.

4. Tell students when you say, "Heads-up, Stand-up, Partner-up," that is a signal that they will immediately stand up, join a partner, and make eye contact with him or her. Then students must follow directions for the discussion topic. Model what *Heads-up, Stand-up, Partner-up* would look and sound like. Then provide time for students to practice with each other. Praise students for their efforts.

Turn and Talk (cont.)

5. Revisit the anchor chart created in Managing Writer's Workshop Lesson 2 to add student insights into what Writer's Workshop looks like, sounds like, and feels like.

Engage

6. Remind students that they practiced how to *Turn and Talk*. Ask students to talk with partners about how they will be expected to conduct themselves as they talk with other students.

Apply

7. Provide students with the *Turn and Talk Notebook Entry* (page 64) to add to their Writer's Notebook. Remind students to follow the guidelines established today when they talk with peers. Encourage students to work on a piece of writing from their folders or begin a new piece of writing as they work today.

Write/Conference

8. Provide time for students to write. Continue to have quick roving conferences until the management of Writer's Workshop is solid and successful. Provide praise to your student writers.

Spotlight Strategy

9. No spotlight strategy today. Celebrating is done through the sharing component instead.

Share

10. Have students meet with partners to share their writing. Provide students approximately two minutes to share what they think about the value of sharing time.

Homework

Ask students to think about how sharing with other students energizes their writing ideas. Also, have them think about how important it is to show respect for every writer in the room by using a two-inch voice during Writer's Workshop.

Turn and Talk Notebook Entry

Turn and Talk

Remember to...

make eye contact with your partner

find your partner quickly

use a soft, two-inch voice

ask questions to clarify thinking

stick to the writing topic

make sure each person has a turn to talk

give only compliments— no put-downs

give a compliment when needed

Guidelines for Writer's Worksho

Procedures

Note: You will need to repeat this lesson many times until procedures are in place. Adjust the guidelines to meet the needs of your class.

Think About Writing

1. Explain to students that getting Writer's Workshop routines in place creates order and efficiency in the classroom.

2. Review mentor texts, if desired. You may also want to begin reading literature from your favorite authors to begin exploring mentor texts.

Teach

3. Tell students, "Today I will show you the guidelines for Writer's Workshop and what you need to be doing to make efficient use of the time scheduled for writing." Explain that after each daily mini-lesson, students will be expected to systematically follow some guidelines.

4. Model and explain the ideas listed on the *Guidelines for Writer's Workshop Notebook Entry* (page 67). Record each idea on a sheet of chart paper as it is discussed with students. Display the anchor chart in the room and refer to it often until students effortlessly follow the guidelines.

Engage

5. Have students turn to partners to review the guidelines for Writer's Workshop. Encourage students to use the anchor chart to guide their discussions.

Guidelines for Writer's Workshop *(cont.)*

Apply

6. Encourage students to think about how the guidelines for writing will help them spend their time more efficiently. Provide students with the *Guidelines for Writer's Workshop Notebook Entry* to add to their Writer's Notebook. Encourage students to work on a piece of writing from their folders or begin a new piece as they write today.

Write/Conference

7. Provide time for students to write. There should be no conferencing about writing until procedures are firmly in place. Begin to increase the amount of sustained writing time according to the developmental levels of your students.

Spotlight Strategy

8. Spotlight a student who immediately gets to work on his/her writing. For example, "Trevor did something brilliant. He went to his seat and immediately started to write in his Writer's Notebook."

Share

9. Have students meet with partners to share what they wrote today. Provide approximately two minutes for students to share. Choose one or two students, and have them share with the whole group.

10. Do a group reflection on how the guidelines will help students become better writers. Continue to add to the anchor chart created in Managing Writer's Workshop Lesson 1.

Homework

Ask students to think about the guidelines introduced today. Have students write two sentences to explain how knowing what is expected of them will make them more disciplined writers.

Guidelines for Writer's Workshop Notebook Er

Guidelines for Writer's Workshop

- You must always be writing or sketching in your Writer's Notebook.

- Always include the date of your work.

- Keep your drafts in your writing folder.

- Work quietly so that everyone can do their best thinking.

- Write on every other line when drafting.

- Request a conference when you are ready for a final draft.

- Use a soft, two-inch voice.

- Use your best handwriting or the computer on a final draft.

- Place your final draft in the editor's basket.

- Record what you have learned as a writer when you have completed a project.

Remember...

A writer's work is never done!

Teacher and Peer Conferences

Standard

Understands the structure of Writer's Workshop

Materials

- *Peer Conference Notebook Entry* (page 70; peerconference.pdf)
- Chart paper
- Markers
- *Compliment and Comment Cards* (page 61; complicommentcards.pdf)
- Writing folder
- Writer's Notebooks

Mentor Texts

- *A Writer's Notebook* by Ralph Fletcher
- *Amelia's Notebook* by Marissa Moss
- See *Mentor Text List* in Appendix C for other suggestions.

Procedures

Note: You may assign writing partners or allow students to form partners on their own. The collective personality of your class should guide your decision. Repeat this lesson until the procedure is in place. Remind students that they should always glue the notebook entry pages on the left side of their notebook.

Think About Writing

1. Explain to students that it is important to build teacher and peer conferencing into Writer's Workshop. Tell students that meeting with another person to share their writing is how they will get compliments and comments for improving their writing.

2. Review mentor texts, if desired.

Teach

3. Tell students, "Today I will show you how to meet with a teacher or partner in an assigned place in the room to review your writing."

4. Explain that getting feedback from another person is a great way to improve writing. Show students a designated area of the room for peer conferences. Then, explicitly model for students how to sit shoulder-to-shoulder with a partner so that they can read each other's work. Review how to give compliments and comments on writing. (See Managing Writer's Workshop Lesson 6.)

5. Review the questions on the *Peer Conference Notebook Entry* (page 70). Add each question to a sheet of chart paper and discuss each one. Model what a teacher conference will look like with a student. Next have students practice peer conferencing. Revisit the anchor chart created in Managing Writer's Workshop Lesson 2 and add student insights about what Writer's Workshop looks like, sounds like, and feels like.

Teacher and Peer Conferences *(cont.)*

Engage

6. Have students meet with partners by the time you count to five with your fingers. Provide lots of praise for students who quickly meet with partners. Remind students to use the *Compliment and Comment Cards* (page 61) in their writing folders to help them make appropriate comments about writing work.

Apply

7. Encourage students to schedule weekly conferences with peers or with you in order to get feedback on their writing work. Provide students with the *Peer Conference Notebook Entry* to add to their Writer's Notebook. Tell students that today they can work on drafting a new piece of writing or continue with something from their folder.

Write/Conference

8. Provide time for students to write. Select two students to move to the designated peer conferencing area of your room and assist them in providing feedback to each other. Continue to select pairs of students to peer conference, paying close attention to the conferencing partners.

Spotlight Strategy

9. Spotlight a student who is revising his/her work based on a peer conference. For example, "Allison is doing something brilliant. She is working on one small detail that was suggested by her partner to improve the quality of her writing."

Share

10. Have students *Turn and Talk* with partners about how providing compliments and comments during conferences will support their writing.

Homework

Ask students to think about the procedures for meeting with a peer to conference. Have students write one compliment and one comment they could give to a partner about his or her writing.

Peer Conference Notebook Entry

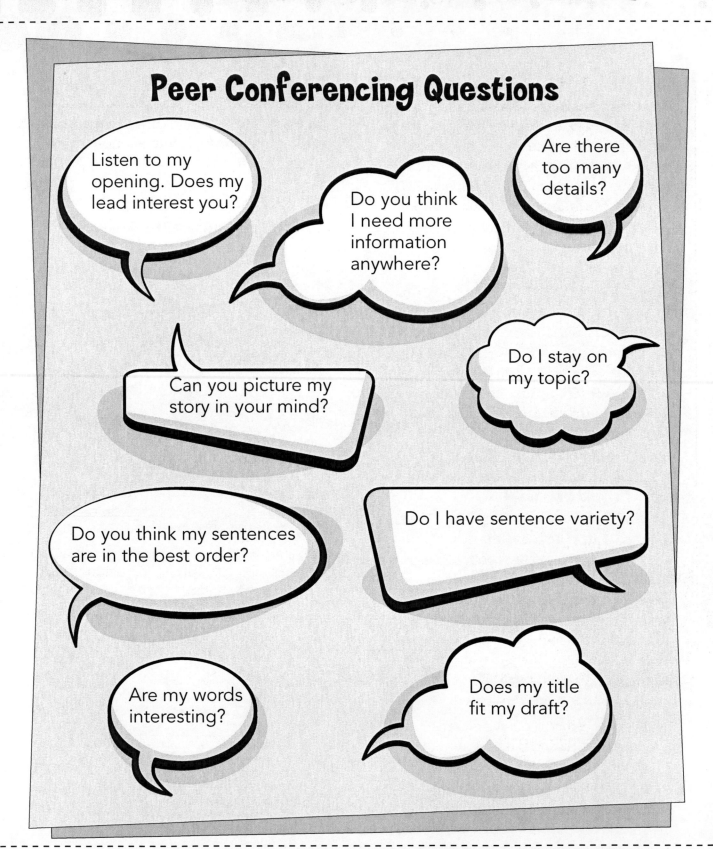

Peer Conferencing Questions

Listen to my opening. Does my lead interest you?

Do you think I need more information anywhere?

Are there too many details?

Can you picture my story in your mind?

Do I stay on my topic?

Do you think my sentences are in the best order?

Do I have sentence variety?

Are my words interesting?

Does my title fit my draft?

The Five-Step Writing Process

Standard

Understands the structure of Writer's Workshop

Materials

- *The Five-Step Writing Process Notebook Entry* (page 73; fivestepprocess.pdf)
- Chart paper
- Markers
- Writer's Notebooks
- Index cards
- Writing samples *(optional)*

Mentor Texts

- *Amelia's Notebook* by Marissa Moss
- *The Sloppy Copy Slip Up* by DyAnne DiSalvo
- *Look at My Book: How Kids Can Write and Illustrate Terrific Books* by Loreen Leedy
- See *Mentor Text List* in Appendix C for other suggestions.

Procedures

Note: Refer to the five-step writing process (prewriting, drafting, revising, editing, and publishing) as students work through the writing process on numerous projects throughout the year.

Think About Writing

1. Remind students that they have been developing their writing by using a variety of ideas and talking about how authors write. Explain that writing can be separated into simple steps that make the process more manageable. These simple steps will help them improve their finished writing.

2. Review mentor texts, if desired.

Teach

3. Tell students, "Today I will show you each step of the Five-Step Writing Process to help you become better writers."

4. Record each step from *The Five-Step Writing Process Notebook Entry* (page 73) onto a sheet of chart paper. Discuss each step with students as you write it. If possible, display student work samples that show each step of the process. For example, for prewriting, you could show a graphic organizer.

Engage

5. Have students talk with partners to name and briefly discuss the steps of the writing process. Encourage students to talk across their five fingers and name each of the five steps. Students may refer to the anchor chart, if necessary. Provide approximately two or three minutes of talk time.

The Five-Step Writing Process (cont.)

Apply

6. Remind students to use the steps of the writing process to make their writing the best it can be. Provide students with *The Five-Step Writing Process Notebook Entry* to add to their Writer's Notebook. Today, students can revise or edit an existing writing piece or begin with a new idea.

Write/Conference

7. Provide students time to write. Prepare index cards with the five steps of the writing process. Gather a small group at a table or the carpet to reteach the steps as needed. Explain and clarify each step. Use concrete samples to demonstrate. Allow four or five minutes to reteach. Then begin to rotate around the room and individually confer.

Spotlight Strategy

8. Spotlight a student who is using an idea from a draft in his/her writing. For example, "Writers, you rock! Notice how Daniel is capturing a moment from an experience in his draft." Echo your thinking from the mini-lesson strategy.

Share

9. Have students share their writing with partners. Provide approximately two minutes for students to talk.

Homework

Ask students to think about how the Five-Step Writing Process can help their writing.

The Five-Step Writing Process

1   **Prewriting:**
Think about your topic:
brainstorm and plan

2   **Drafting:**
Write your thoughts on paper:
rough copy

3   **Revising:**
Reread, rethink, and refine:
check organization and add
details and interesting words

4   **Editing:**
Review and correct:
Capitalization
Usage
Punctuation
Spelling

5   **Publishing:**
Complete the final copy and
share your writing with others

Ideas

Thinking, Thinking, Thinking!

Ideas are the heart of writing. The purpose of this section is to help students generate ideas for writing. The lessons assist students in exploring the ideas of authors through mentor texts and in discovering unique writing ideas in their own lives. Through class-created anchor charts and individually created lists, students will collect plenty of ideas so when they begin to write, they are not at a loss for topics. Students are encouraged to keep their ideas in their writing folders so the ideas are readily at hand. Lessons in this section include the following:

- Lesson 1: My Expert List (page 77)

- Lesson 2: I Can Write Like That! (page 80)

- Lesson 3: Collecting Ideas (page 83)

- Lesson 4: People We Love (page 86)

- Lesson 5: Fabulous Faunae (page 89)

- Lesson 6: Story Seeds (page 92)

- Lesson 7: Famous People I Admire (page 96)

- Lesson 8: What Should I Write? (page 99)

The *Ida, Idea Creator* poster (page 76) can be displayed in the room to provide a visual reminder for students that ideas is one of the traits of writing. You may wish to introduce this poster during the first lesson on ideas. Then, refer to the poster when teaching other lessons on ideas to refresh students' memories and provide them with questions to help hone their writing topics.

Ida
Idea Creator

What is my writing about?

❧ Did I choose an interesting topic?

❧ Did I focus on my idea?

❧ Did I include supporting details?

❧ Did I stick to my topic?

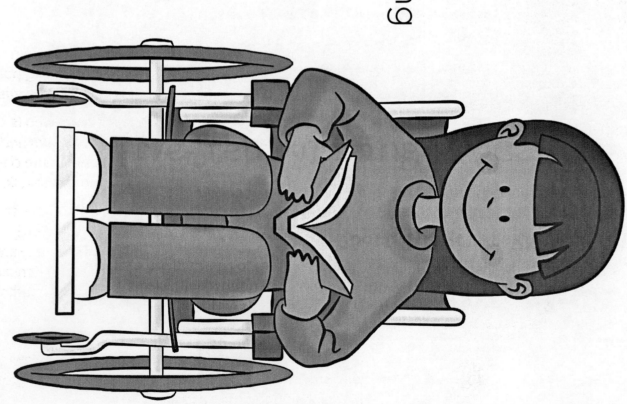

My Expert List

Procedures
Note: Add to this list throughout the year to build an extensive "expert list." Students who have broad interests and wide-ranging lists rarely say, "I don't have anything to write about!"

Think About Writing
1. Remind students that they have been creating a personal Writer's Notebook and developing ideas to write about. Explain that we are experts on the things that happen in our lives, and that many authors write about those things.

2. Review mentor texts if desired, and emphasize the author's area of expertise. For example, "Cynthia Rylant is truly an expert about families, and she turned her expertise into fabulous stories about her life and family."

Teach
3. Tell students, "Today I will show you how to create an expert list so that you will always have a beginning point for writing ideas that will grow and develop into stories."

4. Explain to students that an expert is someone who is knowledgeable about a topic. Have students *Turn and Talk* to partners about some of the experiences the class has shared together. Provide time for students to talk.

5. Write the title *Our Expert List* on a sheet of chart paper. Have students share the experiences they discussed and list them on the chart paper. Tell students that they are experts on those topics because they have experienced them. Explain to students that these are ideas that they can use as writing topics.

6. Remind students that they have had many individual experiences. Share your personal expert list. Review with students that their personal expert lists make great ideas for writing topics as well.

My Expert List (cont.)

Engage

7. Ask students to think of ideas for their personal expert lists. Show students how to use the index finger of one hand to touch each finger of the opposite hand as they name and count their ideas. Encourage students to have at least five ideas. Provide approximately two minutes for students to gather their ideas.

Apply

8. Encourage students to be on the lookout for experiences in their everyday lives. Tell students to jot down their ideas so they can be remembered as writing ideas. Provide students with the *My Expert List Notebook Entry* (page 79) to add to their Writer's Notebook. Have students work on the *Your Turn* section before proceeding to their writing folders.

Write/Conference

9. Provide time for students to create their own expert lists. As students work, rotate among them, asking questions and facilitating student ideas. Remember to make anecdotal notes to share ideas with the class. Notice and engage those students who are reluctant.

Spotlight Strategy

10. Point out examples of students adding worthy ideas to their expert lists. Ask selected students to share with the class. This helps promote ideas for other students.

Share

11. Ask students to meet with a writing partner and share the best items on their expert lists. Encourage students to give a couple of ideas to their writing partners and get a couple of ideas from their partners.

Homework

Have students look for ideas of things that can be added to their expert lists. Encourage them to write down their ideas so the ideas can be added to their Writer's Notebook.

My Expert List Notebook Entry

My Expert List

Think about...

- Family
- Favorite vacations
- Traditions
- Favorite books
- Special moments
- Favorite characters
- Friends
- Favorite places
- Special treasures
- School
- Happy/sad things
- Hobbies
- Movies

- Sports
- Music
- Authors
- Pets/animals
- Famous people
- Funny things
- Scary things
- Best life lessons
- Worst life lessons
- Heroes
- Fair/unfair
- I can…
- I want to…

Your Turn:

Make your own expert list in your Writer's Notebook.

I Can Write Like That!

Standards

- Uses prewriting strategies to plan written work
- Writes expository compositions

Materials

- *I Can Write Like That! Notebook Entry* (page 82; canwritelikethat.pdf)
- Chart paper
- Markers
- Writer's Notebooks

Mentor Texts

- *The Important Book* by Margaret Wise Brown
- *Everybody Needs a Rock* by Byrd Baylor
- Recommended literature for CCSS or Core Reading Program
- See *Mentor Text List* in Appendix C for other suggestions.

Procedures

Note: This lesson uses *The Important Book* as a model; however, any mentor text can be used. Revisit this lesson throughout the year using a variety of literature. Use quality literature to model the author's craft and have students use models and patterns to build the confidence to create their own stories.

Think About Writing

1. Explain to students that authors generate ideas to spin into stories and compositions about their own lives. As writers, they can get writing ideas from studying the craft of other authors. Then, those ideas can be used to develop their own writing.

2. Review mentor texts of your choice, and emphasize the author's use of patterned text. For example, in *The Important Book* the author uses a simple pattern with a main idea statement, details to support the statement, and a wrap-up that connects back to the main idea. Her subjects are simple things in nature—grass, snow, rain, flowers—as well as simple things you need, such as shoes.

Teach

3. Tell students, "Today I will show you how to write like the authors of literature you know. We will use different patterns, but you can build on your own thinking to craft your stories."

4. Display and discuss the *I Can Write Like That! Notebook Entry* (page 82). Ask students to help identify the text pattern in *The Important Book*. Create a template of the text pattern on a sheet of chart paper. For example, the template for *The Important Book* would be:

I Can Write Like That! *(cont.)*

Topic: _____

Opening Statement: The important thing about _____ is that _____.

3 Details:

1. _____

2. _____

3. _____

Closing Statement: But, the important thing about _____ is that _____.

5. Model how to use the text pattern to write about a topic of your choice.

Engage

6. Ask students to think of ideas they can use that follow the same pattern as a mentor text. Have students share their ideas and how they might expand the ideas into stories with partners. Ask students to think of details and rehearse their writing plan using their fingers. Provide approximately three minutes for students to talk.

Apply

7. Tell students that literature, both fiction and nonfiction, gives them room to grow in writing and supports them until they are ready to write independently. Provide students with the *I Can Write Like That! Notebook Entry* to add to their Writer's Notebook. Have students work on the *Your Turn* section before proceeding to their writing folders.

Write/Conference

8. Provide time for students to write. As students work, rotate among them to have conversations with them about their writing. Begin conversations with students by asking, "What is going well in your writing?" Make astute observations in your Conferring Notebook to help you make decisions about your next writing plan.

Spotlight Strategy

9. Spotlight a student who is imitating an author's craft. For example, "Jill has taken an idea from literature and is beginning to expand it into her own story. Just listen to how Jill imitated our author's pattern."

Share

10. Have students share the pattern they used in their writing today. Provide approximately two minutes for students to talk.

Homework

Ask students to make a list of at least two stories they might like to weave into their own stories with a twist.

I Can Write Like That! Notebook Entry

I Can Write Like That!

Studying the writing of your favorite authors gives you ideas and techniques to experiment with in your own writing.

Try this pattern, modified from *The Important Book* by Margaret Wise Brown.

Topic: Bananas

Opening Statement: The important thing about bananas is that they taste great and are very nutritious.

3 Details:

1. Bananas grow in hot, humid, rainy weather, such as jungle.

2. The tiny bananas grow down first, then out, and finally up.

3. In 90 days, the fruit is ready for harvest.

Closing Statement: But the important thing about bananas is that they taste good and are good for you.

Your Turn:

Write about a topic using the text pattern from *The Important Book*. Select a topic like friends, pets, animals, food, or nature.

Collecting Ideas

Standard

Uses prewriting strategies to plan written work

Materials

- Manila envelopes or sheet protectors
- Magazines, photographs, newspapers
- *Collection Pocket Label Template* (page 85; collectionpocket.pdf)
- Writing folders

Mentor Texts

- *A Writer's Notebook* by Ralph Fletcher
- See *Mentor Text List* in Appendix C for other suggestions.

Procedures

Note: You might want to keep a digital camera in the classroom to build a class Collection Pocket.

Think About Writing

1. Tell students that every writing piece begins with an idea. Explain that writers collect ideas for writing in different ways. Many authors' ideas come from their experiences and it is helpful to collect pictures that reflect activities or memories.

2. Review mentor text, if desired, and emphasize the author's writing ideas.

Teach

3. Tell students, "Today I will show you how to build a Collection Pocket of things you are really interested in. The items in the pocket will help you come up with ideas for writing."

4. Display manila envelopes or sheet protectors. Tell students that these will become their Collection Pockets for ideas. Explain that anything that provides an idea for writing can be placed in a Collection Pocket. Magazine pictures, photographs, or articles from newspapers can be saved in students' pockets in case they ever need a writing idea.

Engage

5. Have students *Turn and Talk* to partners about places they may find ideas for their Collection Pockets.

Collecting Ideas (cont.)

Apply

6. Provide students with the *Collection Pocket Label Template* (page 85) and a manila envelope or sleeve protector so that they can make their own Collection Pockets. Remind students that they can continually add items to their Collection Pockets throughout the year so they never run out of ideas. Provide students with Collection Pockets to put in their writing folders and tell them that today they will start to fill their pockets with ideas.

Write/Conference

7. Provide students with magazines, photographs, or newspapers to add ideas to their Collection Pockets. As students work, rotate among them to conference. Ask questions, such as, "What are some ideas that you want to place in your Collection Pocket?" "How will this help you become better at developing ideas?"

Spotlight Strategy

8. Point out examples of students who quickly moved into their activity and knew exactly how to generate a Collection Pocket.

Share

9. Have students meet with partners to share how they are going to collect ideas for their Collection Pockets.

Homework

Have students look for at least five items to place in their Collection Pockets. Remind them to look at magazine pictures, photographs, or newspapers.

Collection Pocket Label Template

Directions: Cut out the Collection Pocket Labels. Provide one for each student and have them glue the label on to their Collection Pocket.

Collection Pocket	**Collection Pocket**
Collection Pocket	**Collection Pocket**
Collection Pocket	**Collection Pocket**

People We Love

Standard

Uses prewriting strategies to plan written work

Materials

- *People I Love Notebook Entry* (page 88; peopleilove.pdf)
- Chart paper
- Markers
- Writer's Notebook

Mentor Texts

- *Thank You, Mr. Falker* by Patricia Polacco
- *The Old Woman Who Named Things* by Cynthia Rylant
- *Love You Forever* by Robert Munsch
- See *Mentor Text List* in Appendix C for other suggestions.

Procedures

Note: Students may continue to build their People I Love list throughout the year. After this mini-lesson, use the narrative paragraph mini-lesson (Organization Lesson 3) to move into drafting. Revisit this lesson in celebration of Mother's Day, Father's Day, Grandparents Day, National Education Day (teachers), and Author's Tea.

Think About Writing

1. Explain to students that they have special people in their lives who influence who they will become. That person may be a parent, grandparent, neighbor, teacher, or someone in the community. These special people and their influence become story seeds that can flourish and grow.

2. Review mentor texts, if desired, and emphasize the author's use of special people in the text.

Teach

3. Tell students, "Today I will show you how to make lists of the people we love so they can be saved as ideas for future writing pieces."

4. Display and discuss the *People I Love Notebook Entry* (page 88).

5. Label a sheet of chart paper *People I Love*. Model how to create a list of special people and two or three points about why each person holds a special place in your heart. Follow the format on the notebook entry.

Engage

6. Have students turn and talk to partners about five important people in their lives. Have students use their fingers to count as they name their important people. Provide approximately two minutes for partners to generate ideas.

People We Love (cont.)

Apply

7. Remind students that the special people in their lives can become ideas for them as they write. Provide students with the *People I Love Notebook Entry* to add to their Writer's Notebook. Have students work on the *Your Turn* section before proceeding to their writing folders.

Write/Conference

8. Have students begin to fill in their People I Love lists with some specific memories or details about each person. Encourage them to follow the format on the notebook entry. As students work, begin working with small groups or hold individual conferences. Make observations of student writing behaviors to help guide your future instruction.

Spotlight Strategy

9. Spotlight lists students have generated. For example, "Writers, you rock! Just listen to this list of special people!" Spotlight one or two students' lists.

Share

10. Have students share their best three ideas with partners. Provide approximately two minutes for students to share.

Homework

Have students make lists of at least five people special to them. Allow time for students to add the new names to their lists the next day.

People I Love Notebook Entry

People I Love

Authors write about special people in their lives. Make a list of special people in your life and list one or two interesting details, such as something you enjoy doing together, or all of those characteristics that make them special.

Name: Esther
Who is he/she? My mom

Interesting Details:
1. loves cats
2. great cook
3. enjoys shopping
4. likes to hike

Your Turn:

Make a list of people you love. Use the form shown above as your model. The details you add can be developed into your own stories.

#50917—Getting to the Core of Writing—Level 3 © Shell Education

Fabulous Faunae

Standards

- Uses prewriting strategies to plan written work
- Uses a variety of strategies to plan research

Materials

- Chart paper
- Markers
- Pictures of animals
- *Fabulous Faunae Notebook Entry* (page 91; fabulousfaunae.pdf)
- Writer's Notebooks

Mentor Texts

- *Diary of a Worm* by Doreen Cronin
- *Crab Moon* by Ruth Horowitz
- See *Mentor Text List* in Appendix C for other suggestions.

Procedures

Note: Use literature to connect to informational texts. The CCSS resource book list or your Core Reading program may provide additional literature resources.

Think About Writing

1. Explain to students that as they become experienced writers, they will be able to add more information to develop and support their writing projects. Tell students that authors use lists and outlines to gather information for writing.

2. Review mentor texts, if desired, and emphasize the author's use of animal life.

Teach

3. Tell students, "Today I will show you how to gather a list of animals that can be used as topics for informative writing or research projects."

4. Label a sheet of chart paper *Fabulous Faunae*. Explain to students that "faunae" means animals. Display the animal pictures. Allow students to briefly comment on each picture. Then, write the name of the animal on the chart.

5. Display and discuss the *Fabulous Faunae Notebook Entry* (page 91).

6. Model how to use the format of the notebook entry to develop an animal facts list. Select an animal from the chart created in Step 4 and add details by answering the questions on the notebook entry page. Model and think aloud each step as you gather and record information on chart paper. If the answers to the questions are not known, discuss with students what resources are available to them to find the information.

Fabulous Faunae *(cont.)*

Engage

7. Have students turn to partners and name animals that are of interest to them. Encourage students to use their fingers to count at least five animals. Remind students that they will need to spend time finding information and writing about the animals they choose, so they should choose only animals that intrigue them. Provide approximately three minutes for students to talk.

Apply

8. Remind students of the importance of making lists to record ideas for future writing pieces. Provide students with the *Fabulous Faunae Notebook Entry* to add to their Writer's Notebook. Have students work on the *Your Turn* section before proceeding to their writing folders.

Write/Conference

9. Provide time for students to make their own faunae lists. Check the group for awareness of task. If necessary, reteach a small group with additional animal pictures to promote excitement and motivation.

Spotlight Strategy

10. Spotlight students who use their time wisely to make a list of animals to research. For example, "Spectacular list-making today. Demetry spent his time wisely and his effort is paying off!"

Share

11. Have students move into teams of four to share. Tell students to share their best ideas. Encourage everyone to give an idea and take an idea from someone. Remind students to use a two-inch voice in the classroom.

Homework

Have students make lists of five additional ideas for fabulous faunae. Encourage students to sort through magazines and newspapers or watch television to find ideas.

Fabulous Faunae Notebook Entry

Fabulous Faunae

Authors make lists and outlines to gather information for their writing. It helps them organize their ideas and make sure they don't leave out any important information in their writing.

Your Turn:

To begin your fabulous faunae research:

1. Make a list of animals that interest you.

2. Think about what you already know about your topic.

3. Decide what you want to learn about your topic.

4. Gather resources to collect information.

5. Use the questions below to guide your research and collect facts and information about your topic.

- What is the name of your animal?
- What does it look like?
- Where does it live?
- What food does it eat?
- How does it survive?
- What are other interesting facts about your animal?

The facts and information you gather can be developed into your own informational stories.

Story Seeds

Standard

Uses prewriting strategies to plan written work

Materials

- *Story Seeds Model Chart* (page 95; storyseedschart.pdf)
- *Story Seeds Notebook Entry* (page 94; storyseeds.pdf)
- Our Expert List anchor chart (from Ideas Lesson 1)
- Writer's Notebook

Mentor Texts

- *Shortcut* by Donald Crews
- *Shoes Like Miss Alice's* by Angela Johnson
- *All the Places to Love* by Patricia MacLachlan
- *A Chair for My Mother* by Vera William
- See *Mentor Text List* in Appendix C for other suggestions.

Procedures

Note: Narrowing topics is a difficult task for many students. Using visual representations or adding kinesthetic movement—for example, big arms for watermelon and pinched fingers for seeds—may support students in understanding how to limit the scope of their topics.

Think About Writing

1. Remind students that they have been developing ideas to write about by creating lists, reading literature, and thinking about their own experiences. Explain that sometimes topics from their lists are too big, so today they will begin to practice narrowing their topics into manageable pieces.

2. Review mentor texts, if desired, and emphasize the author's focus on one specific event.

Teach

3. Tell students, "Today I will show you how to begin with a big idea—like a watermelon—and then narrow that idea down to just a tiny topic, like a tiny seed." Display the *Story Seeds Model Chart* (page 95) for students. Explain that writers understand that readers like to know about small moments—things that happened in 20 minutes or five minutes, or even two minutes, and that readers like to know all the details about those moments.

4. Display and discuss the *Story Seeds Notebook Entry* (page 94).

5. Model how to review the ideas from the Our Expert List anchor chart. Draw a small seed icon next to the small moment topics.

Story Seeds (cont.)

Engage

6. Have students work with partners to look over their writing and decide whether they are big watermelon topic stories or small moment seed stories.

Apply

7. Provide students with the *Story Seeds Notebook Entry* to add to their Writer's Notebook. Have students work on the *Your Turn* section before proceeding to their writing folders. Tell students that today they will each write a personal narrative about a small moment. Encourage students to stop and think before they begin writing their personal narratives—is this a small seed story or a big watermelon story?

Write/Conference

8. Provide time for students to write. As students work, rotate around the room to help them select focused topics. Rove and confer to support student writing in a sequential and detailed fashion.

Spotlight Strategy

9. Spotlight students who clearly understand how to narrow a topic to a small seed story with details that are sequential and focused.

Share

10. Have students turn to partners to share how they tightened up their writing topics using small seed ideas.

Homework

Ask students to make a list of three small moments about their families, neighbors, and friends.

Story Seeds Notebook Entry

Story Seeds

Authors choose specific ideas when selecting their writing topics. They may start with a BIG idea, but they narrow their topic to create a SMALL moment story with descriptive details that capture their readers.

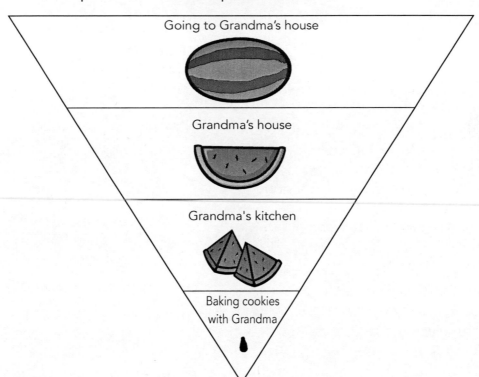

Going to Grandma's house

Grandma's house

Grandma's kitchen

Baking cookies
with Grandma

Your Turn:

Arrange these topic ideas from the BIG watermelon to the SMALL seed. Then narrow your own expert topics into small seed moments.

Example 1	Example 2
Training my dog	I like baseball
My pets	Hitting a home run
Teaching Champ to speak	I like sports
My dog Champ	My baseball team

Story Seeds Model Chart

Directions: Display the chart below for students and explain how readers like to know the details of main events. Use the watermelon example below to explain how a big idea (watermelon) narrows down to a small moment story (seed).

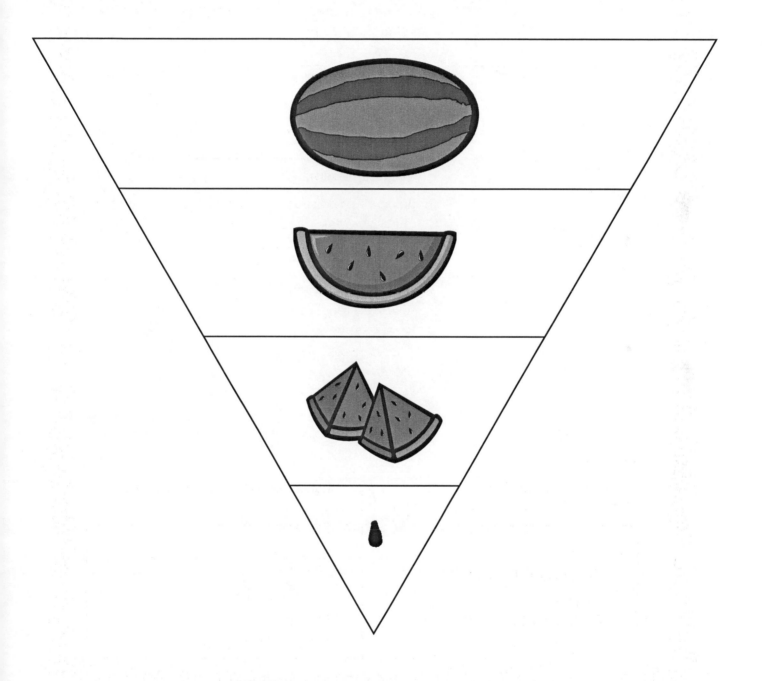

Famous People I Admire

Standard

Uses prewriting strategies to plan written work

Materials

- Chart paper
- Markers
- *Famous People I Admire Notebook Entry* (page 98; famouspeopleadmire.pdf)
- Writer's Notebooks

Mentor Texts

- *50 American Heroes Every Kid Should Meet* by Dennis Denenberg
- *Dare to Dream! 25 Extraordinary Lives* by Sandra McLeod Humphrey
- DK Biography series for kids
- See *Mentor Text List* in Appendix C for other suggestions.

Procedures

Note: Use this lesson to encourage students to dream impossible dreams. Study the lives of famous people to determine how they handled anxiety and pressure while achieving the impossible. Students can make connections to their own lives or the lives of their families. Use literature from CCSS.

Think About Writing

1. Explain to students that writers sometimes look to the lives of famous people they admire and respect to find encouragement.

2. Review mentor texts, if desired, and emphasize the famous people described in the book.

Teach

3. Tell students, "Today I will show you how to gather ideas to write a biographical opinion. A biographical opinion is your view about the life of a famous person."

4. Label a sheet of chart paper *Famous People I Admire*. Add names of people you admire to the list. Think aloud as you add the names of the people and some of the reasons you admire them. List a wide range of famous people, including:

- government officials, such as the president, a senator, a mayor, or a board member
- historical figures, such as Abraham Lincoln or Anne Frank
- scientists, such as Albert Einstein or Marie Curie
- inventors, such as the Wright Brothers
- heroines, such as Amelia Earhart
- sports idols, such as Jackie Robinson
- current-day famous people, such as sports figures or TV and movie personalities

#50917—Getting to the Core of Writing—Level 3 © Shell Education

Famous People I Admire (cont.)

5. Display and discuss the *Famous People I Admire Notebook Entry* (page 98). Model for students how to select a famous person and note a few details about him or her.

Engage

6. Ask students to work with partners to name famous people that they admire and respect. Have students tell their partners reasons for their positive opinions of these people. Provide approximately two minutes for discussion.

Apply

7. Encourage students to think about how important people have influenced the way they think, act, or live. Remind students to give reasons why they admire the famous people they are writing about. Provide students with the *Famous People I Admire Notebook Entry* to add to their Writer's Notebook. Have students work on the *Your Turn* section before proceeding to their writing folders.

Write/Conference

8. Provide time for students to create lists of famous people. Many times, students have little general knowledge beyond their family or community. Work with a small group and assist them by naming important people who influence our lives in significant ways.

Spotlight Strategy

9. Spotlight students who make lists of people they admire with supporting details. For example, "Spotlight on Martin! You're right on target. Listen to this clever list of famous people."

Share

10. Have students share their ideas with partners. Ask students to name three special people from their lists. Then have students choose one person and share two reasons why they respect that person. Provide approximately three minutes for students to share.

Homework

Have students talk with their families about famous people they may want to write about. Ask students to make a list of five people they want to add to their lists in their notebook.

Famous People I Admire Notebook Entry

Famous People I Admire

Authors write about famous people they admire and respect.

George Washington

- military and political leader
- commander of Continental Army
- nation's first president

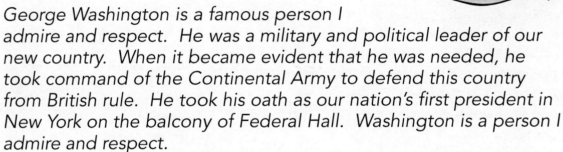

Use your ideas to develop a paragraph or story about your famous person. For example:

George Washington is a famous person I admire and respect. He was a military and political leader of our new country. When it became evident that he was needed, he took command of the Continental Army to defend this country from British rule. He took his oath as our nation's first president in New York on the balcony of Federal Hall. Washington is a person I admire and respect.

Your Turn:

Make a list of important people in your Writer's Notebook. Give two or three reasons to support your thinking. Need an idea? How about…

- Charles Lindbergh
- Oprah Winfrey
- Mahatma Gandhi
- Martin Luther King Jr.
- Bill Gates
- Mae Jemison
- Abraham Lincoln

What Should I Write?

Standards

- Uses prewriting strategies to plan written work
- Uses strategies to write for a variety of purposes

Materials

- Writer's Notebooks
- *What Should I Write? Notebook Entry* (page 101; whatshouldwrite.pdf)
- A variety of writing samples: menus, picture books, ABC books, newspaper and magazine articles, brochures, how-to manuals, letters, etc.

Mentor Texts

- *Read Anything Good Lately?* by Susan Allen
- Other CCSS literature
- See *Mentor Text List* in Appendix C for other suggestions.

Procedures

Note: Providing options for writing purposes and types promotes interest among reluctant writers. Creating travel brochures and alphabet books related to social studies and science themes incorporates writing across the curriculum. Build a bulletin board with types of writing to create enthusiasm and motivation.

Think About Writing

1. Explain that authors write for different purposes and in different formats. They may write a speech to persuade an audience to recycle, a travel brochure to inform readers of a summer camp, or a book of poetry for a reader's entertainment.

2. Review mentor texts, if desired, and emphasize the author's purpose in writing the book.

Teach

3. Tell students, "Today I will show you a variety of writing types that you may wish to explore in your own writing, depending on the purpose." Explain that in Writer's Workshop, students can explore many different types of writing, for example, menus, advertisements, poetry, or letters.

4. Share examples of writing with students, and discuss the author's purpose in each example. Display the various samples on a bulletin board and encourage students to bring in other examples to add to the display.

5. Display and discuss the *What Should I Write? Notebook Entry* (page 101). Review the various purposes for writing and the types of writing within each purpose.

What Should I Write? *(cont.)*

Engage

6. Have students meet with partners to share the type of writing they would like to explore. Remind students to consider the purposes of their writing. Provide approximately two minutes for students to share.

Apply

7. Remind students that there are many different kinds of writing. Explain that the notebook entry for today will help provide them with ideas. Provide students with the *What Should I Write? Notebook Entry* to add to their Writer's Notebook. Have students work on the *Your Turn* section before proceeding to their writing folders.

Write/Conference

8. Provide time for students to write. Scan the room to make certain that all students have a focus and have selected something to work on. Assist students who do not get started right away. Make notes on the success of this lesson and adjust future planning as needed.

Spotlight Strategy

9. Spotlight students who add interesting ideas to their notebook. For example, "Look at all of Samantha's amazing ideas!"

Share

10. Select one or two students who clearly understood the idea and have them share their writing with the whole group.

Homework

Ask students to search for different kinds of writing and think about the author's purpose for writing. Have students bring one example to share with the class.

#50917—Getting to the Core of Writing—Level 3 © Shell Education

What Should I Write? Notebook E:

What Should I Write?

Authors write for different purposes and in different formats. They may write a speech to persuade an audience to recycle, a travel brochure to inform readers of a summer camp, or a book of poetry for a reader's entertainment. Just remember:

P.I.E.

Persuade	Inform	Entertain
Brochure	ABC book	Fairy tale
Commercial	Advertisement	Journal entry
Poster	Invitation	Picture book
	Newspaper article	Short story
	Recipe	
	TV news report	

Your Turn:

Think of other types of writing. Decide on the authors' purposes. Add and label three columns on your notebook page. As you discover purposes for writing, add them to your list. Use these ideas when creating your own writing project.

Sentence Fluency

Getting Started

Sentence fluency helps make writing interesting. It is a trait that allows writers to add interest to their writing. By changing the sentence length, and where words are placed next to each other in the sentence, writers are able to help guide the reader through their work. Authors with good sentence fluency know the techniques needed to construct sentences that flow and have rhythm. The lessons assist students in exploring parts of sentences, ways sentences are built, and ways to expand sentences to develop more interesting ideas. Lessons in this section include the following:

- Lesson 1: Popcorn Sentences (page 105)
- Lesson 2: A Simple Sentence (page 108)
- Lesson 3: The Compound Subject (page 111)
- Lesson 4: Types of Sentences (page 114)
- Lesson 5: The Compound Verb (page 117)
- Lesson 6: The Compound Sentence (page 120)
- Lesson 7: Rubber Band Sentences (page 123)
- Lesson 8: A Complex Sentence (page 127)

The *Simon, Sentence Builder* poster (page 104) can be displayed in the room to provide a visual reminder for students that sentence fluency is one of the traits of writing. You may wish to introduce this poster during the first lesson on sentence fluency. Then, refer to the poster when teaching other lessons on sentence fluency to refresh students' memories and provide them with questions to help guide them as they create sentences.

Simon

Sentence Builder

What kinds of sentences will I use?

✔ Did I use long, medium, and short sentences?

✔ Did I use statements and questions?

✔ Did I use different sentence beginnings?

✔ Do my sentences flow smoothly when I read them aloud?

Popcorn Sentences

Standards

- Uses a variety of sentence structures in writing
- Uses strategies to draft and revise written work

Materials

- Chart paper
- Markers
- Writer's Notebooks
- *Popcorn Sentences Notebook Entry* (page 107; popcornsentences.pdf)

Mentor Texts

- *Bedhead* by Margie Palatini
- Literature from CCSS or Core Reading Program
- See *Mentor Text List* in Appendix C for other suggestions.

Procedures

Think About Writing

1. Explain that by studying sentences, students will become better writers and will learn to express their ideas better.

2. Review mentor texts, if desired, and emphasize the author's use of varying sentence types and lengths.

Teach

3. Tell students, "Today I will show you how to make popcorn sentences to build phrasing and fluency in sentence writing."

4. Write the word *popcorn* on a sheet of chart paper. Have students count the number of letters in the word. Explain that just like the word *popcorn* has seven letters in it, popcorn sentences have seven words in them.

5. Explain to students that writing longer sentences helps with phrasing, fluency, and creating more interesting sentences. Tell students that they will play a game with partners to practice creating popcorn sentences.

6. Tell students that one partner will be the sentence creator and the other the word counter. The sentence creator will create a sentence. The word counter will count the number of words in the sentence using his or her fingers. The goal is to create sentences with seven or more words in them.

7. Model with a student partner how to create a popcorn sentence, such as, "Last night, after dinner, I sat on the porch and read." Be sure to explicitly model how to be both the sentence creator and the word counter. Practice with several sentences.

Popcorn Sentences (cont.)

Engage

8. Have students practice creating popcorn sentences with partners. Allow approximately two minutes for students to practice. Ensure both partners have a chance to be both the sentence creator and the word counter. Use sentence stems to provide a starting point for students, if needed.

Apply

9. Remind students to experiment with sentences and use their ears as tools to establish correctness and fluency in sentence writing. Provide students with the *Popcorn Sentences Notebook Entry* (page 107) to add to their Writer's Notebooks. Have students work on the *Your Turn* section before proceeding to their writing folders.

Write/Conference

10. Provide time for students to write. As students work, scan the room for students who need help. Then, rotate among students to confer with individuals and small groups. Remember to make note in your Conferring Notebook.

Spotlight Strategy

11. Spotlight students who successfully build popcorn sentences. For example, "Listen to this marvelous sentence. Henri used sentences just like Margie Palatini. Smart writing work!"

Share

12. Have students work in triads. Each person should share his or her best sentence. Provide approximately two minutes for students to share.

Homework

Ask students to teach their families how to create popcorn sentences. Have students write two popcorn sentences.

Popcorn Sentences Notebook Entry

Popcorn Sentences

Authors vary their sentence lengths by making some long and some short.

You can use popcorn sentences to add variety and flow to your writing. Count the number of words in your sentence. There should be seven or more words, just like there are seven letters in POPCORN!

Your Turn:

Find a partner and use these sentence starters or sentences from your own writing to build popcorn sentences.

- After school…

- My best friend…

- The neighbor's dog…

- It was after midnight…

- The football player…

For a real challenge, select sentences from your writing. Revise some into short sentences and others into popcorn sentences. Read them aloud to your partner and listen for fluency.

A Simple Sentence

Procedures

Note: Students respond best when a manipulative or visual representation can bring meaning to an abstract concept.

Think About Writing

1. Remind students that they have been practicing building and stretching sentences. Explain that often writers read and rewrite to create just the right balance in their sentences.

2. Review mentor texts, if desired, and emphasize the author's use of sentence structure and variation.

Teach

3. Tell students, "Today I will show you how to recognize simple sentences."

4. Explain there are many different types of sentences; however, today, the focus will be on simple sentences. Tell students that a simple sentence has only one complete thought. It may have a compound subject or a compound predicate, but it is still a simple sentence.

5. Display and discuss the *A Simple Sentence Notebook Entry* (page 110). Write the following sentences on chart paper and discuss and label the parts of each sentence:

   - *My head hurts.*
     (simple subject and simple predicate)

   - *Lanty and John rode bikes on the trail.*
     (compound subject and simple predicate)

   - *My hands and fingers look wrinkly and feel rough.*
     (compound subject and compound predicate)

A Simple Sentence (cont.)

Engage

6. Ask students to work with partners to create two simple sentences. Have students use topics from their notebook to provide them with ideas, if needed. Remind students to give compliments and comments to their partners.

Apply

7. Encourage students to explore, experiment, and play with sentences until they become music to their ears. Remind students to write sentences that sound natural, like speech. Provide students with *A Simple Sentence Notebook Entry* to add to their Writer's Notebook. Have students work on the *Your Turn* section before proceeding to their writing folders.

Write/Conference

8. Provide time for students to write. As students work, scan the classroom to make sure that all students are on task. Then, move out to confer with students. When needed, pull in a small group to a table and provide naming and action cards as manipulatives students can use to build sentences. Remember to use your Conferring Notebook to take anecdotal notes.

Spotlight Strategy

9. Spotlight students who use interesting sentences. For example, "Listen to Bryn's amazing sentence. (Read sentence.) She used interesting sentences, just like Margie Palatini's work in *Bedhead*."

Share

10. Have students meet in triads to share how they improved their writing today. Remind students to use an appropriate noise level as they talk and give compliments and comments.

Homework

Have students look at various writing materials for simple sentences. Ask them to write three simple sentences they find and bring them back to share tomorrow.

A Simple Sentence Notebook Entry

A Simple Sentence

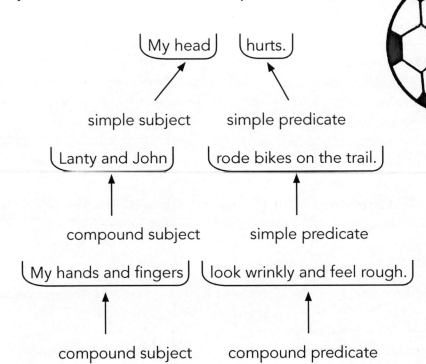

A **simple sentence** has one complete thought.

My head ——→ simple subject
hurts. ——→ simple predicate

Lanty and John ——↑ compound subject
rode bikes on the trail. ——↑ simple predicate

My hands and fingers ——↑ compound subject
look wrinkly and feel rough. ——↑ compound predicate

Your Turn:

Create simple sentences in your notebook from five of these topics. Then, create exciting sentences in other writing projects.

Topics:

soccer	biking	music	school
friend	family	shopping	pets

The Compound Subject

Standards

- Uses a variety of sentence structures in writing
- Uses strategies to draft and revise written work

Materials

- Chart paper
- Markers
- Writer's Notebooks
- *The Compound Subject Notebook Entry* (page 113; compoundsubject.pdf)

Mentor Texts

- *Thank You, Mr. Falker* by Patricia Polacco
- Recommended literature from CCSS or Core Reading Program
- See *Mentor Text List* in Appendix C for other suggestions.

Procedures

Note: This lesson uses the book *Thank You, Mr. Falker*. However, you may use any mentor text that has compound sentences. Revisit this lesson repeatedly until students fully understand and comprehend the use of compound subjects.

Think About Writing

1. Remind students that they have been trying out different ways to improve their writing by looking at how real authors combine parts of sentences. Sentences have two basic parts: the naming part (the subject) and the action part (the predicate). Explain that great authors add additional words to the subjects and the verbs in their sentences to make them more interesting.

2. Review mentor texts, if desired, and emphasize the author's sentence structure.

Teach

3. Tell students, "Today I will show you how to improve and add variety to the subject part of sentences."

4. Display and discuss *The Compound Subject Notebook Entry* (page 113).

5. Write the following sentences from *Thank You, Mr. Falker* on a sheet of chart paper. You can choose to display sentences from a different mentor text, if desired. Have students identify the compound subjects in the sentences:

   Even though her grandma and grandpa were gone, the little girl didn't want to move. Maybe, though, the teachers and the kids in her new school wouldn't know how dumb she was. She and her mother and brother moved across the country in a 1949 Plymouth.

The Compound Subject (cont.)

Engage

6. Write the following sentences on chart paper. Have students work with partners to create sentences with compound subjects by adding subjects.

   - _____ and _____ played basketball in the gym.

   - His _____ and her _____ were thrown into the washing machine.

   - My _____ and his _____ are going out to dinner.

Apply

7. Encourage students to use compound subjects to add sentence variety and fluency to their writing. Provide students with *The Compound Subject Notebook Entry* to add to their Writer's Notebook. Have students work on the *Your Turn* section before proceeding to their writing folders.

Write/Conference

8. Provide time for students to write. As students work, scan the classroom to make sure that all students are working. Rotate among students to confer individually or in small groups.

Spotlight Strategy

9. Spotlight students who add compound subjects to their writing. For example, "Landon created a brilliant sentence. Listen to how he added variety and interest by using a compound subject just like Patricia Polacco."

Share

10. Have students meet with partners to share two of their best sentences. Ask students to reflect on why they selected those sentences.

Homework

Ask students to think of ways to make interesting sentences that contain a compound subject with easy-to-follow ideas. Have students write three sentences with compound subjects.

The Compound Subject Notebook Entry

The Compound Subject

Authors use **compound subjects** to add variety, fluency, and interest to their writing.

A compound subject is a list of two or more nouns that perform the action in the predicate.

(Mary) rode her bike to school.

(Jesse) rode his bike to school.

(Mary and Jesse) rode their bikes to school.

Your Turn:

Add compound subjects to these sentences.

_____ and _____ played baseball in the park.

_____ and _____ went to the movies.

_____ and _____ ran through the forest.

_____, _____, or _____ swim in the ocean.

Types of Sentences

Procedures

Note: You will repeat this lesson throughout the year. Use literature to identify different types of sentences and sentence structure to help students recognize the connection between reading and writing. Activities, such as sentence-finding games, should be motivational, fun, and engaging.

Think About Writing

1. Explain to students that one way to become better writers is to listen to the sentences of authors. By listening, students can hear how authors use creative phrases and word order to make reading feel natural.

2. Review mentor texts, if desired, and emphasize how the writing flows from one idea to another.

Teach

3. Tell students, "Today I will show you the four different types of sentences."

4. Display and discuss the *Types of Sentences Notebook Entry* (page 116). Tell students that using the correct punctuation clarifies the meaning and adds vitality and energy to writing.

5. Model how to create each of the four types of sentences on a sheet of chart paper. Emphasize the ending punctuation that goes with each type of sentence. Review the four types of sentences by saying the names of each. Ask students to name the four types of sentences.

Types of Sentences *(cont.)*

Engage

6. Have students work with partners to practice creating each type of sentence. Write the following sentence stems on chart paper to help get students started:

   - **Declarative**
     The student…
     My mom and dad…

   - **Imperative**
     Everyone get…
     Stop that…

   - **Interrogative**
     What…
     Will you…

   - **Exclamatory**
     Wow…
     Look at…

Apply

7. Encourage students to use a variety of sentences to make their writing more interesting. Provide students with the *Types of Sentences Notebook Entry* to add to their Writer's Notebook. Have students work on the *Your Turn* section before proceeding to their writing folders.

Write/Conference

8. Provide time for students to write. Select two or three students who are having difficulty and meet with them to provide additional support and practice, if needed. Have additional sentence stems ready to provide repetition. Support your observations by making notes in your Conferring Notebook.

Spotlight Strategy

9. Spotlight students who include different types of sentences in their writing. For example, "Jalon did something brilliant. Listen to the rhythm and flow of his sentences."

Share

10. Have students meet with partners to share what they wrote today. Ask students to choose two of their best sentences to share. Then have students move into a quad to share their best sentences.

> ### Homework
> Ask students to find an example in a book or write one of each type of sentence for homework.

Types of Sentences Notebook Entry

Types of Sentences

Authors use different punctuation marks to add variety and interest to their sentence writing.

- A **declarative sentence** makes a statement and ends with a period.

  Justin Sinn was born in Sparta, Illinois.

- An **imperative sentence** gives a command or makes a request. Most imperative sentences end with a period. A strong command ends with an exclamation point.

  Be quiet during the play. (command)

  Please close the door. (request)

  Stop! (strong command)

- An **interrogative sentence** asks a question and ends with a question mark.

  What time are you going to the movies?

- An **exclamatory sentence** shows excitement or expresses strong feeling and ends with an exclamation point.

  Luke won the race!

Your Turn:

Practice writing examples of each sentence type in your notebook. Remember the punctuation!

#50917—Getting to the Core of Writing—Level 3 © Shell Education

The Compound Verb

Standards

- Uses a variety of sentence structures in writing
- Uses strategies to draft and revise written work

Materials

- Chart paper
- Markers
- Writer's Notebooks
- *The Compound Verb Notebook Entry* (page 119; compoundverb.pdf)

Mentor Texts

- *To Root, to Toot, to Parachute: What Is a Verb?* by Brian Cleary
- *The Relatives Came* by Cynthia Rylant
- See *Mentor Text List* in Appendix C for other suggestions.

Procedures

Note: This lesson uses the mentor text *The Relatives Came*. However, any mentor text with good examples of compound verbs can be used. Revisit, practice, and remind students of this strategy in their Writer's Notebook as well as their writing.

Think About Writing

1. Remind students they have been exploring writing sentences that add meaning to their stories. Tell students that saying their sentences out loud will help them decide if they have fluency and variety, which are key qualities of well-constructed sentences.

2. Review mentor texts, if desired, and emphasize the author's sentence construction.

Teach

3. Tell students, "Today I will show you how to create sentences using compound verbs to enrich and enhance the message."

4. Display and discuss *The Compound Verb Notebook Entry* (page 119).

5. Write the following sentence from *The Relatives Came* on a sheet of chart paper. You can choose to display a sentence from a different mentor text, if desired.

   They drank up all their pop, ate up all their crackers, traveled up all those miles and pulled into our yard.

   Have students identify and count all the verbs in the sentence. Discuss how using compound verbs adds interest to the sentence.

The Compound Verb *(cont.)*

Engage

6. Have students work with partners to practice creating sentences with compound verbs. Write the following sentences on chart paper to help get students started:

   - *The substitute teacher _____ her watch and _____ to the principal's office.*
   - *My young son _____ the ball and _____ to first base.*
   - *The busy student _____, _____, and _____ in the library.*

   Allow students to share their sentences with the whole group.

Apply

7. Encourage students to try writing compound verbs in their sentences. Provide students with *The Compound Verb Notebook Entry* to add to their Writer's Notebook. Have students work on the *Your Turn* section before proceeding to their writing folders.

Write/Conference

8. Provide time for students to write. As students work, scan your classroom to make sure that all students are working. Rotate among students to confer individually or in small groups. Have samples of verbs on note cards to support the most students who have a hard time getting started.

Spotlight Strategy

9. Spotlight students who include compound verbs in their writing. For example, "Spotlight! Rajit created an amazing sentence. Listen to how he added compound verbs to his sentence to convey just the right meaning."

Share

10. Have students work with partners to share what they wrote today. Encourage students to share something they learned today to improve the quality of their writing.

Homework

Ask students to write two sentences that have compound verbs in them. Allow students to share their sentences the next day.

The Compound Verb Notebook Entry

The Compound Verb

Authors use **compound verbs** to combine short, choppy sentences and to add rhythm and flow to their writing.

A compound verb is more than one action word, or verb, in the sentence. Compound verbs are connected by conjunctions and commas if there are more than two.

Calee *danced* and *jiggled* her toes to the music.

Elliot *dribbled* down the court and *swished* the basket to tie the score.

Mrs. Cates could *spend*, *save*, or *donate* her money.

Your Turn:

Add verbs to the sentences below.

- Luke and Lindsay _____ and _____ at the mall.
- My friend _____ and _____ during the game.
- The adorable puppy _____ and _____ at the next-door neighbor.
- The children _____, _____, and _____ after school.

The Compound Sentence

Standards

- Uses a variety of sentence structures in writing
- Uses strategies to draft and revise written work

Materials

- Chart paper
- Markers
- Writer's Notebooks
- *The Compound Sentence Notebook Entry* (page 122; compoundsentence.pdf)

Mentor Texts

- *Thank You, Mr. Falker* by Patricia Polacco
- *Just Me and 6,000 Rats: A Tale of Conjunctions* by Rick Walton
- Literature from CCSS resource list or Core Reading Program
- See *Mentor Text List* in Appendix C for other suggestions.

Procedures

Note: Research indicates that students need numerous repetitions to move skills and strategies into short-term and long-term memory. Repeat this lesson many times so that students build flexibility in their writing and create interest and energy by generating sentence variety.

Think About Writing

1. Remind students that to be proficient in writing, they must explore writing different types of sentences.

2. Review mentor texts, if desired, and emphasize the author's use of sentence variation.

Teach

3. Tell students, "Today I will show you how to create a compound sentence." Explain that a compound sentence contains two independent clauses joined by a conjunction.

4. Write the conjunctions on a sheet of chart paper in the following order: *for, and, nor, but, or, yet, so.* Tell students that the first letter from each conjunction can be used to make the word *FANBOYS.* Explain that this is a mnemonic device to aid in remembering all the conjunctions.

5. Display and discuss *The Compound Sentence Notebook Entry* (page 122).

6. Write the following sentences on chart paper and have students identify the conjunctions in the sentences:

   - *All of the pizza was already gone, so we had to settle for breadsticks.*

   - *The elevators were crowded, but we squeezed into the empty space.*

The Compound Sentence *(cont.)*

Engage

7. Have students work with partners to practice creating compound sentences. Write the following sentence stems on chart paper to help students get started:

   - *I've always loved the city, but…*
   - *I biked for two hours, yet…*
   - *Our team won the regional, so…*

   Allow students to share the sentences they created with the whole class.

Apply

8. Encourage students to use sentence variety to express complete thoughts and add energy and rhythm to their stories, essays, and compositions. Provide students with *The Compound Sentence Notebook Entry* to add to their Writer's Notebook. Have students work on the *Your Turn* section before proceeding to their writing folders.

Write/Conference

9. Provide time for students to write. As students write, pull a small group to review the notebook entry. Check for understanding before sending them off to work independently. Be sure to make notes in your Conferring Notebook for planning.

Spotlight Strategy

10. Spotlight students who use compound sentences in their writing. For example, "What aspiring authors! Just listen to David's compound sentence."

Share

11. Have students meet with partners to share their most successful sentences.

Homework

Ask students to write FANBOYS on a sheet of paper and the conjunction that goes with each letter of the word. Have students create two sentences using conjunctions.

The Compound Sentence Notebook Entry

The Compound Sentence

Authors use a variety of sentence structures and lengths to make their writing rhythmic and interesting.

A **compound sentence** contains two independent clauses joined by a coordinating conjunction:

F	**A**	**N**	**B**	**O**	**Y**	**S**
o	n	o	u	r	e	o
r		d	r	t		t

Remember: FANBOYS!

Here are some compound sentences:

- My mom picked up the pizza, but she forgot the salad.
- All of the pizza was gone, so we had to settle for breadsticks.
- Everyone enjoyed the meal, and we rushed off to catch a movie.

Your Turn:

Add an independent clause and coordinating conjunction to these sentence stems to create a compound sentence.

- My friends went to the football game, …
- The monkey reached for the banana, …
- Valerie went to the movies, …
- My dad likes to ski, …

#50917—Getting to the Core of Writing—Level 3 © Shell Education

Rubber Band Sentences

Standards

- Uses a variety of sentence structures in writing
- Uses strategies to draft and revise written work

Materials

- Chart paper
- Markers
- Writer's Notebooks
- Sticky notes
- *Rubber Band Sentences Notebook Entry* (page 125; rubbandsentences.pdf)
- Rubber band
- *Question Word Cards* (page 126; questionwordcards.pdf)

Mentor Texts

- *Bedhead* by Margie Palatini
- See *Mentor Text List* in Appendix C for other suggestions.

Procedures

Note: To model the lesson, have cards prepared showing the question words: who, which, when, what kind, and where. Repeat this often, as it improves sentence length, rhythm, and understanding of sentence variety. You can use a rubber band or other manipulative to represent sentence length.

Think About Writing

1. Explain that authors use varied sentence length—short and long—to add variety and energy to their writing. Too many short or too many long sentences can make writing monotonous or boring.

2. Review mentor texts, if desired, and emphasize the author's use of various sentence lengths. For example, "In the story *Bedhead* by Margie Palatini, the action moves quickly and keeps you interested because of varied sentence lengths." Read several sentences aloud and stretch a rubber band to show the varied sentence lengths.

Teach

3. Tell students, "Today I will show you one way you can build variety in your sentence lengths."

4. Explain to students that adding words to sentences gives the reader more details and will build more interesting sentences. Today, they will add details by asking questions. Display and discuss the *Rubber Band Sentences Notebook Entry* (page 125).

5. Display the *Question Word Cards* (page 126). Write the following sentence on sticky notes, one word per sticky note, and post on a sheet of chart paper:

    The baby cried.

    Stretch a rubber band to show the sentence's length.

Rubber Band Sentences (cont.)

6. Model how to use the *Question Word Cards* to add words and build the sentence. Write the answers to the questions on sticky notes and add the sticky notes to the original sentence:

   - **When?:** this morning
     This morning, the baby cried.

   - **What kind?:** hungry
     This morning, the hungry baby cried.

   - **Who?:** Jamie's
     This morning, Jamie's hungry baby cried.

   - **Where?:** in her crib
     This morning, Jamie's hungry baby cried in her crib.

   After each question, read the new sentence as you stretch a rubber band to provide visual support of the growing sentence. You may need to add additional sticky notes to change previously capitalized words to lowercase; however, remember to keep the focus on expanding sentences.

Engage

7. Have students practice building sentences with partners. Have students ask their partners questions to encourage sentence expansion. Remind students to use the *Question Words Cards* for support. Provide approximately two minutes for students to talk.

Apply

8. Encourage students to use questions to construct more interesting and detailed sentences. Provide students with the *Rubber Band Sentences Notebook Entry* to add to their Writer's Notebook and the *Question Word Cards* to keep in their writing folders. Have students work on the *Your Turn* section before proceeding to their writing folders.

Write/Conference

9. Provide time for students to write. As they work, move around to confer with individual students or provide small-group instruction.

Spotlight Strategy

10. Spotlight students who use both short and long sentences in their writing. For example, "Isabella wrote a brilliant sentence that sounds smooth and rhythmic. Smart work!"

Share

11. Have students meet in triads to share their best sentences. Remind students to give each other compliments. Provide approximately two minutes for students to share.

Homework

Ask students to look in books for examples of how authors vary the lengths of their sentences. Have students copy one long and one short sentence from a book.

Rubber Band Sentences Notebook Entry

Rubber Band Sentences

Authors use both short and long sentences to enhance meaning and vary sentence length.

Example: The baby cried.

When?: this morning
This morning, the baby cried.

What kind?: hungry
This morning, the hungry baby cried.

Where?: in her crib
This morning, the hungry baby cried in her crib.

Who?: Jamie
This morning, Jamie's hungry baby cried in her crib.

Your Turn:

Turn these short sentences into long sentences.

- The car honked.
- The boys ran.
- A dog barked.
- The lion roared.

Question Word Cards

Directions: Cut out the cards. Use the cards to model how to add words to build sentences. Then, have students use the cards to practice building their own sentences.

Who or which?

When?

What kind?

Where?

#50917—Getting to the Core of Writing—Level 3 © Shell Education

A Complex Sentence

Procedures

Note: Complex sentences can be difficult for young students to comprehend. However, repeating this mini-lesson and identifying sentence varieties in literature will enhance student learning.

Think About Writing

1. Explain that many authors make their sentences rhythmic with careful thought about creating just the right image for the reader.

2. Review mentor texts, if desired, and emphasize the author's use of words and phrases to capture just the right idea so the reading feels natural.

Teach

3. Tell students, "Today I will show you how to create complex sentences." Explain that complex sentences are made up of two or more parts.

4. Display and discuss *A Complex Sentence Notebook Entry* (page 129). Use the entry to explain that independent clauses, like parents or other adults, are able to survive or stand on their own. Dependent clauses, like babies, cannot be left alone. Tell students that independent and dependent clauses are connected using subordinating conjunctions. These are words that join phrases together. List the following words on chart paper: *after, as, because, before, if, that, until, when, who.*

5. Write the following sentences on chart paper and have students identify the subordinating conjunctions and the clauses in the sentences:

    - *School was dismissed early because it was snowing.*
    - *After school, the kids made snowmen.*
    - *The fourth grade students, who made a lot of noise, lost their recess.*

    Have students identify the subordinating conjunctions and the clauses in the sentences.

A Complex Sentence (cont.)

Engage

6. Have students work with partners to create three complex sentences. Remind students to use an independent clause and a dependent clause and join both clauses together using a subordinating conjunction.

Apply

7. Encourage students to add complex sentences to their writing to create energy and originality. Remind them to use subordinating conjunctions. Provide students with *A Complex Sentence Notebook Entry* to add to their Writer's Notebook. Have students work on the *Your Turn* section before proceeding to their writing folders.

Write/Conference

8. Provide time for students to write. Work with small groups in a guided writing setting, if needed. Write several complex sentences on paper. Color code the independent and dependent clauses to make them easier to identify.

Spotlight Strategy

9. Spotlight one or two students who have clearly connected to the lesson. This helps to echo the strategy across the writing lesson.

Share

10. Have students meet with partners to share the sentences they created. Remind students to give their partners compliments that specifically identify something in the writing.

Homework

Ask students to write two complex sentences. Remind students to use subordinating conjunctions in their sentences.

#50917—Getting to the Core of Writing—Level 3 © *Shell Education*

A Complex Sentence Notebook Entry

A Complex Sentence

Authors use **complex sentences** to convey ideas clearly and entertain the reader with sentence variety.

A complex sentence can contain an independent clause, a dependent clause, and a subordinating conjunction.

Independent clause: can stand alone

Dependent clause: cannot stand alone

Subordinating conjunction: connects clauses together (after, as, because, before, if, that, until, when, who)

The subordinating clause can be in the beginning, end, or middle of the complex sentence.

- When the rain stopped, we went outside to play.
- We went outside to play when the rain stopped.
- We went, when the rain stopped, outside to play.

Your Turn:

Use these subordinating clauses to practice building complex sentences.

- when the bell rang
- because it was raining
- after the game
- who loves football

Organization

Linking the Pieces Together

Organization provides the structure of writing. It helps readers make connections from one idea to the next. Organization provides the skeletal support for the overall meaning of writing. The lessons help students explore different types of writing and the ways they are organized. Lessons in this section include the following:

- Lesson 1: Name Poetry (page 133)
- Lesson 2: 123 Paragraphs: Opinion (page 136)
- Lesson 3: 123 Paragraphs: Story (page 139)
- Lesson 4: 123 Paragraphs: Informing (page 142)
- Lesson 5: Building a Story Mountain (page 145)
- Lesson 6: Telling a Story (page 152)
- Lesson 7: More Than "Once Upon a Time" (page 155)
- Lesson 8: Circular Endings (page 159)
- Lesson 9: Writing a Letter (page 162)
- Lesson 10: It's My Opinion! (page 166)
- Lesson 11: Just Stating the Facts (page 170)
- Lesson 12: Poetry Fun (page 174)

The *Owen, Organization Conductor* poster (page 132) can be displayed in the room to provide a visual reminder for students that organization is one of the traits of writing. You may wish to introduce this poster during the first lesson on organization. Then, refer to the poster when teaching other lessons on organization to refresh students' memories and provide them with questions in order to guide them as they organize their writing.

Owen
Organization
Conductor

How do I plan my writing?

❧ Did I sequence my thoughts?

❧ Did I have a beginning, middle, and end?

❧ Did I hook my reader?

❧ Did I include transition words?

Name Poetry

Standards

- Uses strategies to draft and revise written work
- Writes narrative accounts, such as poems and stories

Materials

- Chart paper
- Markers
- Writer's Notebooks
- *Name Poetry Notebook Entry* (page 135; namepoetry.pdf)

Mentor Texts

- *African Acrostics: A Word in Edgeways* by Avis Harley
- *Autumn: An Alphabet Acrostic* by Steven Schnur (also *Summer*, *Winter*, and *Spring*)
- See *Mentor Text List* in Appendix C for other suggestions.

Procedures

Note: You may use this mini-lesson to create acrostic poems throughout the year. Acrostics are an excellent way to teach and publish writing across the curriculum. For example, have students write acrostics about themes or units of study.

Think About Writing

1. Tell students that they will be exploring some of the methods authors use to organize their writing.

2. Review mentor texts, if desired, and emphasize the format of the poetry.

Teach

3. Tell students, "Today I will show you two styles of poetry that you can use when writing."

4. Display and discuss the *Name Poetry Notebook Entry* (page 135).

5. Explain that an acrostic poem begins with a word written vertically. Write your last name vertically on a sheet of chart paper. Tell students that each letter is the beginning sound for a word, phrase, or sentence. Model how to turn your name into an acrostic poem using words, phrases, or sentences to describe you.

6. Tell students another type of poem is an All About Me poem. Model on chart paper how to create an All About Me poem following the format in the *Name Poetry Notebook Entry*.

7. Sketch a self-portrait to show characteristics listed in one of the poems. Explain to students that topics from the poems can be ideas to develop into a piece of writing. For example, the All About Me poem on the *Name Poetry Notebook Entry* states that Cynthia is afraid of snakes. Tell students that a topic for a piece of writing could be why Cynthia is afraid of snakes.

Name Poetry (cont.)

Engage

8. Have students work with partners to share ideas about what they might include in their name poems.

Apply

9. Provide students with the *Name Poetry Notebook Entry* to add to their Writer's Notebook. Have students work on the *Your Turn* section before proceeding to their writing folders.

Write/Conference

10. Provide time for students to write. As they write, rotate around the class conferencing with students. Ask questions, such as: "What have you learned as a writer today?" "How can your Writer's Notebook help you?"

Spotlight Strategy

11. Spotlight students who work well together to complete their All About Me poem. For example, "Tatiana and Jenny were working together as a team, helping each other to complete their name poems."

Share

12. Have students meet with partners to share their name poems. Observe students as they share, choose one or two students who clearly understood the format of the poem, and have them share with the whole group.

Homework

Ask students to teach their parents how to create one of the name poems. Have students create a name poem about a family member.

Name Poetry Notebook Entry

Name Poetry

Acrostic Poem

C reative

Y elling soccer fan

N ifty

T houghtful

H appy

I ncredibly fast runner

A wesome soccer player!

All About Me Poem

First Name	Luke
Four words that describe me	Kind, athletic, strong, daring
Who loves...	Who loves biking
Who fears...	Who fears spiders
Who needs...	Who needs a puppy
Who gives...	Who gives hugs to his mom
Who wants to see..	Who wants to see a bike race
Who lives...	Who lives in Bridgeport, WV
Last Name	Nesler

Your Turn:

Create an acrostic or All About Me poem in your Writer's Notebook. Add an illustration to your poem.

123 Paragraphs: Opinion

Procedures

Note: Mentor texts generate rich discussion for students to share ideas and opinions on the validity of family pets or other opinion topics. Repeat this lesson using a variety of topics and literature.

Think About Writing

1. Explain to students that there are many different text types and purposes. Opinion, narrative, and informative are three types of writing used in the real world.

2. Review mentor texts, if desired, and emphasize the author's opinions in the book.

Teach

3. Tell students, "Today I will show you how to develop an opinion paragraph." Review with students the three parts of a paragraph: topic sentence, body, and closing statement.

4. Explain that in an opinion text, the writer is trying to persuade, or convince, the reader to understand and support an issue. After stating an opinion, authors support their opinions with reasons and examples.

5. Write the following prompt on a sheet of chart paper:

    Should classrooms have pets?

    Then, create a table with three horizontal sections labeled: *Topic Sentence*, *Body: Reasons to Support*, and *Closing Statement*. Discuss each section. Then, model how to fill in each section with ideas.

123 Paragraphs: Opinion (cont.)

For example:

Topic Sentence
The way I see it, every classroom should have a pet, right? A pet hamster would teach us to be responsible.
Body: Reasons to Support
Teaches responsibility
• Clean cage • Provide weekend care • Exercise
Closing Statement
During the school year, students need to spend time caring for a classroom pet to learn responsibility.

6. Display and discuss the *123 Paragraphs: Opinion Notebook Entry* (page 138). Read the paragraph modeled in the entry. Remind students that opinion writing is used in the real world—for example, in speeches and book reviews.

Engage

7. Have students work with partners to think of opinions or issues that they feel strongly about, such as free time at school, school lunches, making school more interesting, or homework policies. Provide approximately two minutes for students to talk.

Apply

8. Provide students with the *123 Paragraphs: Opinion Notebook Entry* to add to their Writer's Notebook. Have students work on the *Your Turn* section before proceeding to their writing folders.

Write/Conference

9. Provide time for students to write. As they work, hold a small-group reteach lesson identifying the parts of a paragraph with students who may need extra support. Observe writing behaviors in a Conferring Notebook to plan the next steps.

Spotlight Strategy

10. Spotlight students who have a topic sentence, details, and closing statement. For example, "Writers, you're well on your way. Just listen to Camille's topic sentence, details, and closing statement. Exceptional paragraph work today."

Share

11. Have students work with partners to share what they wrote today. Remind students to take turns and support their partners by being great listeners. Provide approximately two minutes for students to share.

Homework

Ask students to listen to conversations in their homes or to the news to see if they can identify any opinions. Have students write one opinion they hear.

123 Paragraphs: Opinion Notebook Entry

123 Paragraphs: Opinion

In an **opinion paragraph**, you share the way you think or feel about something or someone. It is important to give reasons and examples to support your opinion.

There are three parts to an opinion paragraph—a topic sentence, the body, and a closing statement.

1. A **topic sentence** states your opinion.
The way I see it, every classroom should have a pet, right? A pet hamster would teach us to be responsible.

2. The **body** gives reasons and supporting details.
Responsibility by third graders is required for success in school. A pet hamster would need food and water. The hamster could not be left alone over the weekend, so students would need to offer pet care at home and over holidays. Every animal should have a workout, so our class would need to provide appropriate exercise.

3. A **closing statement** restates your opinion.
So you can see that students would develop responsible behaviors in the classroom if they were required to care for a pet.

Your Turn:

Write your own opinion paragraph. Refer to the Ideas section of your Writer's Notebook for topics.

123 Paragraphs: Story

Standards

- Uses strategies to draft and revise written work
- Writes narrative accounts, such as poems and stories

Materials

- Chart paper
- Markers
- Writer's Notebooks
- *123 Paragraphs: Story Notebook Entry* (page 141; 123story.pdf)

Mentor Texts

- *That Book Woman* by Heather Henson
- *The Relatives Came* by Cynthia Rylant
- See *Mentor Text List* in Appendix C for other suggestions.

Procedures

Note: Writers need multiple opportunities to build their writing skills. This lesson is designed to shape the process of constructing a real or imagined experience with events sequenced in a clear and concise order.

Think About Writing

1. Explain to students that writers acquire skills to organize their thinking and make events and experiences flow from one idea to the next.

2. Review mentor texts, if desired, and emphasize the way the author's writing flows from one idea to the next.

Teach

3. Tell students, "Today I will show you how to develop a narrative paragraph." Explain to students that a narrative paragraph shares a personal experience and has three parts: topic, body, and closing.

4. Display and discuss the *123 Paragraphs: Story Notebook Entry* (page 141). Explain that topics for narrative writing can be experiences in which there is a deep emotional attachment. Write the following sentence stems on chart paper for students to consider:

    - *Last summer, …*
    - *On my birthday, …*
    - *My mom and I shopped…*
    - *My best friend…*
    - *The worst day of my life…*
    - *The scariest time in my life…*

5. Remind students that the details of an event are what make the experience come to life for the reader. Tell students that the more details the author provides, the more the reader will understand the experience. Encourage students to brainstorm at least three details to support their topic sentences.

123 Paragraphs: Story (cont.)

6. Explain to students that conclusions sum up the event and usually tell how the writer feels at the end of the event.

7. Choose one of the sentence stems as a topic for a narrative writing piece and model creating a story. Think aloud as you write so students can hear your thought process as you compose.

Engage

8. Ask students to think about something they would like to write about. Have students talk with partners about a topic and details they can include to create interest. Allow approximately three minutes for students to share.

Apply

9. Provide students with *123 Paragraphs: Story Notebook Entry* to add to their Writer's Notebooks. Have students work on the *Your Turn* section before proceeding to their writing folders.

Write/Conference

10. Provide time for students to write. Work in a small group with students who may need assistance brainstorming ideas for writing. Then, rotate around the classroom, conferencing with individual students.

Spotlight Strategy

11. Spotlight students who are writing narrative paragraphs with a topic sentence supporting events. For example, "Wow! Outstanding effort! Writers, you're right on target with your narrative paragraphs. Listen to Chania's topic sentence and events to support. I feel 'in the moment' of this story."

Share

12. Select two or three students to share their writing in the Author's Chair. Remind students to give compliments to the students who share.

Homework

Ask students to make a list of three topics they may like to write about. Encourage students to talk with their parents or other family members to gather ideas.

123 Paragraphs: Story Notebook Entry

123 Paragraphs: Story

A **narrative paragraph** is a story. It can be about a personal experience or a made-up story (fiction).

There are three parts to a narrative paragraph—a topic sentence, the main body, and a closing sentence.

1. The **topic sentence** introduces the characters and setting.
Last summer, my family decided to drive the four-wheeler back in the mountains around the Blacksnake Trail.

2. The **body** tells the events in the order in which they happened.
We packed the food and my dad gassed up the four-wheeler. As we drove along the trail, we spotted a bobcat sitting on the bank, gazing through the trees. He took off like a shot and disappeared into the underbrush. We moved higher into the mountains. The wind began to increase and the air grew brisk and cold. We rounded a turn and standing in the middle of the road in front of us was a huge black bear. I screamed and Dad gunned the engine. The bear took off like a bullet down the mountain.

3. A **closing sentence** sums up the story.
We drove slowly home, thinking about our exciting adventure. I look forward to future trips across the mountains and around Blacksnake Trail.

Your Turn:

Try writing your own narrative paragraph using one of these topics or one of your own: family, pets, friends, trips, sports, school, animals, or adventures.

123 Paragraphs: Informing

Standards

- Uses strategies to draft and revise written work
- Writes expository compositions

Materials

- Newspapers
- Magazines
- Chart paper
- Markers
- Writer's Notebooks
- *123 Paragraphs: Informing Notebook Entry* (page 144; 123informing.pdf)

Mentor Texts

- *I Face the Wind* by Vicki Cobb
- *Families Change* by Julie Nelson
- See *Mentor Text List* in Appendix C for other suggestions.

Procedures

Note: Use this lesson to prepare students for research. Students need support in selecting facts for research presentations, lab reports, and all aspects of curriculum.

Think About Writing

1. Tell students there are many different types of paragraphs, and today, they will look at informative paragraphs, such as those found in newspapers, magazine articles, and nonfiction books.

2. Review mentor texts, if desired, and emphasize the informational format of the books.

Teach

3. Tell students, "Today I will show you how to develop an informative paragraph." Explain to students that an informative paragraph reports information.

4. Review the parts of a paragraph with students: a hook and topic sentence, a body, and a closing statement. Explain to students that informative paragraphs can follow that same format. Explain that a hook can be used at the beginning to create interest and reel the reader into the message. The topic sentence or main idea creates the organizational structure that will follow. The body includes details. The closing statement summarizes the information within the paragraph.

5. Use chart paper to model the following:

   Hook: *A tree fact*

   Topic sentence: *Trees are one of our greatest natural resources.*

   Body: *Facts to support the topic sentence*
   - *Produce oxygen*
   - *Build homes*
   - *Provide paper*
   - *Produce sap for products*

123 Paragraphs: Informing (cont.)

Closing Statement: *Here's a reminder to all that we need to protect and replenish our trees, one of our greatest natural resources.*

6. Display and discuss the *123 Paragraphs: Informing Notebook Entry* (page 144). Read the paragraph that was created based on the items listed in Step 5.

Engage

7. Have students work with partners to think of something of interest, such as animals, trees, space, elections, seasons, or nature. Encourage students to count on their fingers to identify at least five topics. Remind students to allow both partners time to talk. Provide approximately two minutes for students to talk.

Apply

8. Provide students with the *123 Paragraphs: Informing Notebook Entry* to add to their Writer's Notebook. Have students work on the *Your Turn* section before proceeding to their writing folders.

Write/Conference

9. Observe your audience for confusion. If you notice students having difficulty getting started, immediately pull them into a small group for a reteach. When finished, move into individual conferences, keeping anecdotal observations to plan the next steps.

Spotlight Strategy

10. Spotlight students who show a good understanding of informative text structure. For example, "You must be proud of your work! Just listen to this aspiring young author! Notice how Tammy's writing is building her understanding of informative text. Smart writing!"

Share

11. Have students meet with partners to share their topic sentences and at least three details. Allow approximately two minutes for students to share.

Homework

Ask students to look around their houses for topics that they think might be used as informative writing topics. Have students each make a list of five topics.

123 Paragraphs: Informing Notebook Entry

123 Paragraphs: Informing

An **informative paragraph** informs, describes, explains, or defines a specific subject for the reader.

There are three parts to an informative paragraph—a hook and topic sentence, the body, and a closing statement.

1. The **hook** grabs the reader and the topic sentence or main idea tells the reader what you are going to write about.
Did you know our country, America, is covered by forest? Our trees are one of our greatest natural resources.

2. The **body** gives information the reader needs to understand the topic, such as facts, procedures, and examples.
Two trees produce enough oxygen to support a family of four for a year. Ninety-five percent of homes in our country use lumber (wood) for construction. On average, Americans use approximately 750 pounds of paper products each year. Think of all the paper plates, cups, notebooks, and notebook paper! Even the sap from trees can be used to make syrup, chewing gum, and crayons.

3. A **closing statement** summarizes the information within the paragraph.
Here's a reminder to all that we need to protect and replenish our trees, one of our greatest natural resources.

Your Turn:

Try writing your own informative paragraph. Think about a topic related to health, science, space, nature, animals, history, or presidents.

Building a Story Mountain

Standards

- Uses strategies to draft and revise written work
- Writes narrative accounts, such as poems and stories

Materials

- Chart paper
- Markers
- Writer's Notebooks
- *Building a Story Mountain Notebook Entry* (page 147; buildingstory.pdf)
- *The Princess and the Pea Story Cards* (page 148; princesspeacards.pdf)
- *Little Red Riding Hood Story Cards* (page 149; redridinghoodcards.pdf)

Mentor Texts

- Fairy tales
- *Suggested Story Mountain Texts* (pages 150–151; mountaintexts.pdf)

Procedures

Note: Using a visual representation helps students better understand and remember the narrative story pattern. Identify the story mountain in numerous texts.

Think About Writing

1. Explain that authors develop stories with a beginning, middle, and end. Tell students that many authors use a story pattern tool to keep the reader interested from the first page of the story to the last page. This tool is called a *story mountain*.

2. Review mentor texts, if desired, and emphasize the author's use of beginning, middle, and end.

Teach

3. Tell students, "Today I will show you how to begin organizing narrative writing into a story mountain pattern that will make the reader want to keep reading."

4. Display and discuss the *Building a Story Mountain Notebook Entry* (page 147). Review the parts of the story mountain pattern:

   - The *introduction* hooks the reader while introducing the characters and setting.
   - The *build-up* tells the reader what the characters are doing at the beginning of the story.
   - The *problem* might be a mystery or a dilemma.
   - The *resolution* is the part of the story that tells how the problem is solved.
   - The *wrap-up* is the ending/conclusion and shares what the characters learned or how the characters changed from the beginning of the story.

5. Think aloud as you relate the events from *The Princess and the Pea Story Cards* (page 148) to the story mountain pattern.

Building a Story Mountain (cont.)

Engage

6. Have students Turn and Talk to practice identifying the events in a story. Display and read the events on the *Little Red Riding Hood Story Cards* (page 149) and ask students to think about which section of the story mountain each card relates to.

Apply

7. Encourage students to develop a story mountain narrative that grips the reader right from the introduction and holds the reader to the final conclusion. Provide students with the *Building a Story Mountain Notebook Entry* to add to their Writer's Notebook. Have students work on the *Your Turn* section before proceeding to their writing folders.

Write/Conference

8. Provide time for students to write. Scan your classroom for confusions that need to be settled. Then begin to rotate around the room, conferencing with students.

Spotlight Strategy

9. Spotlight students who are working hard to develop a story mountain. For example, "Ramiel is working to develop a story mountain. Wonderful work ethic!"

Share

10. Have students meet in quads to share their writing for the day. Allow approximately two minutes for students to share.

Homework

Ask students to look and listen at home for funny stories or personal anecdotes that could potentially develop into a story mountain narrative.

Building a Story Mountain Notebook Entr

Building a Story Mountain

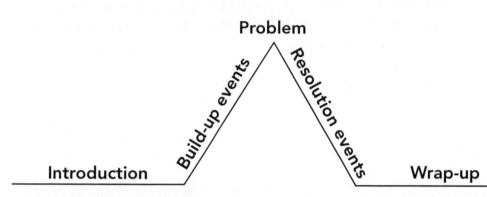

Introduction—Include the character(s), setting, and a "hook" to catch your reader.

Build-up events—These events lead the reader into the problem.

Problem—Something happens; a conflict.

Resolution events—These events sort out and solve the problem.

Wrap-up—The conclusion: What has changed from the beginning of the story?

Your Turn:

Use the story mountain pattern to create your own story. Try these story starters or create your own.

- Imagine you are caring for the class pet and suddenly it starts talking to you.

- On your way home from school, a hot air balloon lands right in front of you and your friend.

The Princess and the Pea Story cards

Directions: Cut out the cards. Use the cards to relate the events to the story mountain pattern.

The Princess and the Pea

Once there was a prince who wanted a "real" princess. He searched far and wide and met many beautiful princesses.

But, he could not be sure they were "real."

He returned home and found at his gate a princess. She was a real mess.

She said she was a "real" princess. But the prince, king, and queen wanted to be absolutely positive she was a princess.

The queen placed a tiny pea under all the bedding—20 mattresses and 20 quilts. That night the princess could not sleep at all.

The royal family was thrilled. Only a real princess could have been disturbed by a tiny pea.

Little Red Riding Hood Story Cards

Directions: Cut out the cards. Use the cards to relate the events to the story mountain pattern.

Little Red Riding Hood

Once there was a little girl named Little Red Riding Hood.

She packed a lunch and headed down the forest path to her grandma's house.

The wolf ran ahead and let himself into Granny's house.

Little Red Riding Hood ran out of Granny's house screaming for help. A woodsman heard her cry for help.

The woodsman knocked out the wolf and carried him deep into the forest. Little Red Riding Hood and Granny enjoyed a delicious lunch.

Suggested Story Mountain Texts

Fairy Tales

Artell, Mike. 2003. *Petite Rouge: A Cajun Red Riding Hood*. New York: Puffin.

Birdseye, Tom. 2003. *Look Out Jack! The Giant is Back!* New York: Holiday House.

Brett, Jan. 1996. *Goldilocks and the Three Bears*. New York: Puffin.

———. 2007. *The Three Snow Bears*. New York: Putnam Juvenile.

———. 2010. *The Three Little Dassies*. New York: Putnam Juvenile.

Ernst, Lisa C. 1998. *Little Red Riding Hood: A New Fangled Prairie Tale*. New York: Simon & Schuster.

———. 2000. *Goldilocks Returns*. New York: Simon & Schuster Books for Young Readers.

Galdone, Paul. 1982. *Jack and the Beanstalk*. New York: Clarion Books.

———. 1985. *The Three Bears*. New York: Clarion Books.

———. 2011. *The Three Little Pigs*. New York: Clarion Books.

Geist, Ken. 2007. *Three Little Fish and the Big Bad Shark*. New York: Cartwheel Books.

Jackson, Ellen. 1998. *Cinder Edna*. New York: HarperCollins.

Kellogg, Steven. 1991. *Jack and the Beanstalk*. New York: HarperCollins.

———. 2002. *The Three Little Pigs*. New York: HarperCollins.

Ketteman, Helen. 2007. *Waynetta and the Cornstalk*. Park Ridge, IL: Albert Whitman & Company.

Louie, Ai-Ling. 1996. *Yeh-Shen: A Cinderella Story from China*. New York: Puffin.

Lowell, Susan. 2000. *Little Red Cowboy Hat*. New York: Henry Holt and Co.

———. 2001. *Cindy Ellen: A Wild Western Cinderella*. New York: HarperCollins.

———. 2004. *Dusty Locks and the Three Bears*. New York: Henry Holt and Co.

Marshall, James. 1993. *Little Red Riding Hood*. New York: Picture Puffins.

———. 1998. *Goldilocks and the Three Bears*. New York: Puffin.

———. 2000. *The Three Little Pigs*. New York: Grosset & Dunlap.

Rising, Luna. 1992. *Three Little Javelinas*. Lanham, MD: Rising Moon Books.

Scieszka, Jon. 1996. *The True Story of the Three Little Pigs*. New York: Puffin.

Thaler, Mike. 1997. *Cinderella Bigfoot*. New York: Cartwheel Books.

Trivizas, Eugene. 1997. *Three Little Wolves and the Big Bad Pig*. New York: Aladdin Paperbacks.

Ward, Nick. 2001. *A Wolf at the Door*. New York: Scholastic Paperbacks.

Young, Ed. 1996. *Lon Po Po: A Little Red Riding Hood Story from China*. New York: Puffin.

Suggested Story Mountain Texts (cont.)

Narratives

Brown, Marcia. 1998. *Cinderella*. New York: Aladdin Paperbacks.

Buehner, Caralyn. 2010. *The Escape of Marvin the Ape*. Logan, IA: Perfection Learning.

Daly, Niki. 2007. *Pretty Salma: A Little Red Riding Hood Story from Africa*. New York: Clarion Books.

Fletcher, Ralph. 2005. *Marshfield Dreams: When I Was A Kid*. New York: Henry Holt and Co.

Gray, Libby. 1999. *My Mama Had a Dancing Heart*. New York: Scholastic.

Havill, Juanita. 1987. *Jamaica's Find*. New York: Houghton Mifflin Company.

Henkes, Kevin. 2007. *Chrysanthemum*. New York: Greenwillow Books.

Keats, Ezra Jack. 1996. *The Snowy Day*. New York: Puffin.

———. 1998. *A Letter to Amy*. New York: Puffin.

———. 1998. *Goggles*. New York: Puffin.

———. 1998. *Peter's Chair*. New York: Puffin.

Laminack, Lester. 2004. *Saturdays and Teacakes*. Atlanta, GA: Peachtree Publishers.

Viorst, Judith. 2009. *Alexander and the Terrible, Horrible, No Good, Very Bad Day*. New York: Atheneum Books for Young Readers.

Willems, Mo. 2007. *Knuffle Bunny Too: A Case of Mistaken Identity*. New York: Hyperion.

William, Vera B. 1984. *A Chair for My Mother*. New York: Greenwillow Books.

Telling a Story

Standards

- Uses strategies to draft and revise written work
- Writes narrative accounts, such as poems and stories

Materials

- Chart paper
- Markers
- Writer's Notebooks
- *Telling a Story Notebook Entry* (page 154; tellingstory.pdf)

Mentor Texts

- *Fireflies* by Julie Brinckloe
- *Roller Coaster* by Marla Frazee
- *The Relatives Came* by Cynthia Rylant
- *Owl Moon* by Jane Yolen
- See *Mentor Text List* in Appendix C for other suggestions.

Procedures

Note: Modeling and creating stories together provides a structure that builds confidence with young writers. Model each section—telling, sketching, and writing—across several days to show students strategies for moving writing from telling the story to writing the story.

Think About Writing

1. Review with students that authors use a variety of organizational techniques as they write. Explain that today students will look at how authors build stories with a beginning, middle, and end.

2. Review mentor texts, if desired, and emphasize the author's use of beginning, middle, and end. For example, in *The Relatives Came*, Cynthia Rylant begins the story with a trip to visit relatives, the middle reflects the fun activities while the relatives were visiting, and the ending includes the return trip home and the dreams about the next visit.

Teach

3. Tell students, "Today I will show you how to build three paragraphs: a brilliant beginning, a mighty middle, and an excellent end." Explain that many authors use this structure for stories.

4. Display and discuss the *Telling a Story Notebook Entry* (page 154).

5. Fold a sheet of paper into three sections (top, middle, and bottom). Name each section as you touch it. The top section will be for the beginning. The middle section will be for the middle, and the bottom section will be for the ending.

Telling a Story (cont.)

6. Model how to create a story by telling, sketching, and writing:

   - Telling—Touch each section of the paper and orally tell the story.
   - Sketching—Draw a quick picture to illustrate what will happen in each section.
   - Writing—Write the story that you told and sketched.

Engage

7. Have students plan a story with partners by touching three fingers to represent the beginning, middle, and end of the story. Remind students to think about the story mountain pattern as they begin developing their own stories. Allow enough time so that both partners have an opportunity to share. Move around, listen in, provide guidance, and take notes.

Apply

8. Encourage students to build stories that are logical, sequenced, and that flow from beginning to end. Provide students with the *Telling a Story Notebook Entry* to add to their Writer's Notebook. Have students work on the *Your Turn* section before proceeding to their writing folders.

Write/Conference

9. Provide time for students to write. Observe the group for any confusion that needs to be addressed.

Spotlight Strategy

10. Spotlight students who have built stories that are well-planned from beginning to end. For example, "Writers, your work is awesome! Just look at Justine's work, with a well thought-out, sketched, and labeled beginning, middle, and end."

Share

11. Have students meet with partners to share their work. Ask students to retell the stories, using their pictures as guides. Allow approximately two minutes for students to share.

Homework

Have students ask their parents for interesting narrative story ideas about their experiences. Have them make a list of three ideas to bring back to Writer's Workshop.

Telling a Story Notebook Entry

Telling a Story

Narrative writing may be a fictional story like *The Wizard of Oz* or a personal story about something that happened to you. The purpose is to entertain the reader. Both have characters, settings, and sequenced events.

Beginning/Introduction The introduction may be one or two paragraphs. It will "hook" your reader and introduce the topic of your story. These paragraphs will include the characters and setting.	**Brilliant Beginning (BB)** • Hook • Characters: Who? • Setting: Where? When?
Middle/Body The middle paragraphs tell the events in the order in which they happened and give the story suspense. They should include enough details to make the experience come to life for the reader.	**Mighty Middle (MM)** What happened? How did it happen? Why did it happen? • Event 1 • Event 2 • Event 3
End/Conclusion The final paragraph sums up the story. It may share your feelings about the experience or event and why it was important to you.	**Excellent Ending (EE)** • Wrap-up • Feelings/Importance

#50917—Getting to the Core of Writing—Level 3 © Shell Education

More Than "Once Upon a Time"

Standards

- Uses strategies to draft and revise written work
- Writes narrative accounts, such as poems and stories

Materials

- Chart paper
- Markers
- Writer's Notebooks
- *The Gingerbread Man Hook Cards* (page 157; gingerbreadmancards.pdf)
- *More Than "Once Upon a Time" Notebook Entry* (page 158; moreonceuponatime.pdf)

Mentor Texts

- *The Gingerbread Man* by Jim Aylesworth
- Other children's story classics
- See *Mentor Text List* in Appendix C for other suggestions.

Procedures

Note: Give students ample time to examine stories and collect hooks, leads, and grabbers. Have students experiment with many children's classics and rewrite the "Once upon a time…" beginning. To extend this writing project, have students rewrite *The Gingerbread Man* or another favorite story.

Think About Writing

1. Explain that authors organize paragraphs in their stories. As proficient writers, we know the reader expects to find the main idea early in the paragraph and details need to support the main idea. However, creating interest for the reader right in the beginning requires that we read good literature, study the author's craft, and practice.

2. Review mentor texts, if desired, and emphasize the first few sentences of the book. Discuss whether the sentences create interest for the reader.

Teach

3. Tell students, "Today I will show you how to create a brilliant beginning to a story." Explain that having a great beginning makes the reader wonder what will happen and want to read more. Tell students exciting beginnings are called *grabbers*, *hooks*, or *leads*.

4. Write the following opening line from *The Gingerbread Man* on a sheet of chart paper:

   Once upon a time there was a little old woman and a little old man, and they lived all alone in a little old house.

   Ask students if they think this beginning is exciting or interesting. Does it make them want to read more?

More Than "Once Upon a Time" *(cont.)*

5. Tell students that there are four types of beginnings they can use to catch the reader's attention: Action, Sound, Question, and Character Description. Explain the four types of hooks using *The Gingerbread Man Hook Cards* (page 157). Display and discuss the *More Than "Once Upon a Time" Notebook Entry* (page 158).

Engage

6. Have students work in quads to change the first line in a familiar story. Ask students to try to create interesting beginning lines for the story using two of the four types of hooks. Use familiar stories such as *The Three Little Pigs*, *Little Red Riding Hood*, or other CCSS literature that you have available.

Apply

7. Encourage students to develop a brilliant beginning in their writing that grabs the reader's attention. Provide students with the *More Than "Once Upon a Time" Notebook Entry* to add to their Writer's Notebooks. Have students work on the *Your Turn* section before proceeding to their writing folders.

Write/Conference

8. Provide time for students to write. Scan your group for potential problems that need to be addressed. Then, rotate around the classroom to conference with individual students or work with small groups. Try to conference with three to five students each day.

Spotlight Strategy

9. Spotlight students who write interesting hooks. For example, "Listen to how Terri has hooked me into the story by creating an incredible lead, just like a real author! Smart writing work today!"

Share

10. Have students meet with partners to review the types of writing hooks. Then have students share the hooks they tried today. Ask them to share briefly and then find a new partner to share with. Allow approximately two minutes for students to share.

Homework

Have students write down the first sentence of three books. Ask students to identify the hooks used in each sentence.

The Gingerbread Man Hook Cards

Directions: Cut out the cards and use them to discuss the four types of hooks.

Action

The little old woman rolled him out, dressed him up and pinched his gingerbread shoes into shape. Now I shall have a little boy of my own!

Sound

Ah! Plunk! Swish! The Gingerbread Man jumped out of the oven and away he ran, out the door, and down the street!

Question

"Can you catch me?" he shouted to the little old woman. "Can you catch me?" he screamed at the little old man.

Character Description

The Gingerbread Man was a rascal. He was determined to outrun everyone who chased him. However, wait until you hear how he was outfoxed by a fox!

More Than "Once Upon a Time Notebook" Entry

More Than "Once Upon a Time"

Authors use a **hook** to grab the attention of their reader.

Try one of these hooks to begin your writing.

Action
The little old woman rolled him out, dressed him up and pinched his gingerbread shoes into shape. "Now I shall have a little boy of my own!"
Sound
Ah! Plunk! Swish! The Gingerbread Man jumped out of the oven and away he ran, out the door, and down the street!
Question
"Can you catch me?" he shouted to the little old woman. "Can you catch me?" he screamed at the little old man.
Character Description
The Gingerbread Man was a rascal. He was determined to outrun everyone who chased him. However, wait until you hear how he was outfoxed by a fox!

Your Turn:

Practice writing hooks by rewriting the beginning of other children's favorites, such as:

- *The Three Little Pigs*
- *Jack and the Beanstalk*

Circular Endings

Standards

- Uses strategies to draft and revise written work
- Writes narrative accounts, such as poems and stories

Materials

- Chart paper
- Markers
- Writer's Notebooks
- *Circular Endings Notebook Entry* (page 161; circularendings.pdf)

Mentor Texts

- *Snowmen at Night* by Caralyn Buehner
- *Shortcut* by Donald Crews
- *Whistle for Willie* by Ezra Jack Keats
- *The Paperboy* by Dav Pilkey
- *The Relatives Came* by Cynthia Rylant
- See *Mentor Text List* in Appendix C for other suggestions.

Procedures

Note: Notice endings in the literature you share with students. Specifically point out other ending types and remind students to collect endings in their notebook.

Think About Writing

1. Explain that authors create brilliant beginnings and mighty middles that lure the reader in to read more of the story. Authors often work just as hard on creating an ending that is perfect for wrapping up their writing.

2. Review mentor texts, if desired, and emphasize the author's use of a circular ending.

Teach

3. Tell students, "Today I will show you how to write a circular ending." Explain that circular endings have similar words, phrases, characters, or settings as the beginning of the story.

4. Display and review the *Circular Endings Notebook Entry* (page 161).

5. Review several mentor texts with students. Reread the first line and the last line of each text and ask students to identify how they are the same. Create a two-column table on chart paper. Label one column *Beginnings* and the other column *Endings*. Record words, phrases, characters, settings, or sentence structure from each mentor text.

Engage

6. Provide mentor texts to quads of students. Have partners decide if the text has a circular ending or a different ending. Ask students to be ready to share the reasoning behind their thinking.

7. Gather students together and allow groups to share. Continue the anchor chart started in Step 5 with student findings.

Circular Endings (cont.)

Apply

8. Encourage students to develop an ending that circles back to the beginning and stays with the reader. Provide students with the *Circular Endings Notebook Entry* to add to their Writer's Notebook. Have students work on the *Your Turn* section before proceeding to their writing folders.

Write/Conference

9. Provide time for students to work. Scan the group to identify students who need assistance getting started. Then, rotate among students to conference. Use your Conferring Notebook for anecdotal notes. Try to conference with three to five students each day.

Spotlight Strategy

10. Spotlight students who write good endings for their stories. For example, "Jana wrote an amazing ending. Listen to how she changed her writing to make it sound just like an author's ending. Smart writing work!"

Share

11. Have students share their writing with partners.

Homework

Have students write the beginning and ending lines of two books. Ask students to identify whether the ending is circular or completely different.

Circular Endings Notebook Entry

Circular Endings

Some authors use **circular endings** to connect their story's beginning to the story's ending by using similar words, phrases, characters, or settings.

Developing a circular ending can help you bring closure to your writing. Try mimicking some of these favorites in your stories.

Whistle for Willie by Ezra Jack Keats

B: Oh, how Peter wished he could whistle!

E: He whistled all the way there, and he whistled all the way home.

The Relatives Came by Cynthia Rylant

B: It was in the summer of the year when the relatives came. They came up from Virginia.

E: And when they were finally home in Virginia, they crawled into their silent, soft beds and dreamed about the next summer.

The Great Kapok Tree by Lynne Cherry

B: Two men walked into the rain forest.

E: Then he dropped the ax and walked out of the rain forest.

The Sunsets of Miss Olivia Wiggins by Lester Laminack

B: Miss Olivia Wiggins sits and looks at nothing and at everything, all at the same time.

E: All the while, Miss Olivia Wiggins sat perfectly still, staring at nothing and at everything, all at the same time.

Your Turn:

Find another book with a circular ending. Write what happens at the beginning and the end.

Writing a Letter

Standards

- Uses strategies to draft and revise written work
- Writes personal letters

Materials

- Chart paper
- Markers
- Writer's Notebooks
- *Writing a Friendly Letter Notebook Entry* (page 164; writingfriendlyletter.pdf)
- Examples of letters
- *Writing a Business Letter Notebook Entry* (page 165; writingbusinessletter.pdf)

Mentor Texts

- *Dear Peter Rabbit* by Alma Flor Ada
- *Yours Truly, Goldilocks* by Alma Flor Ada
- *Amelia's Notebook* by Marissa Moss
- *Thank You, Mr. Falker* by Patricia Polacco
- See *Mentor Text List* in Appendix C for other suggestions.

Procedures

Note: Writing letters to grandparents, school staff, or veterans is an excellent opportunity for a real-world connection.

Think About Writing

1. Remind students that there are many different kinds of writing and each has its own purpose. Tell students that today they will explore different types of letter writing.

2. Review mentor texts, if desired, and emphasize the author's use of letter writing in the book.

Teach

3. Tell students, "Today I will show you how to organize your thinking for writing friendly and business letters."

4. Tell students that friendly letters have five basic parts: date, greeting, body, closing, and signature. Display and review the *Writing a Friendly Letter Notebook Entry* (page 164). Use your fingers as you name each part of the letter. Have students repeat the five parts of a friendly letter. Write a friendly letter on chart paper. Label each of the five parts of the letter.

5. Distribute examples of friendly letters and allow students a few minutes to explore the materials. Samples may include: business letters, letters from friends, thank you notes, letters to the editor, etc. You may wish to place the sample letters in sheet protectors and use wipe-off markers to identify parts of the letters. Gather the class back together and record observations about the letters on a class chart.

6. Repeat Steps 4 and 5, discussing the characteristics of a business letter using the *Writing a Business Letter Notebook Entry* (page 165) and showing student samples.

Writing a Letter (cont.)

Engage

7. Remind students to consider the audience when they write letters. The format of the letter should be adjusted based on who will be receiving the letter. Have students meet with partners to discuss possible audiences for letters which they would like to write.

Apply

8. Encourage students to try writing a letter in the correct format. Provide students with the *Writing a Friendly Letter Notebook Entry* and the *Writing a Business Letter Notebook Entry* to add to their Writer's Notebook. Have students work on the *Your Turn* section before proceeding to their writing folders.

Write/Conference

9. Provide time for students to write. Scan the classroom to check for students who may need assistance getting started. Then, rotate among students to conference with individuals or small groups. Make observations of your instruction.

Spotlight Strategy

10. Spotlight students who understand the format of a letter. For example, "Spotlighting! Look at the brilliant way Gayle is organizing a letter. Be proud that your reader will fully understand this message."

Share

11. Have students share their letters with partners. Tell students, "Let's play TAG today."

> T—Tell a compliment.
> A—Ask a question.
> G—Give a suggestion.

Homework

Ask students to find one example of a letter to bring to school to share. Tell students that they can write one if they cannot find one.

Writing a Friendly Letter Notebook Entry

Writing a Friendly Letter

A **friendly letter** is written to someone you know well, like a grandparent, cousin, or friend.

Friendly letters are written to share an experience, give information, thank someone, offer an invitation, or share words of kindness.

The five parts of a friendly letter include the date, greeting, body, closing, and signature.

March 24, 2012 ← **date**

Dear Dawna, ← **greeting (polite hello)**

I am so happy you and your family will be meeting us at the beach. We will have a great time getting a tan, fishing off the pier, and eating delicious seafood. The key to the beach house will be with Ms. Morrison, the neighbor, at 183 Pacific Drive. We should be arriving around 8 o'clock Sunday evening. Can't wait to see you. ← **body**

Your friend, ← **closing (polite good-bye)**

Xavier ← **signature**

Your Turn:

Write a friendly letter to someone you know well. Be sure to include all five parts of a friendly letter.

Writing a Business Letter Notebook Entry

Writing a Business Letter

A **business letter** may be written to request or share information, or tell someone about a problem. We may write a business letter to persuade or convince someone to consider our ideas or our opinion about a topic, or to request donations for a project.

The seven parts of a business letter include the heading, date, inside address, greeting, body, closing, and signature.

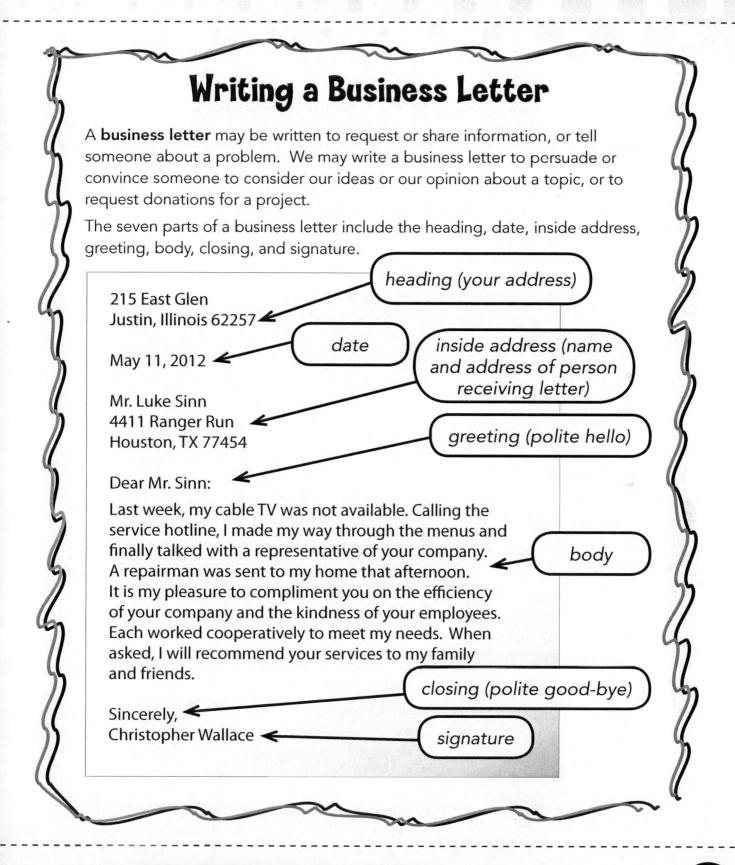

215 East Glen
Justin, Illinois 62257 ← **heading (your address)**

May 11, 2012 ← **date**

Mr. Luke Sinn
4411 Ranger Run
Houston, TX 77454 ← **inside address (name and address of person receiving letter)**

Dear Mr. Sinn: ← **greeting (polite hello)**

Last week, my cable TV was not available. Calling the service hotline, I made my way through the menus and finally talked with a representative of your company. A repairman was sent to my home that afternoon. ← **body**
It is my pleasure to compliment you on the efficiency of your company and the kindness of your employees. Each worked cooperatively to meet my needs. When asked, I will recommend your services to my family and friends.

Sincerely, ← **closing (polite good-bye)**
Christopher Wallace ← **signature**

It's My Opinion!

Standards

- Uses strategies to draft and revise work
- Writes opinion compositions

Materials

- Chart paper
- Markers
- Writer's Notebooks
- *It's My Opinion! Notebook Entry* (page 168; itsmyopinion.pdf)
- *It's My Opinion! Organizer* (page 169; itsmyopinionorganizer.pdf)

Mentor Texts

- *Should We Have Pets?* by Sylvia Lollis
- *I Wanna New Room* by Karen Orloff
- See *Mentor Text List* in Appendix C for other suggestions.

Procedures

Note: Teach this lesson over several days. The first modeling session should be done as a whole class shared writing project.

Think About Writing

1. Remind students there are many types of writing. Explain that today's lesson will be on writing an opinion to try to persuade the reader to agree with the writer's point of view.

2. Review mentor texts, if desired, and emphasize the author's use of opinion in the book.

Teach

3. Say, "Today I will show you how to develop an opinion essay." Tell students that an opinion essay is an essay that tells what you believe.

4. Explain that an opinion essay has three parts. List the three parts on chart paper:

   - *A brilliant beginning states your opinion and grabs the reader's attention.*
   - *A mighty middle states your reasons for the opinion.*
   - *An excellent ending concludes the essay and restates your opinion.*

   You may wish to color code the sections of an essay using green for the beginning, yellow for the middle, and red for the end.

5. Display and discuss the *It's My Opinion! Notebook Entry* (page 168) and *It's My Opinion! Organizer* (page 169).

6. Model how to use the organizer for an opinion essay on chart paper. Consider developing the organizer based on a mentor text or a familiar topic for your class, such as recess time or taking a field trip. Think aloud as you create your organizer.

It's My Opinion! *(cont.)*

7. Model how to use the completed organizer to write an essay. Think aloud as you write the essay to clearly model how you use the organizer to assist you.

Engage

8. Have students meet with partners to share some opinions or issues that they feel strongly about: free time at school, a public office, ideas for making school more interesting, homework policies, etc. Allow approximately two minutes for partners to share.

Apply

9. Encourage students to write persuasive essays to convince the reader of their opinion. Remind students of the parts of an opinion essay: a brilliant beginning, including a topic sentence to explain your opinions, a body to give reasons why you think the way you do, and a concluding statement restating your opinion. Provide students with the *It's My Opinion! Notebook Entry* to add to their Writer's Notebooks and the *It's My Opinion! Organizer* for their writing folders. Have students work on the *Your Turn* section of the notebook entry before proceeding to their writing folders.

Write/Conference

10. Provide time for students to write. Scan the classroom for students who need assistance getting started. Then, rotate around the room to conference with students. Record your observations in your Conferring Notebook.

Spotlight Strategy

11. Spotlight students who understand opinion writing. For example, "Spotlight! Anneka understands that an opinion essay convinces someone of her view. Her writing has reasons to support her thoughts. Brilliant thinking!"

Share

12. Have students share their ideas with partners. Remind students to give a compliment and make a comment. Choose one or two who understood the idea and have them share with the whole group.

Homework

Ask students to make lists of three new topics they can use to write opinion essays. Encourage them to talk with their parents to get some ideas.

It's My Opinion! Notebook Entry

It's My Opinion!

Authors use **opinion writing** to persuade, or convince, the reader to agree with his/her point of view.

Opinion writing contains supporting facts and reasons organized from the strongest to the weakest. Many times, opinion writing is written in the form of a letter and includes:

Beginning/Introduction

The beginning paragraph includes a focus sentence that states your opinion. It should grab the reader's attention through building background information.

Middle/Body

The middle paragraphs each begin with a topic sentence that states the reasons for your opinion. Each reason should be supported by facts and examples. This section is also referred to as the argument of the paper.

End/Conclusion

The final paragraph summarizes key points and restates your opinion. It may include a "last plea" to win the reader over to your thinking.

Know the difference!

Opinion: a belief that is based on what someone thinks

> "Cats make great pets."

Fact: a statement that you can prove to be true

> "Cats have 290 bones in their bodies."

Your Turn:

Think of three topics on which you have strong opinions. Make a list of your opinions that you might want to develop in your writing, then begin completing your organizer.

Name: _____ Date: _____

It's My Opinion! Organizer

Directions: Use the organizer below to help you organize your opinion writing.

Beginning	• Position/opinion • Hook • Summary of reasons Remember: Use only words and phrases to organize your thoughts and ideas.	
Middle	Reason #1	Fact/Example: Fact/Example: Fact/Example:
	Reason #2	Fact/Example: Fact/Example: Fact/Example:
End	• Restate position/ opinion • Last plea • End on a positive note	

Just Stating the Facts

Standards

- Uses strategies to draft and revise written work
- Writes expository compositions

Materials

- Chart paper
- Markers
- Writer's Notebooks
- *Just Stating the Facts Notebook Entry* (page 172; juststatingfacts.pdf)
- *Just Stating the Facts Organizer* (page 173; statingfactsorganizer.pdf)

Mentor Texts

- Select nonfiction titles based on your theme, e.g., magnets, electricity, storms, people. Seymour Simon and Jim Arnosky are two of the many recognized authors of nonfiction for young children. *National Geographic Kids* and *Eye Wonder: DK Publishing* are also excellent resources for young researchers.
- See *Mentor Text List* in Appendix C for other suggestions.

Procedures

Note: This mini-lesson works best when presented as a shared writing exercise, with teacher and students collaborating on text content. Once modeling is complete, students may create additional pieces of writing with a partner.

Think About Writing

1. Review with students that there are many types of informative writing. Tell students that informative writing sometimes describes a process, such as a how-to. It can be a report, or a collection of information to share our knowledge. Informative writing can be found in newspapers, magazine articles, and nonfiction books.

2. Review mentor texts, if desired, and emphasize the type of informative writing.

Teach

3. Tell students, "Today I will show you how to develop an informative essay, sometimes called an *expository essay*."

4. Tell students that an informative essay also has three parts. List the three parts on chart paper:

   - *A beginning or introduction gains the reader's interest.*

   - *A middle or body contains facts, reasons, or details.*

   - *An end, conclusion, or wrap-up summarizes all the main points.*

   You may wish to color code the sections of an essay, using green for the beginning, yellow for the middle, and red for the end.

5. Display and discuss the *Just Stating the Facts Notebook Entry* (page 172) and the *Just Stating the Facts Organizer* (page 173).

6. On chart paper, model how to use the organizer for an informative essay. Think aloud as you create your organizer.

Just Stating the Facts *(cont.)*

7. Model how to use the completed organizer to write an essay. Think aloud as you write the essay to clearly model how you use the organizer to assist you.

Engage

8. Have students think about something they can write about to explain or give directions. Tell them that as they talk with their partners, they should think about the three main parts: a hook and an introduction or opening statement, a body that tells important reasons or steps, and a concluding paragraph that gives a feeling of completion. Have them brainstorm some ideas they might include in their informative writing.

Apply

9. Remind students that informative writing allows us to share knowledge about a variety of subjects. Scientists and journalists use it every day. Provide students with the *Just Stating the Facts Notebook Entry* to add to their Writer's Notebooks and the *Just Stating the Facts Organizer* for their writing folders. Have students work on the *Your Turn* section of the notebook entry before proceeding to their writing folders.

Write/Conference

10. Provide time for students to write. Problem solve with students who are having difficulties getting started, before moving off to provide individual or small group conferences. Pull a small group to reteach, if needed.

Spotlight Strategy

11. Spotlight students who begin planning their writing immediately. For example, "Trajan is moving into his writing plan with no wasted time. Excellent work ethic."

Share

12. Have students meet in triads to share their writing. Observe and take notes to plan future instruction. Share successes you notice with the whole class.

> ### Homework
> Have students search around their homes for forms of informative writing. Ask students to bring at least one form of informative writing to school to share with the class.

Just Stating the Facts Notebook Entry

Just Stating the Facts

Authors use **informative** writing to tell or teach their reader about a topic.

Informative writing identifies a subject or topic, uses specific vocabulary, and uses facts to teach the reader. It contains:

Beginning/Introduction

The introduction states the subject, includes a topic sentence, and gains the reader's interest in the writing.

Middle/Body

The middle paragraphs begin with a topic sentence that states the main idea. These paragraphs contain facts, reasons, or details to support the subject.

End/Conclusion

The final paragraph summarizes and restates the main points to remind the reader of the important points/steps of the writing piece.

Your Turn:

Make a list of three topics you know a lot about and may want to develop into a writing piece.

Name: _____ Date: _____

Just Stating the Facts Organizer

Directions: Use the organizer below to help you organize your informative writing.

Beginning	**Hook**—Strong topic sentence	
Middle	**Main idea**—State reason #1 Use facts and examples to support	
	Main idea—State reason #2 Use facts and examples to support	
End	**Wrap up**—Restate important points	

Poetry Fun

Standards

- Uses strategies to draft and revise written work
- Writes narrative accounts, such as poems and stories

Materials

- Chart paper
- Markers
- Writer's Notebooks
- *Poetry Fun Notebook Entry* (page 176; poetryfun.pdf)

Mentor Texts

- *A Kick in the Head* by Paul Janeczko
- *Kids' Poems: Teaching Third & Fourth Graders to Love Writing Poetry* by Regie Routman
- See *Mentor Text List* in Appendix C for other suggestions.

Procedures

Note: Four types of poetry are provided in this lesson. Introduce one type at a time. Allow students to become familiar with each type before introducing other types. Once children are comfortable with poetry patterns, move to free verse poetry.

Think About Writing

1. Tell students that poetry is a fun style of writing. Explain that you will be teaching them some poetry patterns. Once students have had a chance to create several types of poems, the class will publish an anthology, or collection, of poetry.

2. Review mentor texts, if desired, and emphasize the various types of poetry.

Teach

3. Tell students, "Today I will show you a poetry pattern." Explain that poetry patterns are a fun, simple, and easy way to begin writing in the genre of poetry.

4. Select a poetry pattern to model for students. Use the *Poetry Fun Notebook Entry* (page 176) as a guide for each type of poetry pattern.

5. Write the poetry pattern on chart paper. Then, model how to fill in the pattern with words to create a poem. Add illustrations to expand understanding and publish a class poetry anthology.

Poetry Fun (cont.)

Cinquain	5 Ws Poetry
Noun	Each line answers a question:
Two adjectives	Who?
Three verbs	What?
Four feeling words	Where?
Repeat title or synonym	When?
	Why?
Diamante	**Couplet**
Noun	Two lines
Two adjectives	Last word of each line rhymes
Three-word sentence	
Four -ing verbs	
Three-word sentence	
Two adjectives	
Synonym for line 1	

Write/Conference

8. Provide time for students to write. Today, keep yourself free to rove and confer. Make suggestions on topics, words, and phrases. Make observations in your Conferring Notebook to determine what needs reteaching and plan future small-group instruction.

Spotlight Strategy

9. Spotlight students who work together to write poems. For example, "Allison and Emily are working together, helping each other create poems."

Share

10. Have students meet with partners to share their poetry. Based on teacher observation, select a couple of poems to share with the group.

Engage

6. Have students work with partners to brainstorm topics for poetry. Gather students together and have them share their ideas with the whole class. Create a class idea chart to support students as they write their poetry.

Apply

7. Provide students with the *Poetry Fun Notebook Entry* to add to their Writer's Notebook. Have students work on the *Your Turn* section before proceeding to their writing folders. Encourage students to try the different types of poetry listed on the notebook entry once they have all been introduced.

Homework

Have students make lists of three words or topics that they would like to use when writing poetry.

Poetry Fun Notebook Entry

Poetry Fun

Cinquain Line 1: Noun Line 2: Two adjectives Line 3: Three verbs Line 4: Four feeling words Line 5: Repeat title or synonym	**5 Ws Poetry** Each line answers a question: Who? What? Where? When? Why?
Diamante Noun Two adjectives Three-word sentence Four -ing verbs Three-word sentence Two adjectives Synonym for line 1	**Couplet** Two lines Last word of each line rhymes

Your Turn:

Write a poem about a topic of your choice using the types of poetry above.

Word Choice

Showing Your Story

The use of rich, descriptive words by the writer can show the reader a mental image. By studying word choice, students will learn how to use vivid, colorful, and dynamic words to enrich their writing and make it as precise as possible. The use of amazing words is encouraged; however, everyday words used correctly are also celebrated. The lessons help students explore different types of words and the ways they can be used to create interest in writing pieces. Lessons in this section include the following:

- Lesson 1: Be Specific! (page 179)

- Lesson 2: Vivid Verbs (page 182)

- Lesson 3: Amazing Adjectives (page 185)

- Lesson 4: Banished, Boring Words (page 188)

- Lesson 5: Transition Words (page 193)

- Lesson 6: Super Similes (page 198)

- Lesson 7: Awesome Adverbs (page 201)

- Lesson 8: Interesting Idioms (page 206)

The *Wally, Word Choice Detective* poster (page 178) can be displayed in the room to provide a visual reminder for students that word choice is one of the traits of writing. You may wish to introduce this poster during the first lesson on word choice. Then, refer to the poster when teaching other lessons on word choice to refresh students' memories and provide them with questions to help guide them as they make choices for words they use in their writing.

Wally
Word Choice Detective

What words will paint a picture for my reader?

✔ Did I use some amazing words?

✔ Did I use sensory words?

✔ Did I use action words?

✔ Did I use a variety of words?

Be Specific!

Procedures

Note: This lesson will require repetition to build understanding of how parts of speech impact the written message. Build understanding through practice in the Writer's Notebook and revising writing projects.

Think About Writing

1. Explain that authors organize their writing and create sentences with variety and fluency. The words we use create the pictures we paint for our readers. Share the following quote from Ruth Culham: "Pay attention to the little things. Don't shut things out. Your memory is smarter than you think. There are interesting bits and pieces in there. Let them come to the surface."

2. Review mentor texts, if desired, and emphasize the author's use of proper nouns and adjectives in the book.

Teach

3. Tell students, "Today I will show you how to use words to paint a picture for your reader by giving specific details." Explain that authors do this by expanding common nouns into proper nouns and by adding descriptive words or adjectives. Review the terms *common noun*, *proper noun*, and *adjective* with students.

4. Write the following sentence on chart paper:

   The car raced down the street.

   Tell students they can create a better picture in the reader's mind by being more specific about the kind of car. Have students brainstorm various types of cars they know. Make a list on chart paper. Rewrite the sentence with a specific type of car mentioned in it. For example:

   The Ford Thunderbird raced down the street.

   Guide students through additional brainstorming to add a proper noun to name the street. For example:

   The Ford Thunderbird raced down Washington Avenue.

Be Specific! *(cont.)*

5. Ask students to be more specific about the car or street by adding adjectives to describe them. Have students brainstorm adjectives to describe the car. Make a list on chart paper. Rewrite the sentence with adjectives added to it. For example:

   The candy apple red Ford Thunderbird raced down congested Washington Avenue.

6. Display and discuss the *Be Specific! Notebook Entry* (page 181).

Engage

7. Encourage students to paint pictures with words in their writing. Have students talk with partners to practice adding proper nouns and adjectives to the following sentences:

   • *The boy got a lot of stuff for his birthday.*

   • *The queen lived in a castle.*

Apply

8. Encourage students to be specific in their writing. Provide students with the *Be Specific! Notebook Entry* to add to their Writer's Notebook. Have students work on the *Your Turn* section before proceeding to their writing folders.

Write/Conference

9. Provide time for students to write. Select a small group and write common nouns on sticky notes. Have students generate proper nouns and adjectives to describe the nouns. Make astute observations to determine future planning. Allow four or five minutes to work with the small group and then begin rotating among the class to conference with students as they write.

Spotlight Strategy

10. Spotlight students who use good descriptive words in their writing. For example, "Spotlighting! Isaiah has truly used his memory to write specific words that paint a picture for his reader. Such clever, skillful writing!"

Share

11. Have students meet in quads to share. Ask each student to share his or her detailed sentences. Provide approximately two minutes for students to share.

Homework

Ask students to pay close attention to the proper nouns and adjectives they hear and read tonight. Have them write a list of three proper nouns and three adjectives.

Be Specific! Notebook Entry

Be Specific!

Authors use specific words, such as proper nouns, to create a clear picture in the reader's mind.

A **common noun** is a person, place, or thing.

A **proper noun** is the specific name of a person, place, or thing and always begins with a capital letter.

Common Noun	Proper Noun	Descriptive Words
car	Ford Thunderbird	1955 candy apple red convertible
street	Washington Avenue	narrow congested

- The car raced down the street.

- The 1955 candy apple red Ford Thunderbird convertible raced down narrow, congested Washington Avenue.

Your Turn:

Writers, be specific using these words. Then, create and add new sentences to your notebook. Remember to capitalize the proper nouns.

Common Noun	Proper Noun	Descriptive Words
hamburger		
store		
teacher		
band		
dog		

Vivid Verbs

Standards

- Uses descriptive and precise language that clarifies and enhances ideas
- Uses verbs in written compositions

Materials

- Chart paper
- Markers
- Writer's Notebooks
- *Vivid Verbs Notebook Entry* (page 184; vividverbs.pdf)

Mentor Texts

- *Kites Sail High* by Ruth Heller
- *Nouns and Verbs Have a Field Day* by Robin Pulver
- *Nothing Ever Happens on 90th Street* by Roni Schotter
- See *Mentor Text List* in Appendix C for other suggestions.

Procedures

Note: Understanding parts of speech through explicit instruction and concrete manipulatives moves students toward independence in writing stories, essays, and compositions. Repetition of this lesson stores information in students' short-term and long-term memory. Build an ongoing anchor chart and continue to add vivid verbs.

Think About Writing

1. Explain that authors use interesting verbs to give power to their message. Read aloud the opening sentences of *Nothing Ever Happens on 90th Street* and ask students to notice how they are drawn into the action immediately: "Eva unwrapped a cinnamon Danish, opened her notebook, and stared helplessly at the wide, white pages."

2. Review mentor texts, if desired, and emphasize the author's use of interesting verbs.

Teach

3. Tell students, "Today I will show you how to make your sentences interesting using vibrant, vivid verbs."

4. Write the following pairs of nouns and verbs on chart paper:

   - *puppy whined*
   - *children bounced*
   - *car screeched*

   Model how to orally create a sentence with each pair of words. For example, "The puppy whined because it was hungry."

5. With students, think of other vivid verbs to use in each sentence. For example, "The puppy howled..." or, "The car skidded...." Begin a new chart titled *Vivid Verbs* and add some vivid verbs to this chart. Ask students to look for verbs as they read books to add to the chart. This chart should be added to continually in order to give students a list of interesting verbs.

Vivid Verbs (cont.)

Engage

6. Write the following sentences on chart paper. Have students work with partners to think of vivid verbs for each sentence:

   - My cousin _____ the fence.
   - The bear _____ the beehive.
   - That airplane _____ above the trees.

   Listen as students practice creating sentences. Gather the group back together to have students share their sentences out loud.

Apply

7. Encourage students to include vivid verbs as a powerful way to give the reader a strong picture of action. Provide students with the *Vivid Verbs Notebook Entry* (page 184) to add to their Writer's Notebook. Have students work on the *Your Turn* section before proceeding to their writing folders.

Write/Conference

8. Provide time for students to write. Write vivid verbs on sticky notes and be prepared to pull in a small guided writing group. Suggested verbs include: *moan, measure, protect, wobble,* and *wrestle.* Work with the small group for four or five minutes and then rotate around the classroom to conference with individual students.

Spotlight Strategy

9. Spotlight students who use verbs to paint vivid pictures in the reader's mind. For example, "Writers, listen to this idea! Henrique has delivered a powerful punch with a brilliant example of vibrant verbs! Remarkable sentence work."

Share

10. Invite two or three students to share their work in the Author's Chair. Select students who have clearly included vivid verbs in their writing. Allow the other students to comment and question.

Homework

Have students listen for vivid verbs. Ask students to make a list of five vivid verbs they hear tonight. Encourage them to add the verbs to the chart tomorrow.

Vivid Verbs Notebook Entry

Vivid Verbs

Authors conjure up just the right vivid **verbs** to paint powerful pictures for their readers.

A verb is a word that expresses an act, occurrence, or state of being.

- It <u>thundered</u> last night.
- Last night, the thunder <u>boomed</u> in the quiet night, <u>startling</u> me from my sleep.

In your Writer's Notebook, select vivid verbs and create a few sentences. Then, examine and revise your draft writing and conjure up vivid verbs.

- screech
- challenge
- bubble
- crash
- capture

- embarrass
- irritate
- interrupt
- whirl
- squirm

- devour
- collide
- grin
- hurl
- tremble

Remember: Show, don't tell!

Your Turn:

Write sentences using at least four of the verbs from the list above.

Amazing Adjectives

Standards

- Uses descriptive and precise language that clarifies and enhances ideas
- Uses adjectives in written compositions

Materials

- Chart paper
- Markers
- Writer's Notebooks
- *Amazing Adjectives Notebook Entry* (page 187; amazingadjectives.pdf)

Mentor Texts

- *Hairy, Scary, Ordinary* by Brian Cleary
- *Bedhead* by Margie Palatini
- See *Mentor Text List* in Appendix C for other suggestions.

Procedures

Note: Adjectives should be used sparingly, but sprinkled in to add flavor and energy. Repeat this lesson as often as necessary using a variety of literature to show examples of adjectives.

Think About Writing

1. Explain to students that authors use adjectives to create pictures in the reader's mind.

2. Review mentor texts, if desired, and emphasize the author's use of adjectives. For example, in *Bedhead*, Margie Palatini got right to work in the first paragraph with mighty images. Notice how the following phrases get you interested: "bleary-eyed Oliver," "soapy silver soap dish," "foggy shaving mirror," and "his hair looked like a coughed-up fur ball."

Teach

3. Tell students, "Today I will show you how adjectives can be used to paint pictures with words." Explain that an adjective modifies, or tells about, a noun or pronoun.

4. Write the following examples of adjectives and nouns on chart paper:

   - *angry child*
   - *damaged book*
   - *handsome boy*
   - *adorable kitten*
   - *glamorous lady*
   - *sticky fingers*

   Model how to create a sentence from each word pair. For example, "The angry child stomped her feet." Write the sentences on chart paper. Discuss with students how the adjective provides a better picture of the noun.

Amazing Adjectives (cont.)

5. Create a new chart titled *Amazing Adjectives* and, with students, list some alternative adjectives for each noun listed above, for example, *furious* for *angry*, or *elegant* for *glamorous*. Ask students to look for adjectives as they read books to add to the chart. This chart should be added to continually in order to give students a list of interesting adjectives.

Engage

6. Have students work with partners to think of adjectives for the following sentences:

- *I ate the _____ apple.*
- *This is my _____ brother.*
- *Look at the _____ lightning!*

Allow two or three minutes for students to work. Have students share adjectives and add them to the *Amazing Adjectives* chart.

Apply

7. Encourage students to use adjectives sparingly and wisely. Remind students that well-chosen adjectives create interest, but overuse adds little meaning to a sentence. Provide students with the *Amazing Adjectives Notebook Entry* (page 187) to add to their Writer's Notebook. Have students work on the *Your Turn* section before proceeding to their writing folders.

Write/Conference

8. Provide time for students to write. Have a few adjectives on sticky notes to work with in small groups, or reteach using the notebook entry. Spend several minutes working with the small group and then rotate around the room and individually conference. Remember to make astute observations to plan future instruction.

Spotlight Strategy

9. Spotlight students who use adjectives to add interest to their writing. For example, "Spotlighting! Listen to the great use of adjectives in the following sentences."

Share

10. Have students work in triads to share their use of adjectives in sentences. Allow approximately two minutes for students to share.

> ### Homework
>
> Ask students to spend some time this evening talking with their parents about amazing adjectives. Have students make a list of five nouns and amazing adjectives to match each noun.

Amazing Adjectives Notebook Entry

Amazing Adjectives

Authors use **adjectives** sparingly and wisely to provide details and clarity in their writing.

An adjective describes or tells more about a person, place, or thing.

- Mom made a cake.

- Mom made a pineapple upside-down cake.

Here are a few amazing adjectives to get you started. Notice others in the stories you read and record them in your Writer's Notebook.

• exotic	• gracious	• grungy
• fascinating	• fancy	• innovative
• miniscule	• drab	• squishy
• sizzling	• curly	• murky
• gloomy	• tangled	• empty
• tedious	• radiant	• screeching
• exceptional	• dreary	• thundering

Your Turn:

Create sentences using at least four of the amazing adjectives above.

Banished, Boring Words

Standard

Uses descriptive and precise language that clarifies and enhances ideas

Materials

- Chart paper
- Markers
- Writer's Notebooks
- *Banished Word Cards* (pages 191–192; banishedwordcards.pdf)
- *Banished, Boring Words Notebook Entry* (page 190; banishedboringwords.pdf)

Mentor Texts

- *Bedhead* by Margie Palatini
- Literature from CCSS or Core Reading Program
- See *Mentor Text List* in Appendix C for other suggestions.

Procedures

Note: Remind students that worn-out, overused words should be banished and rarely used. Repeat this lesson several times, banishing a different word each time, to remind students to challenge their thinking and vary their vocabulary.

Think About Writing

1. Explain that authors stretch out their stories and use clear, vivid word choice to spice up their texts and make them more interesting. Tell students that some words do not provide richness and excitement, and authors challenge themselves to throw out old, worn-out words and add rich, energetic words to hold the reader's attention.

2. Review mentor texts, if desired, and emphasize the author's use of rich, interesting vocabulary.

Teach

3. Tell students, "Today I will show you how to use more interesting words in the place of words that are commonly used." Explain to students that this simple substitution will make their writing more understandable and more interesting for their readers.

4. Choose a word to banish, such as *bad*. Display the *Banished Word Cards* (pages 191–192) for the chosen word. Explain to students that this word is often overused and should be banished. Use great fanfare to get rid of the word. Consider burying it in the schoolyard, throwing it away, or displaying it on a *Banished Words* bulletin board to remind students that it is a banished word.

5. Create a list on chart paper of other words that can be used instead of the word *bad*. Provide several examples, such as *disgusting*, *horrible*, and *lousy*. Have students help brainstorm words, too. This list should be displayed and continually added to as students encounter synonyms in reading.

Banished, Boring Words (cont.)

6. Model how using more interesting words helps make a sentence more interesting. Write a sentence on the chart paper using the banished word. For example:

    It was a <u>bad</u> day.

    Then change the banished word to a more interesting one and discuss how the change improved the sentence. For example:

    It was a <u>lousy</u> day.

Engage

7. Tell students that their job as a writer is to check their work for old, weak, worn-out words. Ask them to see if they can exchange those words for something more exciting, thrilling, and challenging. Read aloud each sentence below or write it on a sentence strip:

    - *Josh had a <u>nice</u> time.*
    - *I got <u>stuff</u> for my birthday.*

    Have them turn to their partners and practice making some brilliant sentences, substituting words for the underlined word.

Apply

8. Remind students to try different words in the place of those words that have been banished. Provide students with the *Banished, Boring Words Notebook Entry* (page 190) to add to their Writer's Notebook. Have students work on the *Your Turn* section before proceeding to their writing folders.

Write/Conference

9. Provide time for students to write. Scan your group to see if anyone needs assistance getting started. Then, rotate around the room to conference with individual students or meet with a small group to quickly reteach or practice a concept.

Spotlight Strategy

10. Spotlight students who use interesting words to make their writing better. For example, "Spotlight! Look at all of your brilliant sentences. You have challenged yourselves and must be proud of the way you're making important changes in word choice. Smart writing!"

Share

11. Have students meet with partners to share their writing. Encourage students to TAG today—Tell a compliment, Ask a question, and Give a suggestion. Provide approximately two to three minutes for students to share.

Homework

Ask students to tell their parents the banished words they learned. Have students work with their parents to create a list of at least three other words that can be used in place of the banished words.

Banished, Boring Words Notebook Entry

Banished, Boring Words

Authors select words that enhance and add meaning to their writing. They revise their writing and add words that are more interesting to readers.

You can revise your writing by finding words from the list below that need to be banished. Replace them with strong, descriptive words that will grab your reader's attention.

Banished Word	Interesting Words
good	amazing, incredible, phenomenal
bad	disgusting, horrible, lousy, terrible
went	strolled, dashed, jogged, scampered
happy	delighted, ecstatic, cheerful, glad
sad	awful, miserable, blue, gloomy
big	enormous, jumbo, gigantic, mammoth
little	miniature, petite, puny, wee
a lot	often, many, several, countless
fun	enjoyable, playful, exciting, amusing
nice	kind, polite, caring, pleasant

Your Turn:

Create new sentences by replacing the underlined words with more descriptive words.

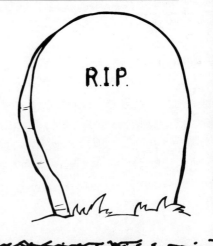

- Playing with my sister is <u>fun</u>.
- I ate <u>a lot</u> of food.
- Jesse <u>went</u> to the store.
- We had a <u>good</u> day.

#50917—Getting to the Core of Writing—Level 3 © Shell Education

Banished Word Cards

Directions: Cut out the cards. Display the cards for students, explaining that the words are often overused in writing.

Banished Word Cards (cont.)

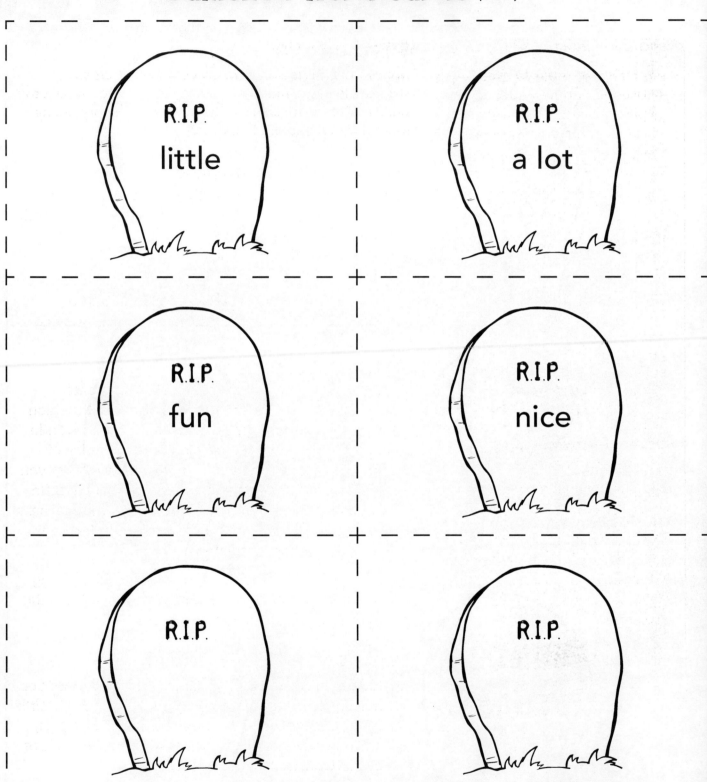

R.I.P.
little

R.I.P.
a lot

R.I.P.
fun

R.I.P.
nice

R.I.P.

R.I.P.

#50917—Getting to the Core of Writing—Level 3 © Shell Education

Transition Words

Standards

- Uses descriptive and precise language that clarifies and enhances ideas
- Links ideas using connecting words

Materials

- Chart paper
- Markers
- Writer's Notebooks
- *Transition Word Cards* (pages 196–197; transitionwordcards.pdf)
- *Transition Words Notebook Entry* (page 195; transitionwords.pdf)

Mentor Texts

- *How Groundhog's Garden Grew* by Lynne Cherry
- Literature from CCSS or Core Reading Program
- See *Mentor Text List* in Appendix C for other suggestions.

Procedures

Note: Apply this lesson to many writing projects so students learn to indicate a shift in sequencing. Repeat to build repetition for short- and long-term memory. Many repetitions are required for mastery.

Think About Writing

1. Explain to students that authors use special words called *transition words* to allow the text to flow smoothly from one point to the next.

Teach

2. Tell students, "Today I will show you how to use transition words to signal the reader you are moving to a new idea."

3. Display the *Transition Word Cards* (pages 196–197). Read each word to students, and have students repeat the words. Ask students to listen for transition words as you read parts of a mentor text that include transition words. For example, at the beginning of *How Groundhog's Garden Grew*, Squirrel says, "First, you need seeds." A few lines later, a paragraph begins, "In February," signaling a change in time. On the very next page, the author wrote, "weeks later," and a few pages later, the author wrote, "The next day."

4. Review the *Transition Word Cards* again, emphasizing that transition words are like road signs that guide the reader to understand the message.

Engage

5. Have students retell an old familiar children's classic or a nursery rhyme using transition words. *Mary Had a Little Lamb, Goldilocks and the Three Bears, Three Little Pigs,* and other well-known stories with a clear sequence of events work well for this activity.

Transition Words (cont.)

Apply

6. Remind students that transition words can be used to show relationships between paragraphs. Provide students with the *Transition Words Notebook Entry* (page 195) to add to their Writer's Notebook. Have students work on the *Your Turn* section before proceeding to their writing folders.

Write/Conference

7. Provide time for students to write. Rotate around the room and conference with students to check for understanding. Pay a compliment when appropriate, and use the conference as an opportunity to teach. Make observations in your Conferring Notebook.

Spotlight Strategy

8. Spotlight students who use transition words in their writing. For example, "You're well on your way. Just listen to this sophisticated use of signal words."

Share

9. Have students work together to share the writing they did today.

Homework

Ask students to identify an activity that they do at home in a sequence. Have them write down the activity sequence using transition words. For example, *First, I feed the dog. Next, I help mom with dinner. After that, I complete my homework. Last, I get ready for bed and prepare my book bag for tomorrow's school day.*

Transition Words Notebook Entry

Transition Words

Authors add **transition words or phrases** to signal and change from one idea to another. Some transition words or phrases are used to show the sequence or order in which things happen.

Here are some transition words you can use in your writing.

- first
- next
- after
- meanwhile
- during

- second
- then
- soon
- now
- finally

- third
- before
- since
- earlier
- at last

Your Turn:

Rewrite and revise this paragraph in your Writer's Notebook, using transition words to show the sequence of the story.

> Dan was getting ready for school. He picked up a red object and put it in his lunchbox. He knew that his teacher, Miss Hoover, would like it very much. He walked to the corner to catch his bus. Dan stepped into the classroom and walked to his teacher's desk. He handed her the red object. Miss Hoover replied, "Thank you very much, Dan!" Dan was thankful that his teacher appreciated the gift.

Remember to use transition words in your writing projects to signal a change from one idea to another.

Transition Word Cards

Directions: Cut out the cards. Read each word with students, emphasing how the words signal a change in time to help the reader understand the sequence of events.

first	next
then	before
after	soon

Transition Word Cards (cont.)

at last	finally
during	earlier
meanwhile	now

Super Similes

Standard

Uses descriptive and precise language that clarifies and enhances ideas

Materials

- Chart paper
- Markers
- Writer's Notebooks
- *Super Similes Notebook Entry* (page 200; supersimiles.pdf)

Mentor Texts

- *Crazy Like a Fox: A Simile Story* by Loreen Leedy
- *All the Places to Love* by Patricia MacLachlan
- *Owl Moon* by Jane Yolen
- See *Mentor Text List* in Appendix C for other suggestions.

Procedures

Note: Use this lesson often to build rich vocabulary and vivid descriptions.

Think About Writing

1. Explain that authors write descriptive sentences with language that flows smoothly and words that convey meaning for readers.

Teach

2. Tell students, "Today I will show you how to use similes to craft imagery for your readers." Explain that a simile is used to compare two things with the words *like* or *as*.

3. Give several examples of similes that are used regularly, for example, "He was sleeping like a log," or "My hands are as cold as ice."

4. Review a mentor text with similes, such as *Owl Moon* by Jane Yolen. Ask students to listen for similes in the book. Begin an anchor chart titled *Similes* and record similes from the text on the chart paper.

Engage

5. Write these simile starters on chart paper:

   - *hard as …*
   - *quick as …*
   - *moves like …*
   - *soft like …*
   - *angry as …*
   - *quiet like …*

   Group students in quads. Assign each group a simile starter and have the groups create at least five similes.

6. Gather the groups back together and have each group share its best simile.

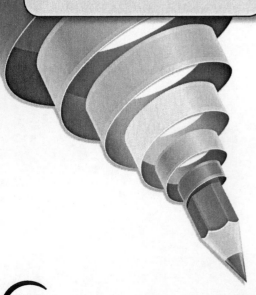

Super Similes (cont.)

Apply

7. Encourage students to use similes to make descriptions more vivid for their readers. Provide students with the *Super Similes Notebook Entry* (page 200) to add to their Writer's Notebook. Have students work on the *Your Turn* section before proceeding to their writing folders.

Write/Conference

8. Provide time for students to write. Scan the group to identify any students who may need assistance getting started. Then, begin conferencing with small groups or individuals. Use your Conferring Notebook to make anecdotal notes and provide teaching points.

Spotlight Strategy

9. Spotlight students who use similes in their writing to paint a picture for the reader. For example, "Sabrina, look at all your super similes. You have selected just the right words to paint a picture for your reader. Excellent thinking and writing."

Share

10. Have students select one simile they want to share with the group. Add each simile to the anchor chart for students to refer to as they write.

Homework

Ask students to listen for similes in the language around you. Have students make a list of at least two similes they hear or find in books. Add the ideas to the anchor chart.

Super Similes Notebook Entry

Super Similes

Authors experiment with language to create vivid descriptions. Using **similes** helps to paint a word picture for the reader.

A simile is used to compare two things that are not completely alike but are alike in one significant way. The words *like* or *as* are included in the comparison.

- My hands are <u>as</u> cold <u>as</u> ice.

- This bread is <u>as</u> hard <u>as</u> a rock!

- Cole is sleeping <u>like</u> a log.

Your Turn:

Practice creating descriptive sentences using similes from the list below, or create your own using the pattern:

_____ like _____   as _____ as

- swims like a fish
- laughs like a hyena
- works like a horse
- teeth like razors
- runs like the wind

- as hungry as a bear
- as white as a ghost
- as sick as a dog
- as cool as a cucumber
- as quick as a wink

#50917—*Getting to the Core of Writing—Level 3* © Shell Education

Awesome Adverbs

Standards

- Uses descriptive and precise language that clarifies and enhances ideas
- Uses adverbs in written compositions

Materials

- Chart paper
- Markers
- *Adverb Picture Cards* (page 204; adverbpicturecards.pdf)
- *Adverb Word Cards* (page 205; adverbwordcards.pdf)
- Writer's Notebooks
- *Awesome Adverbs Notebook Entry* (page 203; awesomeadverbs.pdf)

Mentor Texts

- *Up, Up and Away: A Book About Adverbs* by Ruth Heller
- See *Mentor Text List* in Appendix C for other suggestions.

Procedures

Note: When adverbs are overused, writing sounds stilted and artificial. Remind students to use adverbs sparingly to add details and clarity.

Think About Writing

1. Remind students that authors carefully choose the words they write so their message is accurately expressed.

2. Review mentor texts, if desired, and emphasize the author's use of adverbs.

Teach

3. Tell students, "Today I will show you how to use adverbs to help improve the quality of your writing." Explain that adverbs clarify by telling how, when, where, and how often.

4. Display the *Adverb Picture Cards* (page 204). Work with students to identify the adverbs in the sentences. Discuss the power of interesting adverbs to provide additional information to the reader.

Engage

5. Display the *Adverb Word Cards* (page 205), one card at a time. Have students work with partners to create sentences using the adverbs. Allow several groups to share their sentences for each adverb and record the sentences on chart paper.

Awesome Adverbs *(cont.)*

Apply

6. Encourage students to improve the quality of their writing by using adverbs in their sentences. Provide students with the *Awesome Adverbs Notebook Entry* (page 203) to add to their Writer's Notebook. Have students work on the *Your Turn* section before proceeding to their writing folders.

Write/Conference

7. Provide time for students to write. Meet with the most at-risk students to provide additional support in incorporating adverbs into their writing. Encourage students to use the words on the *Awesome Adverbs Notebook Entry* in their writing. Keep records of your meeting in your Conferring Notebook.

Spotlight Strategy

8. Spotlight students who use adverbs to add descriptive details to their writing. For example, "Extraordinary word work today. Your adverbs are tremendous! Pay close attention to this adverb included in Trina and Raj's work."

Share

9. Have students meet with partners to share their work. Encourage students to listen for adverbs in their partner's writing.

Homework

Ask students to listen for adverbs used in conversation at home. Have students make a list of five adverbs they hear.

Awesome Adverbs Notebook Entry

Awesome Adverbs

An **adverb** can tell the reader how, where, when, or how often. Most adverbs end with –ly.

Authors use adverbs to emphasize information and add descriptive details to their writing.

- Luke skied <u>expertly</u> down the mountain. (How did Luke ski? Expertly.)

- He liked to ski <u>frequently</u>. (How often did he ski? Frequently.)

- Lindsay <u>carefully</u> boarded the ski lift. (How did Lindsay board the lift? Carefully.)

Here are some awesome adverbs you can use in your writing.

• suddenly	• hungrily	• loudly
• angrily	• carefully	• greedily
• quickly	• steadily	• gently
• bravely	• silently	• happily
• slowly	• timidly	• neatly
• safely	• finally	• easily

Remember to reread and revise using adverbs to add emphasis and details in your writing!

Your Turn:

Write sentences using at least four of the adverbs listed above.

Adverb Picture Cards

Directions: Cut out the cards. Have students identify the adverbs in each sentence.

The bee quickly flew to the flower and landed quietly to get a sip of delicious nectar.

The horse stomped noisily at the gate, waiting impatiently for the farmer to bring his oats.

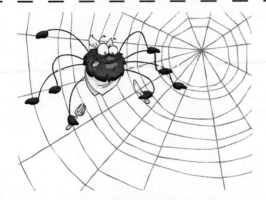

The plump spider waited impatiently for a fat fly to land clumsily on his sticky web.

Certainly, a kind-hearted child will choose to lovingly adopt this adorable puppy.

Slowly, the snake slithered through the grass and hungrily attacked the oblivious mouse.

Waiting eagerly to pounce on its prey, the tiger moved soundlessly through the tall grass.

Adverb Word Cards

Directions: Cut out the cards. Display the cards for students. Have them find partners and create sentences using the adverbs

loudly	neatly
greedily	easily
gently	silently
happily	timidly

Interesting Idioms

Standard

Uses descriptive and precise language that clarifies and enhances ideas

Materials

- Chart paper
- Markers
- Writer's Notebooks
- *Interesting Idioms Notebook Entry* (page 208; interestingidioms.pdf)
- Drawing paper
- Crayons

Mentor Texts

- *More Parts* and *Even More Parts* by Tedd Arnold
- *Amelia Bedelia* by Peggy Parish
- *Why the Banana Split* by Rick Walton
- See *Mentor Text List* in Appendix C for other Appendix C for other suggestions.

Procedures

Note: Create an *Interesting Idioms* wall chart so students can post idioms they find in their reading.

Think About Writing

1. Remind students that authors use vivid, descriptive words in their writing. Authors also listen and use the natural language they hear in their everyday lives. Explain that, as writers, we must listen for language in conversations, literature, and media that create mental images.

2. Review mentor texts, if desired, and emphasize the author's use of idioms.

Teach

3. Tell students, "Today I will show you how to use idioms to add interest to your writing." Explain that an idiom is a phrase that has a meaning different from what the words suggest.

4. Write the following sentence on chart paper:

   She was so distraught that <u>she cried her eyes out</u>.

   Discuss the literal meaning and the true meaning of the underlined idiom.

5. Select and share three to five other idioms from mentor texts or from the *Interesting Idioms Notebook Entry* (page 208). Discuss the literal and true meaning of each idiom with students. Label a sheet of chart paper *Interesting Idioms* and list the idioms the class discusses. Ask students to look for other idioms in books to add to the chart.

Interesting Idioms (cont.)

Engage

6. Write the following idioms on chart paper:

   - *hit the sack*
   - *cat got your tongue*
   - *in the doghouse*

7. Provide students with drawing paper. Have them fold the drawing paper in half and then open it back up. Ask students to select one of the idioms from the chart paper. On one side of the paper, have students draw the literal meaning of the idiom. On the other side of the paper, have students draw the true meaning of the idiom. Allow students to share their illustrations with the class.

Apply

8. Provide students with the *Interesting Idioms Notebook Entry* to add to their Writer's Notebook. Have students work on the *Your Turn* section before proceeding to their writing folders. Encourage students to try to include one idiom from the notebook entry in their writing.

Write/Conference

9. Provide time for students to write. As students work, rotate around the room to conference with individual students.

Spotlight Strategy

10. Spotlight students who include idioms in their writing. For example, "I love the way you included a figure of speech in your writing. The idiom makes your writing so interesting to read. Brilliant thinking."

Share

11. Have students work together to share their writing with partners. Remind students to share the sentences that include idioms.

Homework

Ask students to listen for idioms in the language around them. Have students make a list of at least three idioms they hear. Encourage students to talk to their parents to get help if they do not hear any idioms. Add the idioms students bring back to school to the anchor chart.

Interesting Idioms Notebook Entry

Interesting Idioms

Authors use figurative language such as **idioms** to add color and spice to their writing and to stir the reader's imagination. An idiom is a phrase that has a meaning different from what the words suggest. Idioms are used in our language every day. For example;

Joe is a barrel of laughs.

Joe is not actually a barrel, he is just fun to be around.

Your Turn:

Practice creating colorful sentences using idioms from the list below or others you have discovered in literature, conversations, or media.

- caught his eye
- blow your top
- crocodile tears
- piece of cake
- read my mind
- pull my leg
- I'm all ears

- chewing the fat
- money talks
- spill the beans
- breaks my heart
- in the doghouse
- cost an arm and a leg
- it rings a bell

- sharp as a tack
- climb the walls
- cry your eyes out
- frog in my throat
- go bananas
- hit the sack

#50917—*Getting to the Core of Writing—Level 3* © Shell Education

Voice

Expressing Your Feelings

Voice is the most elusive of the traits of quality writing. It is uniquely the passion, experiences, and creativity that are brought to the reader's attention through the writer's exceptional ability to convey his or her own observations gleaned from experiences. Voice grows as the writer grows! Donald Murray in *Write to Learn* (2004) describes voice as "the person in the writing." Donald Graves in his early work, *Writing: Teachers and Children at Work* (2003) writes a detailed explanation of how to listen for voice in student writing. When students are able to put their speech in writing, the fingerprint of their personality shines through.

Voice is evident in the stories and literature we share with our students every day. It is in those books that we can barely tear ourselves away from, the ones we want to keep reading and can hardly wait to turn the page. Think about the texts you pull out to read to your students again and again. You want to share them because the author's voice connects in some way to you personally. To call attention to voice, collect examples on anchor charts and help students recognize and value its purpose through your read alouds and student writing. As you model writing, use conventions to show emotions and transfer passion from speech to print.

Voice is what makes writing come alive. It is the personality of the writer coming through in the writing. Although sometimes difficult to teach, it is recognizable in writing through the personal tone and feeling of the writing piece. This section contains lessons that focus on how students can connect with their readers to compel them to continue reading. Lessons in this section include the following:

- Lesson 1: How Do You Feel? (page 211)

- Lesson 2: Looking and Listening for Voice (page 216)

- Lesson 3: Informing Interjections (page 219)

- Lesson 4: Know Your Audience (page 222)

The *Val and Van, Voice* poster (page 210) can be displayed in the room to provide a visual reminder for students that voice is one of the traits of writing. You may wish to introduce this poster during the first lesson on voice. Then, refer to the poster when teaching other lessons on voice to refresh students' memories and provide them with questions to help guide them as they make an effort to show voice in their writing.

Val and Van

Voice

What is the purpose of my writing?

✔ Did I write to an audience?

✔ Did I share my feelings?

✔ Did I make my reader smile, cry, or think?

✔ Does my writing sound like me?

How Do You Feel?

Standard
Writes expressive compositions

Materials
- Chart paper
- Markers
- Writer's Notebooks
- *How Do You Feel? Notebook Entry* (page 213; howfeel.pdf)
- *Voice Cards* (pages 214–215; voicecards.pdf)

Mentor Texts
- *The Way I Feel* by Janan Cain
- *How Are You Peeling? Foods with Moods* by Saxton Freymann
- *My Rotten Redheaded Older Brother* by Patricia Polacco
- See *Mentor Text List* in Appendix C for other suggestions.

Procedures

Note: Young writers need to explore emotions beyond happy and sad. Explore literature and build a class chart that identifies other emotions and moods.

Think About Writing

1. Remind students that authors gather and organize their thoughts to create just the right words and passages to express their thoughts and ideas. They also share their emotions and feelings in their writing.

Teach

2. Tell students, "Today I will show you how to explore different emotions, feelings, and attitudes you might use in your writing." Explain to students that the stories we like to read over and over have become favorites because of the way they make us feel.

3. Use a mentor text or the *How Do You Feel? Notebook Entry* (page 213) to introduce students to different emotions. Discuss when you might feel that emotion, or what would it look like if someone had that emotion. Create and display a chart for student writing support. For example:

Emotion/Feeling	Show Me
angry	red face
	clenched fists
	tight lips
	big veins in neck
	glaring eyes

Be sure to compare different levels of emotion, e.g., how is mad different from angry? You may wish to start with three or four different emotions, and as students become familiar with how to use them in their writing, add additional examples to your chart.

How Do You Feel? (cont.)

Engage

4. Have students meet with partners. Provide each student with a *Voice Card* (pages 214-215). Ask them not to show their partner the card. Have one student act out the emotion on the card. He or she may act out the emotion and even talk, but may not say the word on the card. Ask the other student to guess which emotion his or her partner is acting out. Then, have students trade roles.

5. Gather students back together and have them share observations. Add any new emotions to the class chart.

Apply

6. Remind students to capture emotions to draw the reader into their stories. Challenge students to add emotion and feeling into their writing using voice. Provide students with the *How Do You Feel? Notebook Entry* to add to their Writer's Notebook. Have students work on the *Your Turn* section before proceeding to their writing folders.

Write/Conference

7. Provide time for students to write. Scan the classroom to see if any students need assistance getting started. Then begin conferencing with individual students or small groups. Make observations in your Conferring Notebook.

Spotlight Strategy

8. Spotlight students who use voice to create an emotion or feeling in their story. For example, "Listen to these words Roger has written. What kind of voice is he sharing with his readers?"

Share

9. Have students meet with partners to share their writing. Encourage them to listen for voice. Ask the listeners to share how they feel after hearing their partners' writing.

Homework

Ask students to think about their favorite stories. Have students make a list of three stories and the emotions they feel when they hear the stories.

How Do You Feel? Notebook Entry

How Do You Feel?

Voice affects the way we feel or react to an author's writing. The author creates an emotion or feeling through the story and characters.

These are emotions you may discover in your reading. Explore how authors use words to "show" you an emotion. Use these ideas to show emotion in your own writing. For example:

- It made me feel sad: A puppy was lost and alone.
- The character was lonely: He sat on the bench, shoulders slumped, looking down the road, and knew no one would be coming to the park that day.

angry

annoyed

disappointed

excited

happy

sad

confused

shocked

worried

Your Turn:

Select at least three of these or other emotions to create "show me" sentences.

Voice Cards

Directions: Cut out the cards. Distribute one card to each student and have him or her act out the emotion for his or her partner to guess.

angry	annoyed
disappointed	excited
happy	sad

Voice Cards (cont.)

scared

shocked

worried

confused

curious

surprised

Looking and Listening for Voice

Standard
Writes expressive compositions

Materials
- Chart paper
- Markers
- Writer's Notebooks
- *Looking and Listening for Voice Notebook Entry* (page 218; lookinglisteningvoice.pdf)

Mentor Texts
- *Straight to the Pole* by Kevin O'Malley
- *Thank You, Mr. Falker* by Patricia Polacco
- *The Relatives Came* by Cynthia Rylant
- See *Mentor Text List* in Appendix C for other suggestions.

Procedures
Note: This lesson uses *The Relatives Came* by Cynthia Rylant for specific examples; however, voice should be an ongoing learning process through the exploration of literature. Highlight and identify voice as it occurs in literature.

Think About Writing
1. Explain to students that authors use specific details and just the right words to tell their amazing stories, and brilliant authors also use a bit of magic called *voice*. Tell students that voice is what makes us laugh out loud or feel unhappy.

Teach
2. Tell students, "Today I will show you how to explore the way authors use voice in their stories to capture the emotions of the reader." Explain the voice in *The Three Little Pigs*. Voice is what shows us the pigs are frightened and we should be afraid of the wolf. Voice shows up in writing in many different ways and one way is through using feelings and emotions in our writing.

3. Read aloud from selected literature, and ask students to think about the different emotions they feel or that characters display in the stories. Remind students of the emotions chart displayed previously (Voice Lesson 1).

4. Create an anchor chart to specifically identify the characters, events, and related emotions/feelings. Be sure to point out how emotions can change throughout a story. Also note how authors show the reader the emotions. Add to the chart as you explore emotions and feelings in additional literature.

Character and/or Event	Emotion/Feeling
relatives leaving for their trip	happiness
	joy
	excitement

Looking and Listening for Voice *(cont.)*

Engage

5. Provide students with the *Looking and Listening for Voice Notebook Entry* (page 218) to add to their Writer's Notebook. Provide partners with texts to review and look for voice. Have students record their findings on the notebook entry page. Allow partners time to work. Then, gather the class back together so they can share their findings.

Apply

6. Remind students that there are many emotions and feelings that can be used in writing. Encourage students to use more than happy, sad, and mad. Tell students to revisit some writing work in their folders to add emotions and feelings or begin a new piece of writing today.

Write/Conference

7. Provide time for students to write. Scan for and resolve any confusion. Then, begin to conference with individual students or work with small groups. Make observations in your Conferring Notebook.

Spotlight Strategy

8. Spotlight students who use voice to convey emotions of characters. For example, "Shanai, you have clearly used voice in your writing. Listen to how Shanai used descriptive language to show the emotion of the character."

Share

9. Select three students to share their work in the Author's Chair. Provide affirmations as students share their writing with the whole group.

Homework

Ask students to listen for voice in stories in books or on TV. Have students write down at least one example they find and bring it to share with the class tomorrow.

Looking and Listening for Voice Notebook Entry

Looking and Listening for Voice

Authors use descriptive language to create emotions or feelings in their readers.

As you read new stories, think about how you are feeling. Does the story make you laugh, cry, or maybe give you goose bumps? Does something a character does or says make you want to giggle or shout out loud? Is the writing silly or serious? These are all signs of **voice**.

Your Turn:

Select and explore a favorite fairy tale, like *The Three Little Pigs* or *Little Red Riding Hood*, and see how many different emotions or feelings you can identify throughout the story.

Character and/or Event	Emotion/Feeling

Informing Interjections

© Shell Education #50917—Getting to the Core of Writing—Level 3

Standard
Writes expressive compositions

Materials
- Chart paper
- Markers
- Writer's Notebooks
- *Informing Interjections Notebook Entry* (page 221; informinginterjections.pdf)

Mentor Texts
- *Fantastic! Wow! and Unreal!* by Ruth Heller
- *If You Were an Interjection* by Nancy Loewen
- *The Recess Queen* by Alexis O'Neill
- *No, David!* and *Good Boy, Fergus!* by David Shannon
- See *Mentor Text List* in Appendix C for other suggestions.

Procedures
Note: Repeat this lesson and identify interjections in literature to develop an understanding of the use of interjections.

Think About Writing
1. Explain that one way authors express their feelings or emotions is by using specific utterances to keep the reader interested and wondering. These special words, sounds, or expressions are called *interjections*.

2. Review mentor texts if desired, and emphasize the author's use of interjections.

Teach
3. Tell students, "Today I will show you how to add feelings to sentences and stories." Explain that interjections help inform the reader of how a character is feeling, such as excited, tired, or upset. Interjections should not be overused, but can add flavor and energy to a story that might be less than interesting.

4. Write the following sentences on chart paper, chalkboard, or sentence strips:

   - *Oh, no! My mother is on her way home from work.*
   - *Yikes! I'm not finished with my homework.*

   Explain that *Oh*, *no*, and *yikes* show strong emotion. Ask students to imagine the consequences of not being done with homework.

   Yuck! This sandwich is so gross!

   Notice how disappointed and dismayed you might be with a gross sandwich for lunch.

   Drat! My parents won't let me spend the night with a friend.

   How might you feel?

Informing Interjections (cont.)

Engage

5. Have students work with partners to create sentences using the following interjections: *Ooops!*, *Brrrr!*, *Ouch!*, *Good grief!*, and *Oh no!* Allow approximately two or three minutes for students to practice orally.

Apply

6. Encourage students to add interest and feelings to their writing by sprinkling in a few interesting interjections. Remind students not to overuse interjections or their writing will sound unnatural and artificial. Provide students with the *Informing Interjections Notebook Entry* (page 221) to add to their Writer's Notebook. Have students work on the *Your Turn* section before proceeding to their writing folders.

Write/Conference

7. Provide time for students to write. Bring a small group to a conferring area and use additional examples from a list of interjections. Check for understanding and make notes in your Conferring Notebook.

Spotlight Strategy

8. Spotlight students who use interjections to express strong emotions. For example, "Wow! Outstanding effort! Just listen to the following sentences."

Share

9. Have students work with partners to share two of their best sentences with interjections.

Homework

Ask students to listen to TV, and to adults and children talking at home. Have them write down three interjections they hear.

Informing Interjections Notebook Entry

Informing Interjections

Authors use **interjections** to express strong emotions to the reader. Interjections are usually at the beginning of a sentence. They are followed by an exclamation point when showing strong emotion and a comma when using less emotion.

- Oh, no! I lost my yo-yo!

- Ah, here it is.

Here are some interjections you can use in your writing.

- Ahh!
- Boo!
- Eeek!
- Hey!
- Oh, no!
- Shh!
- Whoa!

- Awesome!
- Cool!
- Gross!
- Hurray!
- Ouch!
- Super!
- Wow!

- Bravo!
- Congratulations!
- Good grief!
- Huh?
- Rats!
- Ugh!
- Yuck!

Your Turn:

Create at least three sentences in your notebook using interjections from the list above.

Know Your Audience

Procedures

Note: Voice can be recognized in all forms of media as related to the purpose of the writing.

Think About Writing

1. Explain that authors write for different purposes—to persuade, inform, or entertain. Another key to great writing is knowing who your reader is. This helps determine what voice can be used to share ideas and information.

2. Review mentor texts, if desired, and emphasize the author's purpose and the intended audience.

Teach

3. Tell students, "Today I will show you how to match your writing voice to your readers."

4. Develop a chart that shows different texts and the different kind of voice that may be associated with each. As you read various texts, add to the chart with your findings.

Kind of Text	Purpose	Voice
postcard from a friend at the beach	inform	excitement, happiness
comic strip	entertain	humorous, happiness
lost puppy ad	inform	concern, worry, sadness

Engage

5. Provide students with a variety of text types. Have them work in small groups of four or five to sort through each type of writing and record the type of text, the purpose, and the voice represented in the writing. Allow time for groups to explore texts, and then share a few findings from each group.

Know Your Audience (cont.)

Apply

6. Remind students that emotions and feelings are determined by the purpose for writing and audience. Provide students with the *Know Your Audience Notebook Entry* (page 224) to add to their Writer's Notebook. Have students work on the *Your Turn* section before proceeding to their writing folders.

Write/Conference

7. Provide time for students to write. As students work, rotate around the room. Check to see that students stay focused and understand the purpose of the mini-lesson.

Spotlight Strategy

8. Spotlight students who use different voice for different types of text. For example, "You are to be commended for challenging yourself today! You've poured your heart and head into this work. Spotlighting your effort."

Share

9. Have students work with partners to share their writing.

Homework

Ask students to listen for author's purpose in stories from books or magazines and on TV. Have students write down two sources and what the author's purpose is.

Know Your Audience Notebook Entry

Know Your Audience

Authors consider their audience when they are writing. They decide what voice they will use to persuade, inform, or entertain their reader.

Here are a few examples:

Kind of text	Voice
a thank you note to Grandma	gratitude, kindness
a letter to Mom asking for a new pet	confidence, hope, love, excitement
a note to a friend that you got a new pet	ecstatic, happy
a card from camp, saying that you miss your family	lonely, sad, nervous
a card from camp, saying that you are having a great time	excited, happy

Your Turn:

Choose two of the characters listed below and write a note to each one. Did your voice change from one note to the other?

- sports figure
- friend
- scientist
- alien
- teacher

Conventions

Checking Your Writing

Writing that does not follow standard conventions is difficult to read. The use of correct capitalization, punctuation, spelling, and grammar is what makes writing consistent and easy to read. Students need to have reasonable control over the conventions of writing. This section provides lessons that help students internalize conventions as they write and check their work for conventions after they have written a piece. Lessons in this section include the following:

- Lesson 1: The Capital Rap (page 227)

- Lesson 2: Punctuation Takes a Holiday (page 230)

- Lesson 3: See It! Say It! Spell It! Write It! Check It! (page 233)

- Lesson 4: Editing with CUPS (page 236)

- Lesson 5: Quotation Marks: "Who Said That?" (page 240)

- Lesson 6: Caution Comma Chant (page 243)

- Lesson 7: Using Editing Marks (page 246)

- Lesson 8: Writing Traits Checklist (page 250)

The *Callie, Super Conventions Checker* poster (page 226) can be displayed in the room to provide a visual reminder for students that conventions is one of the traits of writing. You may wish to introduce this poster during the first lesson on conventions. Then, refer to the poster when teaching other lessons on conventions to refresh students' memories and provide them questions to help guide them as they make an effort to use correct conventions in their writing.

Callie
Super Conventions Checker

How do I edit my paper?

✔ Did I check my capitalization?

✔ Did I check my punctuation?

✔ Did I check my spelling?

✔ Did I use good spacing?

✔ Did I read over my story?

The Capital Rap

Standards

- Uses strategies to edit and publish written work
- Uses conventions of capitalization in written compositions

Materials

- Chart paper
- Markers
- Writer's Notebooks
- *The Capital Rap Notebook Entry* (page 229; capitalrap.pdf)

Mentor Texts

- *Amelia's Notebook* by Marissa Moss
- *Bedhead* by Margie Palatini
- *Punctuation Takes a Vacation* by Robin Pulver
- *One Monday Morning* by Uri Shulevitz
- See *Mentor Text List* in Appendix C for other suggestions.

Procedures

Note: Revisit this lesson over several days and revisit regularly until the capitalization skill has been mastered. Each day, implement a different section of the rap.

Think About Writing

1. Tell students that writers are like busy bees. They fly around the page, using capitals everywhere. Every sentence begins with a capital letter! As students work on writing projects, they should listen, talk, and write like the authors they know and love.

2. Share mentor texts with students. Point out everywhere that the authors have used capital letters.

Teach

3. Tell students, "Today I will show you how to use a rap to remember capitalization rules."

4. Display *The Capital Rap Notebook Entry* (page 229) or write the words on chart paper so students can see them. Use a soft voice and snap fingers to a rhythmic beat. Chant the first verse of the rap several times. Have students echo the verses until they feel comfortable enough with the words to join you.

5. On chart paper, write the example sentences that go with the first verse. Review each sentence with students, emphasizing the capitalization rule.

6. Repeat Steps 3 and 4 with the remaining verses.

Engage

7. Have students work with partners to practice *The Capital Rap*. Then have students explain the capitalization rules reviewed in the rap using their own words.

The Capital Rap (cont.)

Apply

8. Remind students to use and check for the capitalization in their writing in order to make their messages clear for the reader. Provide students with *The Capital Rap Notebook Entry* to add to their Writer's Notebook. Encourage students to look at work from their writing folder and add capitals using *The Capital Rap* to remember the rules.

Write/Conference

9. Provide students with time to write. As students work, rotate around the room conferencing with individual students. The classroom environment can only be successful if you are well-prepared. Be ready for any eventuality. Conferencing is the result of your observation of student writing behaviors. Be ready to jot down what you notice to plan the next instruction.

Spotlight Strategy

10. Spotlight students who are checking for capital letters in their writing. For example, "You are doing such important work. Does anyone have a spotlight they would like to share? Remarkable remembering of *The Capital Rap*."

Share

11. Have students meet with partners to share their work. Encourage students to share the words they capitalized and explain why.

Homework

Have students share *The Capital Rap* with their parents. Encourage students to teach the rap to their family.

The Capital Rap Notebook Entry

 **The Capital Rap**

Capital Rap, Capital Rap
"I" am important
So are you,
The beginning of a sentence
is important, too.
Capital Rap, Capital Rap
	• Capitalize the word "I."
	    Richard and **I** are friends.
	• Capitalize a person's name.
	    Mrs. **G**aston is our teacher.
	• Capitalize the first letter in a sentence.
	    We like to write and read stories.

Capital Rap, Capital Rap
Days of the week
and months of the year,
Cities and states
Need capitals, it's clear!
Capital Rap, Capital Rap
	• Capitalize the days of the week.
	    Today is **S**aturday!
	• Capitalize the months of the year.
	    My birthday is in **A**pril.
	• Capitalize the names of cities and states.
	    I live in **C**hicago, **I**llinois.

Capital Rap, Capital Rap
Titles of a book,
Movie or TV,
A special place or holiday,
Need capitals, you see!
Capital Rap, Capital Rap
	• Capitalize the important words in a title.
	    I read **T**he **P**rincess and the **P**ea.
	• Capitalize the names of special places.
	    My family went to **D**isneyland.
	• Capitalize names of holidays.
	    We have a picnic on the **F**ourth of **J**uly.

Punctuation Takes a Holiday

Standards

- Uses strategies to edit and publish written work
- Uses conventions of punctuation in written compositions

Materials

- Chart paper
- Markers
- Writer's Notebooks
- *Punctuation Takes a Holiday Notebook Entry* (page 232; punctuationholiday.pdf)

Mentor Texts

- *Punk-tuation Celebration* by Pamela Hall
- *Amelia's Notebook* by Marissa Moss
- *Bedhead* by Margie Palatini
- *Twenty-Odd Ducks: Why, every punctuation mark counts!* by Lynne Truss
- See *Mentor Text List* in Appendix C for other suggestions.

Procedures

Note: Over several days, emphasize types of punctuation. Use literature to show how punctuation can alter meaning.

Think About Writing

1. Explain to students that authors understand the importance of punctuation. Punctuation can help tell the story.

2. Review mentor texts, if desired, and emphasize the author's use of punctuation.

Teach

3. Tell students, "Today I will show you how punctuation can help improve the rhythm and flow of sentences for the reader." Explain that effective writers practice and experiment with punctuation to improve meaning and make their writing pleasing.

4. Write the following sentences on chart paper without any ending marks:

   - *We played outside in the snow.* (telling/declarative)

   - *How did you build that snowman?* (asking/interrogative)

   - *Wow, a snowman is really cool!* (excitement/exclamatory)

   Tell students that punctuation has taken a holiday and gone on vacation! It is up to the class to put the punctuation marks where they belong. Discuss each sentence with students. Decide on the type of sentence and the ending mark that is appropriate.

5. On subsequent days, discuss other punctuation, such as quotation marks and commas. Use examples from literature or create your own examples on chart paper to use as discussion points.

Punctuation Takes a Holiday *(cont.)*

Engage

6. Have students tell partners how punctuation builds meaningful sentences. Ask them to share how they will use punctuation in their writing. Provide approximately two to three minutes for discussion.

Apply

7. Provide students with the *Punctuation Takes a Holiday Notebook Entry* (page 232) to add to their Writer's Notebook. Have students work on the *Your Turn* section before proceeding to their writing folders.

Write/Conference

8. Provide time for students to write. Stop by the desk of at least three or four students and conference with them about punctuation. As you look over their work, remember to have only one teaching point, and be certain that you start your conference with praise.

Spotlight Strategy

9. Spotlight students who are using different punctuation in their writing. For example, "You are so smart to use your resources to help you with your work. Ray and his partner are becoming very familiar with punctuation and are polishing up their writing."

Share

10. Have students share with partners any punctuation changes they made to their writing. From your observations, select two or three students who have clearly understood this lesson and can provide an important model for others. Have those students share their work in the Author's Chair.

Homework

Ask students to look for punctuation in writing at home. Have them ask their parents to help them locate three pieces of writing with punctuation. Ask students to bring three samples or write three with the focus on punctuation.

Punctuation Takes a Holiday Notebook Entry

Punctuation Takes a Holiday

Yikes! We are in trouble because punctuation has taken a holiday and gone on vacation! Punctuation helps guide us through our reading like signs on a road. Help save the day and add the missing punctuation in each sentence.

Period. A period ends a declarative or imperative sentence.	My name is Kim
Question Mark? A question mark ends an interrogative sentence.	Do you like the beach
Exclamation Point! An exclamation point ends an exclamatory sentence.	Hurray Stop We are finally here
Comma, A comma separates phrases or items in a list.	Mike Luke and Justin jump the waves.
"Quotation Marks" Quotation marks enclose the exact words a person says or writes.	Chris said, Watch out for sharks!

Your Turn:

In your notebook, use each punctuation mark in a sentence. Work on editing for punctuation in your writing.

#50917—Getting to the Core of Writing—Level 3 © Shell Education

See It! Say It! Spell It! Write It! Check It!

Standards

- Uses strategies to edit and publish written work
- Uses conventions of spelling in written compositions

Materials

- Chart paper
- Markers
- Writer's Notebooks
- *See It! Say It! Spell It! Write It! Check It! Notebook Entry* (page 235; seespellwritecheckit.pdf)

Mentor Texts

- Student writing samples or literature you are using in your classroom
- See *Mentor Text List* in Appendix C for other suggestions.

Procedures

Note: Use this lesson frequently so students build automaticity with high-frequency words.

Think About Writing

1. Explain to students that as they write, it is useful to have a list of words that they can write automatically. Writers use strategies and tools to spell, find, and build words.

2. Review mentor texts, if desired, and emphasize words students should be able to spell independently that are appropriate for third grade.

Teach

3. Tell students, "Today I will show you a simple strategy to help build a core of words you can write quickly and smoothly." Select a word you want students to be able to spell quickly and independently, such as the word *always*. Write the word on a sheet of chart paper.

4. Follow the procedures below to practice the word:

   - **Look!** Have students look at the word and notice the spelling.

   - **Say!** Slide your finger under the word and say the word out loud.

   - **Spell!** Cover the word and then write the word quickly and smoothly on scratch paper.

   - **Write!** Use the index finger of one hand as a pretend pencil. Write the word on the palm of the other hand. Practice writing the word three times.

   - **Check!** Return to the chart paper with the word written on it to check the spelling.

See It! Say It! Spell It! Write It! Check It! *(cont.)*

5. As students work, move around and observe, providing corrective feedback to any student making incorrect letter strokes. List each step of the procedure for learning new words on chart paper so students can easily refer to it.

6. Practice additional words using the same procedure.

Engage

7. Have students work with partners to practice other words using the procedure. Remind students to practice each step. Provide students with additional words to practice. Monitor partners and provide support when needed.

Apply

8. Remind students that being able to write words automatically will help make their writing easier and make them good spellers for other writing projects. Provide students with the *See It! Say It! Spell It! Write It! Check It! Notebook Entry* (page 235) to add to their Writer's Notebook. Have students work on the *Your Turn* section before proceeding to their writing folders.

Write/Conference

9. Provide time for students to write. Scan the room to be sure students are working independently and then begin to rotate among students to support them with questions and comments.

Spotlight Strategy

10. Spotlight students who are using the resources around them to help them write. For example, "What a genius! Paul is using the word chart and is practicing *See it! Say it! Spell it! Write it! Check it!* Good writers use all the tools around them to help them write words."

Share

11. Have students meet with partners to show each other some of the words they can write smoothly and quickly.

> ## Homework
>
> Ask students to think about how letters, sounds, words, and language surround them. Encourage students to increase their knowledge of words by finding words in newspapers, magazines, and other places. Have students make a list of three words they would like to be able to write automatically.

See It! Say It! Spell It! Write It! Check It! Notebook Entry

See It! Say It! Spell It! Write It! Check It!

Authors who can spell words can more easily write their stories. Readers can read and understand the message more clearly when words are spelled correctly.

Try this strategy to learn words you use frequently.

Look!	Look closely! What letters, patterns or familiar parts do you notice?	
Say!	Slide your finger under the word. Say the word out loud.	
Spell!	Cover the word and then write the word quickly and smoothly on scratch paper.	
Write!	Use the index finger of one hand as a pretend pencil and write the word on the palm of your other hand. Write the word three times.	
Check!	Check the word on the chart to see if you spelled it correctly!	

Your Turn:

Practice these words using the steps above.

- always
- every
- their
- were

- favorite
- know
- some
- was

- because
- friend
- through
- where

Editing with CUPS

Standards

- Uses strategies to edit and publish written work
- Uses conventions of spelling in written compositions
- Uses conventions of capitalization in written compositions
- Uses conventions of punctuation in written compositions

Materials

- Chart paper
- Different-colored markers
- Writer's Notebooks
- CUPS Writing Sample (page 239; cupswritingsample.pdf)
- *Editing with CUPS Notebook Entry* (page 238; editingcups.pdf)

Mentor Texts

- *Punctuation Takes a Vacation* by Robin Pulver
- See *Mentor Text List* in Appendix C for other

Procedures

Note: Repeat this mini-lesson over several days, demonstrating each component of CUPS.

Think About Writing

1. Explain that authors check their work carefully before others read it. In fact, it is so important for published authors to have their work correct that they have someone called an *editor* review their work and make sure everything is just right.

2. Review mentor texts, if desired, and emphasize the author's use of punctuation.

Teach

3. Tell students, "Today I will show you a step-by-step method to edit your writing called *CUPS.*"

4. Write the word *CUPS* vertically on a sheet of chart paper. Explain that each letter refers to one of the conventions of writing:

   C *apitalization*

   U *sage and grammar*

   P *unctuation*

   S *pelling*

   Briefly review each of the conventions.

5. Distribute and display the *CUPS Writing Sample* (page 239). Write the word CUPS vertically in a corner of the bottom of the page. Demonstrate how to review the sample for each of the conventions. It is helpful to use a different-colored pen for each of the conventions. Have students follow along with you on their own papers.

Editing with CUPS (cont.)

You may wish to use the following schedule to introduce this process to students:

- Day 1: Check only for capitalization
- Day 2: Confirm correct grammar usage
- Day 3: Verify the accuracy of punctuation
- Day 4: Examine for accurate or conventional spelling
- Day 5: Perform a holistic check of the writing sample and CUPS the paper

Engage

6. Have students work with partners to review what each letter in CUPS stands for and what types of things they will check for in their own writing. Provide approximately two minutes for students to talk.

Apply

7. Remind students to use CUPS to help them remember the steps in the editing process. Provide students with the *Editing with CUPS Notebook Entry* (page 238) to add to their Writer's Notebook. Have students work on the *Your Turn* section before proceeding to their writing folders.

Write/Conference

8. Provide time for students to write. Scan the room to be certain that all students are working independently. Pull a small group for further explanation of CUPS, if necessary. Then, conduct conferences with individual students.

Spotlight Strategy

9. Spotlight students who are using CUPS to edit their work. For example, "Look at the brilliant way you are checking over your work. You must be so proud of how you are beginning to take charge just like a real author. It appears that many of you are preparing yourselves for careers as editors. Smart writing work today!"

Share

10. Have students work with partners to review how they will use CUPS as they check their work.

Homework

Ask students to talk with their parents about the importance of editing writing before publishing. Have students ask their parents if they edit their checkbooks, grocery lists, contracts, etc.

Editing with CUPS Notebook Entry

Editing with CUPS

CUPS your papers!

C is for **capitalization**
Are the **first words** in each sentence, as well as proper **names**, capitalized? Remember **"I"**!

U is for **usage and grammar**
Does your writing sound right? Check for **correct** word choice and **complete** sentences.

P is for **punctuation**
Is the punctuation correct? Check for **periods** (.), **question marks** (?), **exclamation points** (!) and **commas** (,).

S is for **spelling**
Are all the words **spelled correctly?** Use your resources such as word walls, word lists, and a dictionary.

Your Turn:

Choose a piece of writing from your writing folder. Write the word CUPS vertically at the top or bottom of the page. Check for each of the CUPS conventions.

#50917—Getting to the Core of Writing—Level 3 © Shell Education

Name: _____ Date: _____

CUPS Writing Sample

Directions: Use CUPS to edit this paragragh.

Football Fun

On wednesday, luke whent over to Justins house to play

video games after school they play a gam of football. Luke

one the first game bute justin winned the next two games.

Then, thay went outside and throwed the football around.

Football is grat fun

Quotation Marks: "Who Said That?"

Procedures

Note: Repeat this mini-lesson to emphasize the value and use of quotation marks.

Think About Writing

1. Remind students that authors record their feelings, thoughts, sadness, and excitement in their writing. Explain that a resource writers use to make their writing flow along smoothly is quotation marks. These marks are used to enclose the words of a speaker. They work with other punctuation to clarify the writer's message.

2. Review mentor texts, if desired, and emphasize the author's use of quotation marks.

Teach

3. Tell students, "Today I will show you how to use quotation marks to show a speaker's words." Explain to students that quotation marks are used to show the exact words a person says.

4. Write the following text from *Bedhead* on a sheet of chart paper:

   "Is everything all right, Oliver?" she whispered. "Come now, dear. Open the door and let us in." "Please?" said Mom. "Pretty, please?...Pretty, pretty, pretty please?..."

   Review the short conversation that Mom has with Oliver. Use a colored marker to trace over the quotation marks showing what Mom said.

5. Write the *Quotation Mark Chant* from the *Quotation Marks: "Who Said That?"* Notebook Entry (page 242) on chart paper. Teach the chant to students.

Quotation Marks: "Who Said That?" *(cont.)*

Engage

6. On sentence strips, write sentences in which characters speak. Do not include the quotation marks. Have student volunteers come up to the sentence strip and cup their hands around the exact words that the person says. Use the following sentences or your own:

   - *"We're going to the park," yelled Dad.*
   - *"Let's make grilled cheese for dinner," said Ryan.*
   - *"Hey, kid!" said the grouchy man.*

7. Show a picture with two people in it. Have partners determine what conversation might take place. Have students share their responses and record them on chart paper, including the quotation marks.

Apply

8. Distribute pictures with two people in them to students. Have students work with partners to add their own conversation to the pictures using quotation marks.

9. Provide students with the *Quotation Marks: "Who Said That?" Notebook Entry* to add to their Writer's Notebook Have students work on the *Your Turn* section before proceeding to their writing folders.

Write/Conference

10. Provide time for students to write. As students work, gather a small group to reteach the concept.

Spotlight Strategy

11. Spotlight students who added dialogue to their writing to add interest. For example, "What sophisticated writers! You continually amaze me! Just listen to how Alexandra added dialogue to create interest and action."

Share

12. Have students meet with partners to share their writing, especially where they added dialogue and quotation marks. Provide approximately two minutes for students to share.

Homework

Ask students to listen to the flow of conversation around them. Have them write three sentences that show what people said in their houses.

Quotation Marks: "Who Said That?" Notebook Entry

Quotation Marks: "Who Said That?"

Authors add **quotation marks** to let the reader know exactly what someone has spoken or written.

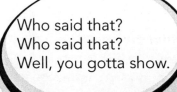

Who said that?
Who said that?
Well, you gotta show.

Put quotation marks around those words, you know...

Quotation marks...'Round the words that are spoken...

Quotation marks... No, I'm not jokin'!

Quotation Mark Chant

Your Turn:

Select two characters from the list below or create your own. Illustrate a conversation between the characters and write what they say in speech bubbles. Then, write a paragraph about their conversation and use quotation marks to show what they say.

cat	Mom/woman	Dad/man	coach
dog	principal/teacher	cowboy	sports player
mouse	daughter/son	bandit	dancer
pig	wolf	bears	Goldilocks
knight	prince/princess	dragon	wizard

Caution Comma Chant

Standards

- Uses strategies to edit and publish written work
- Uses conventions of punctuation in written compositions

Materials

- Chart paper
- Markers
- Writer's Notebooks
- *Caution Comma Chant Notebook Entry* (page 245; cautioncommachant.pdf)
- unedited writing samples without commas

Mentor Texts

- *Grandpa's Teeth* by Rod Clement
- *Eats, Shoots & Leaves: Why, Commas Really Do Make a Difference!* by Lynne Truss
- See *Mentor Text List* in Appendix C for other suggestions.

Procedures

Note: Provide repetition of this lesson over several days and repeat regularly so writers understand that commas clarify messages in writing stories, essays, and compositions, as well as in technology.

Think About Writing

1. Explain that authors use commas to show the reader how to read the words. Commas signal the reader to pause before moving on. Think of taking a trip and the use of stoplights to signal safe travels. Commas are like the yellow caution light, signaling to the reader to slow down and check, but not come to a complete stop.

2. Review mentor texts, if desired, and emphasize the author's use of commas.

Teach

3. Tell students, "Today I will show you a chant to help you remember how to use commas in your writing."

4. Display the *Caution Comma Chant* from the *Caution Comma Chant Notebook Entry* (page 245) or write the words on chart paper. Teach the chant to students, one section at a time. Practice the chant several times with students until they are comfortable. You may wish to teach individual sections of the chant on separate days.

5. Write the samples provided for each section of the chant on chart paper. Discuss the use of commas in each sample.

6. Display an unedited writing sample and use the chant to model how to check for comma use.

Caution Comma Chant (cont.)

Engage

7. Have students practice the *Caution Comma Chant* with partners. Encourage students to create a hand jive, movements, or simply snap their fingers to a steady beat as they chant. Provide approximately three or four minutes for students to practice.

Apply

8. Remind students to use the correct conventions of written language so that their messages are not muddled. Provide students with the *Caution Comma Chant Notebook Entry* to add to their Writer's Notebook. Have students work on the *Your Turn* section before proceeding to their writing folders.

Write/Conference

9. Provide time for students to write. As students work, be available for individual conferences. Make notes to determine those students who would benefit from small group instruction at your next Writer's Workshop session.

Spotlight Strategy

10. Spotlight students who are including commas in their writing. For example, "Tristan has done a great job of adding commas to his writing to tell the reader when to pause. Nice work!"

Share

11. Have students meet with partners to share an idea from their writing and to gain an idea from their partner's writing.

Homework

Ask students to find examples of commas in their homes. Have students write three examples that they find.

Caution Comma Chant Notebook Entry

Caution Comma Chant

Authors use **commas** to tell the reader to slow down, just like a yellow light warns a driver to proceed with caution and slow down.

Caution comma, Caution comma, Commas help the reader know where to pause. They separate a series, And separate a clause.	**Separate a series:** Josh picked up eggs, milk, bread, and chili. **Separate a clause:** I'm tired today, but I will do my homework.
Caution comma, Caution comma, Commas are important In addresses and in dates, Commands and dialogue, like "Oh no, we might be late!"	**Addresses:** 16 Rudosa Street Hillsboro, WV 24946 **Dates:** March 24, 1981 **Commands:** Michael, clean your room! **Dialogue:** Mom said, "It's time for dinner."
Caution comma, Caution comma, Commas are essential, You use them in a letter. When you use them well, Your writing will get better! Oh, yeah!	**In a Letter:** Greeting: Dear Jo, Closing: Best wishes,

Your Turn:

Write three to four sentences using comma, to tell the reader when to pause.

Using Editing Marks

Standards

- Uses strategies to edit and publish written work
- Uses conventions of spelling in written compositions
- Uses conventions of capitalization in written compositions
- Uses conventions of punctuation in written compositions

Materials

- Chart paper
- Markers
- Writer's Notebooks
- *Using Editing Marks Notebook Entry* (page 248; editingmarks.pdf)
- *Using Editing Marks Writing Sample* (page 249; editingmarkssample.pdf
- Colored pens

Mentor Text

- *Look at My Book* by Loreen Leedy
- Other CCSS literature
- See *Mentor Text List* in Appendix C for other suggestions.

Procedures

Note: Divide this mini-lesson into segments so students will not become overwhelmed. Use a different colored pen for each skill: green/capitalization, orange/usage, red/punctuation, blue/spelling.

Think About Writing

1. Tell students that authors pay particular attention to the way their writing is published. Explain that this means they prepare their writing for public viewing.

2. Review mentor texts, if desired, and emphasize the author's use of correct conventions.

Teach

3. Tell students, "Today I will show you how to get a piece of writing ready for presentation." Explain that each time we publish a piece of writing, it needs to be edited for capitalization, usage, punctuation, and spelling. Each of these conventions has special marks that can be used to fix up the writing.

4. Model using a sample writing piece. Edit one convention each day. Create an anchor chart with the editing marks listed on it. Explicitly model by thinking aloud how to edit using the following procedures:

   Day 1—Capitalization: Use a green pen for "go." Check the writing sample for capitals: beginning of a sentence, names, months, cities, days, etc.

   Day 2—Usage: Use an orange pen as you reread the sentences to make sure each sentence makes sense.

   Day 3—Punctuation: Use a red pen for ending punctuation to "stop." Clap when you get to the end of a sentence.

   Day 4—Spelling: Use a blue pen as you check for spelling.

Using Editing Marks (cont.)

Engage

5. Have students talk with partners about how they will edit their writing. Provide approximately two minutes for students to talk.

Apply

6. Remind students that making sure their writing is accurate will help the reader as he or she reads. Provide students with the *Using Editing Marks Notebook Entry* (page 248) to add to their Writer's Notebook.

7. Provide students with the *Using Editing Marks Writing Sample* (page 249) and have them practice editing using the editing marks from the notebook entry. Allow several minutes for students to practice editing then review.

Write/Conference

8. Provide time for students to write or edit. Scan the room for students who may need help getting started. Provide a three- or four-minute reteach for students who may need additional repetitions.

Spotlight Strategy

9. Spotlight students who are using editing marks to edit their writing. For example, "Wow! Writers, well done! Janie is using her eyes and ears to notice and dig out errors. Spotlight on Janie!"

Share

10. Have students meet with partners to talk about how they are preparing their writing for publication.

Homework

Ask students to notice how other authors have prepared their writing for publication.

Using Editing Marks Notebook Entry

Using Editing Marks

Authors reread and ask friends to read their writing. This helps authors find errors in their writing.

Editing Mark	Meaning	Example
≡	Capitalize	david gobbled up the grapes.
/	Change to lower case	My mother hugged Me when I came Home.
⊙	Insert a period	The clouds danced in the sky ⊙
sp ◯	Check spelling	I (laffed) at the story.
∿	Transpose words or letters	How you are?
∧	Add a word or letter	Would you please pass the pizza?
∧,	Insert a comma	I have two cats, two dogs and a goldfish.
⸎	Delete	Will you call call me on the phone tonight?
¶	New paragraph	… in the tree.¶ After lunch, I spent the day…

#50917—Getting to the Core of Writing—Level 3 © Shell Education

Name: _____ Date: _____

Using Editing Marks Writing Sample

Directions: Use the editing marks from your notebook entry to improve this piece of writing.

Batter Up!

Did you know baseball considered is the national sport of the

united states? The first Baseball game was played on June 19

1846 in New jersey Although there were miny different forms of

the game, Alexander Cartwright is credited for inventing the style

of Baseball still played today In Apral of 1910, president william

howard taft began the year's Baseball season by throwing out the

first pitch of the game. That tradition has continued for more than a

century. You can take me out to the ballgame anytime. batter up!

Writing Traits Checklist

Standard
Uses strategies to edit and publish written work

Materials
- Chart paper
- Markers
- Writer's Notebooks
- *Writing Traits Checklist Notebook Entry* (page 252; writingtraitschecklist.pdf)
- Traits Team posters (pages 76, 104, 132, 178, 210, 226; ida.pdf, simon.pdf, owen.pdf, wally.pdf, valvan.pdf, callie.pdf)
- Writing samples

Mentor Texts
- *Look at My Book* by Loreen Leedy
- Other CCSS literature
- See *Mentor Text List* in Appendix C for other suggestions.

Procedures
Note: Teach this lesson over several days, so students feel comfortable using the checklist with peer/adult support and independently. You may also teach the entire lesson in one day and then revisit each trait over time. Writers need to bring their folders to the community meeting area.

Think About Writing
1. Tell students that they have made great accomplishments and have become experts in such a short amount of time. They are choosing topics and including enough information so that the quantity of writing is increasing. They have listened to responses from other writers and teachers. Now, they are going to focus on the entire Traits Team, one trait at a time.

Teach
2. Tell students, "Today I will show you how to check your writing for the traits of good writing." Explain that students will choose one piece of writing to prepare for publishing. Published writing should have all the traits. Post the Traits Team posters in a visible place.

3. Have students select a piece of writing they would like to publish.

4. Make a list of the traits of writing on a sheet of chart paper. Discuss each trait by asking the questions listed on the *Writing Traits Checklist Notebook Entry* (page 252). Provide time in between each trait for students to quickly check and adjust their writing.

Writing Traits Checklist (cont.)

Engage

5. Have students tell partners each of the traits of writing. Ask students to share with partners how they used each trait in their writing. Provide approximately three minutes for students to talk. As students talk, move around the room, listen in on conversations, make comments, and jot down ideas for sharing on sticky notes.

Apply

6. Remind students that being sure their writing includes all the writing traits will help improve their writing. Provide students with the *Writing Traits Checklist Notebook Entry* to add to their Writer's Notebook. Tell students that during writing time today they should use the checklist to check and edit a piece of writing.

Write/Conference

7. Provide time for students to write. As they write, rotate among them and take notes on their process. Note on which traits students may need additional mini-lessons.

Spotlight Strategy

8. Spotlight anyone who took responsibility for his or her writing checklist and attempted to search his or her work.

Share

9. No sharing today. This lesson is intensely focused and requires students to challenge their thinking to new heights.

Homework

Ask students to tell each writing trait to their parents and explain how each trait helps improve their writing. Have students make a list of the six writing traits.

Writing Traits Checklist Notebook Entry

Writing Traits Checklist

Authors reread their writing to make revisions and edits. This writing traits checklist can help you polish your writing.

Ideas
☐ I have a focused topic.
☐ I use supporting details.

Sentence Structure
☐ I include complete and correct sentences.
☐ I include a variety of sentence types and lengths.
☐ My sentences begin in different ways.
☐ My story sounds good when read aloud.

Organization
☐ My introduction hooks the reader.
☐ I have a sequence with a beginning, middle, and end.
☐ I include transition words to link ideas.
☐ I have a strong conclusion.

Word Choice
☐ My words paint a picture in my reader's mind.
☐ I use a variety of words.
☐ I use strong and lively verbs.

Voice
☐ My writing sounds like me.
☐ I "talk" to the reader/audience in my writing.

Conventions
☐ My capitalization is correct.
☐ I use correct grammar.
☐ My punctuation is correct.
☐ My words are spelled correctly.

#50917—Getting to the Core of Writing—Level 3 © Shell Education

Essential Materials

Create a toolkit of items you can carry around with you as you conference with students. The toolkit can be a shoebox, a plastic tote, or anything you are comfortable carrying around from student to student. Any supplies that will help make your conference run smoothly are appropriate to put in the tote. Suggested items are listed below:

- Teacher Conferring Notebook
- Mentor text used for daily writing lesson (changes regularly)
- Highlighters or highlighting tape (to draw attention to words)
- Scissors, glue, tape, or a small stapler for revision, cutting, pasting, and moving around
- Sticky notes for making suggestions
- Colored pens for editing (green, red, blue, black, orange)
  - Green—capitalization
  - Red—ending punctuation
  - Blue—spelling
  - Black—inserting
  - Orange—usage
- Rubber band for stretching sentences
- Whiteboard or magnetic board with markers for modeling
- Magnetic chips or large colored buttons
- 1 package of correction tape or correction fluid
- Assorted paper

Conferring Notebook
Getting to the Core of Writing

Mini-Lesson Log

Date	Mini-Lesson Instructional Focus

conference Log

P: Praise—What strategies did I notice the child using independently?

TP: Teaching Point—What teaching point will move this child forward in his or her development as a writer?

Name: **Date:** P: TP:	**Name:** **Date:** P: TP:	**Name:** **Date:** P: TP:	**Name:** **Date:** P: TP:
Name: **Date:** P: TP:	**Name:** **Date:** P: TP:	**Name:** **Date:** P: TP:	**Name:** **Date:** P: TP:
Name: **Date:** P: TP:	**Name:** **Date:** P: TP:	**Name:** **Date:** P: TP:	**Name:** **Date:** P: TP:

Conference Countdown

10 Conversation—The conversation should feel like a friendly chat with the student doing the most talking. Keep in mind, the person doing the most talking is doing the most learning.

9 It's about the WRITER, not the Writing—Teach the strategy that will support the writer after he or she is finished with this particular piece of writing. For example, do not just spell a word for a child, but teach him or her to segment the sounds to spell many words.

8 Focus on the Content—You are not there to simply fix up the conventions of a writing piece. When possible, have the student read the piece aloud before you even look at it and focus purely on the content. It's a challenge!

7 Observe, Praise, Guide, Connect—Establish a routine to become effective and efficient.

6 Begin with Praise!—Everyone likes a compliment. Beginning with a compliment gives students a sense of joy and pride in their work as well as recognizes developing writing skills.

5 Talk Like a Writer to a Writer—Use the language and vocabulary of a writer and respect the student's developmental level of writing.

4 Connect or not to Connect?—When conferring, only make connections to your daily mini-lesson when appropriate for the student's piece of writing.

3 Record and Reflect—Use your Conferring Notebook to monitor the progress of writing in your classroom and individual students. The information is valuable in defining your focus for writing instruction.

2 Variety—Incorporate a variety of activities that meet the multiple learning modalities of your students, like varying your conferring group sizes and using manipulatives.

1 Be There!—Your face and eyes tell it all. Let students know you truly care about the writing they are sharing with you.

Conferring Step-by-Step

The four phases of a conference structure are:

1. Observe
2. Praise
3. Guide
4. Connect

Observe—Use observation as a chance to build your background knowledge of the writer. During this element of the conference, you will determine what the writer knows and can do independently, and what the writer can do with support, called the zone of proximal development (Vygotsky 1978). Begin by asking yourself:

- What do I already know about this student's developmental level of writing and past writing from my conference notes and previous observations?

- What can I learn from the student's current writing piece and writing behaviors?

- What can I learn through questioning and listening to the writer?

When asking students about their writing work, open-ended questions provide guidance and support for students to begin reflecting on their writing. A close-ended question, such as, "Is this you in the picture?" elicits a simple one- or two-word response. An open-ended question, such as, "What can you tell me about your picture?" offers opportunities for the writer to explain and describe ideas, motives, and feelings about his or her work, ultimately gaining clarity and developing a deeper understanding of his or her writing. You might ask the writer:

- So, what are you working on in your writing today?

- What can you tell me about your important writing work?

Through your observation, you should determine a successful writing point and one teaching point that will help this child become a more independent writer. Selecting a teaching point can be daunting as we analyze a young writer's work. Teachers often ask, "How do you know what to work on when there are so many things?" The truth is there is no right answer. Here are some ideas to guide you as you select teaching points:

- Use what you know about the growth of this writer. Where is this writer developmentally?

- Consider what the student is working on at this time. What is the student's focus in his or her writing?

- Use the current writing curriculum and the Common Core State Standards.

- Use what is being taught in mini-lessons and whole-group instruction.

Where we ourselves are as writers, as well as where we are as teachers of writing, greatly affect our decisions. As you become more knowledgeable about the developmental phases of writers and the understanding of quality writing instruction, your decisions become more sophisticated. The more you confer with your writers, the more effective you become at making decisions during conferring. Most importantly, select one teaching point that will support each writer during your conference. Calkins, Hartman, and White (2003) reminds us to teach to the writer and not to the writing.

Conferring Step-by-Step (cont.)

Praise—Recognize the writer for work well done. Always begin a conference with a positive comment. This praise provides positive feedback intended to identify what the student is doing correctly and to encourage the writer to repeat that accomplishment in future writing. Isolate and identify the successful writing strategy in the student's writing piece. When praises are authentic and specific, they become a teachable moment. Below are some examples of powerful praise:

- "Something I really like that you've done is how you shared the setting with your reader. That's exactly what good writers do!"

- "I see here in your writing you chose to use color words to give your reader more details in your story. Wonderful words!"

- "Just like the authors we have been studying, you have an excellent picture that helps your reader visualize exactly what is happening in your story."

- "I am so impressed with the way you just got right to work and accomplished so much writing in such a short amount of time."

Guide—Personalize and scaffold instruction to meet the writer's needs. The instruction includes sharing the writing strategy you will teach the writer, demonstrating the strategy, and then guiding the writer through practicing the process. Teach the writer a personalized strategy based on your earlier decisions. When the decision is based on a previously taught mini-lesson, writers make additional connections and greater achievement is gained. As part of the routine of the mini-lesson, you must explicitly state what you will teach the student.

- Mentor texts and writing samples are excellent resources to weave into your conference instruction. Writers can visualize the craft you are teaching when they are exposed to concrete examples, particularly from real literature.

- Initial teaching remarks may include, "Let me show you something that good writers do…" and, "Sometimes in my writing, I try to…"

By offering support while the student practices the strategy, you increase the chances of success. Any time you engage students in the application of new strategies, you enhance the probability they will recall that strategy in future writing. Once the writer is engaged in practice, you may move on to confer with another writer. However, leave the writer with expectations until you return, such as, "When I get back, I want to see …" Upon your return, provide specific feedback relative to your expectations. For example, "Well done! Now I really have a picture in my mind of your character."

Conferring Step-by-Step *(cont.)*

Connect—Make connections between teaching and future writing. First, clearly restate what the writer learned and practiced. Then, remind and encourage the writer to use the strategy in future writing. As students become familiar with the conference structure, you may ask the student to share the new learning to get a sense of his or her understanding of your teaching. Making connections may begin as follows:

- "Remember, good writers always…"

- "Tell me what you just learned as a writer."

Writer's Workshop conferences will vary in length and type based on the time of year and the needs of your class. Conferences are most successful when routines and expectations have been established and young writers can manage their own writing time. At the beginning of the year, while establishing routines, drop-by conferences provide a quick glimpse into what each student is working on and what kind of help is needed. Once routines are established, meet with students in individual and/or small group conferences that are focused around specific needs. You may also include peer conferences, but this requires modeling, experience, and practice. For young writers, we use *Compliment and Question*. The compliment should be more than a general statement, such as, "I like your story." It should be specific to the writing, for example, "I like the way you ask a question to begin your story." A question should be something the peer would like to know more about or something that needs clarification.

The conference should be brief and reflect the child's age and development. Small group conferences may be as long as 8–10 minutes as you will be checking in with each student. Hold the conference wherever you prefer. Some teachers prefer moving desk to desk or table to table while others prefer that students join them at a small conference table or on the floor. Remember these two points:

- *Have a seat!* Wherever you decide to hold your conferences, it is important that students know you are committed to giving them your attention. By sitting down, you are sending the message that you are there with them at that moment.

- *Be prepared!* Have materials readily available to you during the conference. You may wish to compile a Conferring Toolkit of essential materials (see page 253 of Appendix A) that can be carried with you or placed in your conference area.

Continuing to provide meaningful and relevant conferences requires some form of keeping notes during your writing conferences. A simple, but thorough conference summary can identify areas of writing deficiencies and strengths as you plan future mini-lessons, select students for small group conferences, and report student progress to parents. To support you as you make conferring a priority in Writer's Workshop, pages for the *Conferring Notebook* are included on pages 254–257.

Benchmark Assessment Overview

Administering a Benchmark (page 255) is a guide to assist you as you begin giving benchmarks. It is important that the prompt is uniform across classrooms when measuring growth at a school level. Third grade benchmark prompts should be simple and attainable, for example:

- Have you ever met someone famous? Think about what might happen if you ran into a famous person you admire. Create a real or imaginary situation and write a story to tell about your experience.

- Which of the four seasons is your favorite? Tell about a perfect day in your favorite season. In your opinion, what makes it perfect?

- Have you ever thought of building and designing your own home? Explain how you might plan it on the inside, outside and why it would be special to you.

The Writing Rubric (pages 263–264; writingrubric.pdf) is a tool to analyze student writing skills.

The Writing Report (page 265; writingreport.pdf) serves as a summative report of a student's writing benchmarks. The completed form along with the beginning-, middle-, and end-of-year benchmarks are placed in the student's record folder at the end of the year.

The Grouping Mat (page 266, groupingmat.pdf) is an at-a-glance chart showing which students in your classroom have attained particular benchmarks. Simply circle the current benchmark period, and complete the chart by recording your students' names in the boxes. Your goal is to see the students' names progressively move upward on the rubric report.

The core of writing instruction is the desire to support young writers as they explore, discover, and learn the writing process. It also involves determining what knowledge and skills young writers have developed over a period of time. Assessment is a continuous process and, when used properly, benefits teachers as well as students.

Administering a Benchmark

Writing Benchmarks are usually administered at the beginning, middle, and end of the school year to measure improvements and determine the writer's strengths and deficits in writing development. To get started, follow these guidelines:

- Administer the Writing Benchmark Prompt in small groups. This allows the teacher to observe and take anecdotal notes of individual student behaviors.

- It is important not to practice the prompt prior to the writing benchmark session.

- Do not provide teacher support. Your goal is to determine what students are able to do independently. If a student demonstrates frustration, he or she may just draw a picture, but you may wish to redirect the student to the prompt. Compliment the drawing and invite the student to write something about the drawing as best he or she can.

- Allow students to use classroom displays such as word walls. Note words copied from the word wall.

- Distribute paper to each student. Use paper familiar to the students. Students should write their name and the date on the back so that it is not seen prior to scoring the writing. This will help you to stay objective as you grade the writing piece .

- Supply pencils and crayons when necessary.

- Explain to your class that this process will show how much they have grown as writers and that a prompt will be given at the beginning, middle, and end of the year.

- Read the prompt to your students. Paraphrase the prompt when necessary to clarify understanding. You may wish to display the prompt on chart paper or on a whiteboard.

- Have each student read you his or her story upon completion. Keep a record of what each student wrote in your own writing so that you will be able to identify the words that he or she used. If some words are unreadable due to invented spelling, write them down at the bottom of the writing piece or on a sticky note.

Third Grade Writing Rubric

		Ideas	Sentence Fluency	Organization	Word Choice
3	**Advanced**	• Maintains main idea; narrowed and focused topic • Supports main idea with descriptive details, anecdotes, and examples	• Writes sentences that are smooth with effective flow and rhythm • Includes a variety of sentence lengths: simple, compound, complex • Includes variety of sentence types: declarative, interrogative, exclamatory, imperative • Includes varied sentence beginnings	• Writes in a logical and purposeful sequence • Includes an inviting introduction • Uses transition words to connect ideas • Includes a conclusion that satisfies the reader • Includes paragraph breaks that are purposefully organized	• Uses descriptive, colorful language to evoke strong visual images, including figurative language • Includes vocabulary that is varied yet purposeful to topic and audience
2	**Proficient**	• Expresses main idea; fairly broad topic • Uses some descriptive details and examples	• Writes sentences that are mostly smooth • Includes some sentence variety in length and type • Includes some variation in sentence beginnings	• Shows some evidence of logical sequence • Shows some evidence of an introduction • Uses some transition words • Includes a conclusion • Shows some evidence of paragraph breaks	• Makes some attempts at descriptive language • Uses some variation in vocabulary; mostly common words and phrases
1	**Basic**	• Attempts to present main idea; unclear topic • Develops few, if any, details; somewhat random	• Writes sentences that are difficult to follow or read aloud • Includes choppy, basic, simple sentences, sentence fragments, and/or run-on sentences • Lacks variety in sentence type • Repeats sentence beginnings	• Lacks evidence of logical sequence; random string of thoughts • Lacks inviting beginning • Lacks use of transition words to connect ideas • Lacks satisfying conclusion • Shows little evidence of paragraph breaks	• Lacks descriptive language • Uses limited vocabulary; monotonous and repetitious
0	**Below Basic**	Student attempts to write, but result is off-topic, illegible, insufficient, or otherwise fails to meet criteria for a score of 1			

Third Grade Writing Rubric (cont.)

		Voice	Conventions
3	Advanced	• Shows originality, excitement, and commitment to topic • Speaks to and connects with audience and purpose; engages reader	• Little, if any, need for editing • Capitalization is correct, errors may be minor • Consistently correct usage of grammar • Effective and correct use of punctuation • Few errors in spelling
2	Proficient	• Shows some originality, excitement, and commitment to topic • Writes with some sense of the audience	• Some need for editing • Capitalization may be inconsistent • Correct grammar usage is fairly consistent • Inconsistent use of punctuation • Most common words spelled correctly
1	Basic	• Shows little of writer's personality or commitment to topic • Reads rather dull and mechanical; connecting to no particular audience	• Extensive editing necessary • Capitalization appears random; sparse • Grammar and usage interfere with readability • Little use of correct punctuation • Frequent spelling errors
0	Below Basic	Student attempts to write, but result is off-topic, illegible, insufficient, or otherwise fails to meet criteria for a score of 1	

Third Grade Writing Report

Student Writing: _____ **Teacher:** _____ **Year:** _____

Beginning of the Year Writing Benchmark 1 Date:				Total	Summary
Ideas	Sentence Fluency	Organization	Word Choice		Advanced: 15–18
3 2 1 0	3 2 1 0	3 2 1 0	3 2 1 0		Proficient: 11–14
Voice		Conventions			Basic: 6–10
3 2 1 0		3 2 1 0			Below Basic: 0–5

Notes: _____

_____

Middle of the Year Writing Benchmark 2 Date:				Total	Summary
Ideas	Sentence Fluency	Organization	Word Choice		Advanced: 15–18
3 2 1 0	3 2 1 0	3 2 1 0	3 2 1 0		Proficient: 11–14
Voice		Conventions			Basic: 6–10
3 2 1 0		3 2 1 0			Below Basic: 0–5

Notes: _____

_____

End of the Year Writing Benchmark 3 Date:				Total	Summary
Ideas	Sentence Fluency	Organization	Word Choice		Advanced: 15–18
3 2 1 0	3 2 1 0	3 2 1 0	3 2 1 0		Proficient: 11–14
Voice		Conventions			Basic: 6–10
3 2 1 0		3 2 1 0			Below Basic: 0–5

Notes: _____

_____

Third Grade Writing Grouping Mat

	Ideas	Sentence Fluency	Organization	Word Choice	Voice	Conventions
3 Advanced						
2 Proficient						
1 Basic						
0 Below Basic						

Benchmark Writing Samples

Beginning of the Year

Prompt: Have you ever met someone famous? Think about what might happen if you ran into a famous person you admire. Create a real or imaginary situation and write a story to tell about your experience.

Last summer, I was sitting in my bed looking at my football cards and I heard someone pull in the driveway. Then someone punched a gigantic hole in the wall and it was Brian Urlacher! "Hey!" he said "Hello?" I said. Then about 2 seconds later I realized it was really Brian Urlacher! "You're Brian Urlacher," I said.

Then, Brian asked if I would go to the stadeim with him. "Yes!" I said. So we went to the stadium. "We are playing the Lions," Brian said. "But its in the middle of summer it's not football season!" I replied. Then they had a game instead. After that, me and Brian went to the sidelines. Suddenly a KFC man came and we ordered lunch. I ordered 5 wings, 2 legs, mashed potatoes, and green beans. Brian ordered the same thing. Before I knew it, the game was over.

After that, me and Brian went back to my house and played. First, we played Madden NFL 07 and Call of Duty: World at War on my Playstation. Then we had a paintball fight with M-16 paintball guns and multi color paintballs and we had a team battle in the woods. After that, we watched T.V. and we watched Pawn Stars and Deadliest Warrior. Finally, we watched movies wich were Windtalkers and Forest Gump.

Last, we had a backyard football game with the Bears against the Packers. In the first few minutes both teams had lots of peanatys. Most was facemasks and offsides. The Packers had lots of tough people like Clay Mathews. Finally, the game was over it was 56–55 and the Bears won.

In conclusion an orange and blue Ford Rapter pulled up in the driveway and a guy came out and it was Deven Hester! After that I shook both their hands and they went back to Chicago.

Benchmark Writing Samples (cont.)

Beginning of the Year (cont.)

Beginning of the Year Benchmark 1 Date:				Total	Summary
Ideas	Sentence Fluency	Organization	Word Choice	10 Basic	Advanced: 15–18
3 ②　1　0	3 ②　1　0	3 ②　1　0	3　2 ①　0		Proficient: 11–14
Voice		Conventions			Basic: 6–10
3　2 ①　0		3 ②　1　0			Below Basic: 0–5

Notes:

- Uses some descriptive details and examples (Ideas)
- Includes some sentence variety in length and type (Sentence Fluency)
- Includes some variation in sentence beginnings (Sentence Fluency)
- Shows some evidence of logical sequence (Organization)
- Shows some evidence of an introduction (Organization)
- Includes a conclusion (Organization)
- Lacks descriptive language (Word Choice)
- Uses limited vocabulary (Word Choice)
- Shows little or writer's personality or commitment to topic (Voice)
- Some need for editing (Conventions)
- Most common words spelled correctly (Conventions)

Benchmark Writing Samples (cont.)

Middle of the Year

Prompt: Which of the four seasons is your favorite? Tell about a perfect day in your favorite season. In your opinion, what makes it perfect?

Have you ever had a perfect summer day? Well I have. My perfect day was at a soccer field day in Hillsboro. As I arrived at the field, I saw a younger age group playing. Then it was our team's turn to play. The ref blew his whistle, which signaled me to kick.

People were sitting in fold up chairs. There were tons of people. We played with a flouresent green ball in the daytime and a glow in the dark ball at night. Tony and I were the team captains, and our jerseys were red and black with spider web desighns on them. Dave's jersy, our referee, was yellow with skinny, black lines on them. The other teams arrived. My opponents were Marlinton, White Sulphur, and Frankford, the team who outscored us. The goals were neon yellow, but they didn't glow in the dark. My dad, which is my team's coach, was wearing his Coach Bruce shirt. There were lots of people walking and walking there dogs on the blacktop. Before the second half, the younger age group was playing.

A ref's whistle made a very high pitch noise. When I looked over at the other team, I heard somebody crying because he got knocked over. That sound was really disturbing! Do you think he will go to the hospital? I doubt he will. He got back up and the game continued. Then my team started. I heard a noise that went THUMP when I kicked the ball. There were lots of bystanders cheering and yelling hoot like noises. My coach was yelling directions on what to do. Tony passed the ball to me and I scored. The ball made a weird noise then it hit the net. The other team got the ball and nearly scored, but it hit the crossbar and went PING! I got switched to defender and heard lots of thundering cars that were annoying. The ball came to me and I kicked it, but it hit somebody's fingers and went CRACK!

If you were at this game, the aroma of power ade left open and really stinky feet would probably make you sick. Moms were spraying sunscreen. Our ref's jersey was clean. People's moms were using there perfoom that was strong and it was sweet and flowery. Saundra had just mowed the grass, and it was really refreshing. At the end of the game, Faith, our goalie, took off her goalie gloves witch were very sweaty.

In my opinion, my perfect summer day is a soccer field day. The best thing was surely the flouresent green ball. The loudest thing was Dave's whistle, witch was realy high pitch. The freshly cut grass was an important part of my day. These details I listed were what made my perfect summer day the best in the world.

Benchmark Writing Samples (cont.)

Middle of the Year (cont.)

Middle of the Year Benchmark 2 Date:				Total	Summary
Ideas	Sentence Fluency	Organization	Word Choice		Advanced: 15–18
③ 2 1 0	③ 2 1 0	3 ② 1 0	③ 2 1 0	17 Advanced	Proficient: 11–14
Voice		Conventions			Basic: 6–10
③ 2 1 0		③ 2 1 0			Below Basic: 0–5

Notes:

- Supports main idea with descriptive details, anecdotes, and examples (Ideas)
- Writes sentences that are smooth with effective flow and rhythm (Sentence Fluency)
- Includes a variety of sentence lengths and structures: simple, compound, and complex (Sentence Fluency)
- Shows some evidence of logical sequences (Organization)
- Shows some evidence of an introduction (Organization)
- Includes a conclusion (Organization)
- Uses descriptive, colorful language to evoke strong visual images; includes figurative language (Word Choice)
- Includes vocabulary that is varied yet purposeful to topic and audience (Word Choice)
- Shows originality, excitement, and commitment to topic (Voice)
- Speaks to and connects with audience; engages reader (Voice)
- Little, if any, need for editing (Conventions)
- Effective and correct use of punctuation (Conventions)

Benchmark Writing Samples (cont.)

End of the Year

Prompt: Have you ever thought of building and designing your own home? Explain how you might plan it on the inside, outside, and why it would be special to you.

To plan and design my house I need a arcatect. My dream house would be the coolest place to hang out with my friends in my girl cave. The girl cave is a place where my friends and I can have sleepovers, watch movies, and have pillow fights. My house will be the coolest place on the block. I will have a jell-o castle that I can jump up and down on. When I get off, it makes my stomach feel all squishy. I'll be telling you more about the outside and inside of my dream house throught out the story, if that's okay with you. What do you want your dream house to be like?

First of all, I will have all kinds of things like sports cars, so I need a guraj. A chocolate hottub will be on my pateo. My fish pond will be right next to my gigantic swimming pool. I just love going outside, and eating and picking apples off the apple trees in my yard. I will plant a strawberry patch to make a scholputure out of the yummy strawberries. Outside, I made my own wishing faintain except it is made out of chocolate, and you can still wish in the chocolate wishing well. There's this awesome maze outside that you go through and at the end there's a barn. Right next to the barn is a butterfly garden, the most relaxing place to be. You can watch the butterflies go past as you read a book because as I said, "It is the most relaxing place to be."

In the inside of my house, my spa room was built so when I get stressed out I can just walk in and they start my message and just relax. My dancing room is called my disko room. The house is made out of glass so that I can see introoders. The biggest room in the house is the living room. My shark tank covers one side of the wall in the living room. I also have 5 bedrooms, and 4 bathrooms that are moolte colored.

Next, my huge grand tour! I have a secret candy shop that kids can come over, and get all kinds of candy. I have a gigantic kitchen for making cakes. I even have a privet chief that cooks everything that I want to eat. Then I have this awesome room where famous people can come and have dances and listen to the music.

As I have shown, my house was planned and designed complete. I had all the things that I wanted to have. My chocolate hottub, sports cars, my peace sign bedroom, and all of the rest. My disko room to party in, and my acquarium! My concert room, the coolest of everything! I love having my own dream house. You can come anytime day or night. Now my house is complete.

Benchmark Writing Samples (cont.)

End of the Year (cont.)

End of the Year Benchmark 3 Date:				Total	Summary
Ideas	Sentence Fluency	Organization	Word Choice	17 Advanced	Advanced: 15–18 Proficient: 11–14 Basic: 6–10 Below Basic: 0–5
③ 2 1 0	③ 2 1 0	③ 2 1 0	③ 2 1 0		
Voice		Conventions			
③ 2 1 0		3 ② 1 0			

Notes:

- Supports main idea with descriptive details, anecdotes, and examples (Ideas)
- Writes sentences that are smooth with effective flow and rhythm (Sentence Fluency)
- Includes a variety of sentence lengths and structures: simple, compound, and complex (Sentence Fluency)
- Includes a variety of sentence types: declarative, interrogative, exclamatory, and imperative (Sentence Fluency)
- Includes varied sentence beginnings (Sentence Fluency)
- Writes in a logical and purposeful sequence (Organization)
- Uses transition words to connect ideas (Organization)
- Uses descriptive, colorful language to evoke strong visual images (Word Choice)
- Includes vocabulary that is varied yet purposeful to topic and audience (Word Choice)
- Shows originality, excitement, and commitment to topic (Voice)
- Speaks to and connects with audience; engages reader (Voice)
- Some need for editing (Conventions)
- Correct grammar usage fairly consistent (Conventions)

Mentor Text List

Managing Writer's Workshop

DiSalvo, DyAnne. 2008. *The Sloppy Copy Slipup*. New York: Holiday House.

Fletcher, Ralph. 1996. *A Writer's Notebook: Unlocking the Writer Within You*. New York: HarperCollins.

———. 2005. *Marshfield Dreams: When I Was A Kid*. New York: Henry Holt and Company.

Leedy, Loreen. 2005. *Look at My Book: How Kids Can Write & Illustrate Terrific Books*. New York: Holiday House.

Lionni, Leo. 1973. *Swimmy*. New York: Dragonfly Books.

McGovern, Ann. 1992. *Too Much Noise*. Boston: Sandpiper.

Moss, Marissa. 2006. *Amelia's Notebook*. New York: Simon & Schuster.

Schotter, Roni. 1999. *Nothing Ever Happens on 90th Street*. New York: Scholastic.

Ideas

Allen, Susan. 2006. *Read Anything Good Lately?* Minneapolis, MN: Millbrook Press.

———. 2010. *Written Anything Good Lately?* Minneapolis, MN: Millbrook Press.

Baylor, Byrd. 1985. *Everybody Needs a Rock*. New York: Aladdin.

———. 1998. *The Table Where Rich People Sit*. New York: Aladdin.

Brinckloe, Julie. 1986. *Fireflies*. New York: Aladdin.

Brown, Margaret W. 1990. *The Important Book*. New York: HarperCollins.

Bunting, Eve. 1992. *The Wall*. Boston: Sandpiper.

———. 2000. *The Memory String*. New York: Clarion Books.

Crews, Donald. 1996. *Shortcut*. New York: Greenwillow Books.

Cronin, Doreen. 2003. *Diary of a Worm*. New York: HarperCollins.

Denenberg, Dennis. 2005. *50 American Heroes Every Kid Should Meet*. Minneapolis, MN: Millbrook Press.

DiCamillo, Kate. 2009. *The Miraculous Journey of Edward Tulane*. Somerville, MA: Candlewick.

Ewald, Wendy. 2002. *The Best Part of Me*. New York: Little, Brown Books for Young Readers.

Fletcher, Ralph. 1996. *A Writer's Notebook: Unlocking the Writer Within You*. New York: HarperCollins.

Horowitz, Ruth. 2004. *Crab Moon*. Somerville, MA: Candlewick.

Humphrey, Sandra M. 2005. *Dare to Dream! 25 Extraordinary Lives*. Amherst, NY: Prometheus Books.

Johnson, Angela. 1995. *Shoes Like Miss Alice's*. New York: Scholastic.

Kalman, Bobbie. 1997. *How a Plant Grows*. New York: Crabtree Publishing Company.

Kellogg, Steven. 1992. *Johnny Appleseed*. New York: HarperCollins, 1988.Kellogg, Steven. *Pecos Bill*. New York: HarperCollins.

Mentor Text List (cont.)

Ideas (cont.)

MacLachlan, Patricia. 1994. *All the Places to Love*. New York: HarperCollins.

———. 1998. *What You Know First*. New York: HarperCollins.

Munsch, Robert. 1995. *Love You Forever*. Ontario: Firefly Books Ltd.

Polacco, Patricia. 1998. *Chicken Sunday*. New York: Puffin.

———. 1999. *My Ol' Man*. New York: Puffin.

———. 2001. *Thank You, Mr. Falker*. New York: Philomel Books.

Rosenthal, Amy K. 2006. *One of Those Days*. New York: Putnam Juvenile.

Rylant, Cynthia. 2000. *The Old Woman Who Named Things*. Boston: Sandpiper.

———. 2004. *The Relatives Came*. Pine Plains, NY: Live Oaks Media.

Schaefer, Carole. 1999. *The Squiggle*. New York: Dragonfly Books.

Schotter, Roni. 1999. *Nothing Ever Happens on 90th Street*. New York: Scholastic.

Simon, Seymour. 1992. *Our Solar System*. New York: William Morrow and Company.

———. 2001. *Tornadoes*. New York: HarperCollins.

Spinelli, Eileen. 2008. *The Best Story*. New York: Dial.

Stevens, Janet. 1999. *From Pictures to Words: A Book about Making a Book*. New York: Holiday House.

Viorst, Judith. 2009. *Alexander and the Terrible, Horrible, No Good, Very Bad Day*. New York: Atheneum Books for Young Readers.

William, Vera B. 1984. *A Chair for My Mother*. New York: Greenwillow Books.

Wong, Janet S. 2002. *You Have to Write*. New York: New York: Margaret K. McElderry Books.

Sentence Fluency

Allen, Debbie. 2003. *Dancing in the Wings*. New York: Puffin.

Bunting, Eve. 2004. *Whales Passing*. New York: Scholastic Inc.

Clearly, Brian P. 2001. *To Root, to Toot, to Parachute: What Is a Verb?* Minneapolis, MN: Carolrhoda Books.

Dahl, Roald. 2007. *The Twits*. New York: Puffin.

Fletcher, Ralph. 1997. *Twilight Comes Twice*. New York: Clarion Books.

MacLachlan, Patricia. 1994. *All the Places to Love*. New York: HarperCollins.

Palatini, Margie. 2003. *Bedhead*. New York: Simon & Schuster Books for Young Readers.

Polacco, Patricia. 2001. *Thank You, Mr. Falker*. New York: Philomel Books.

Rylant, Cynthia. 1993. *When I Was Young in the Mountains*. New York: Puffin.

Mentor Text List (cont.)

Sentence Fluency (cont.)

Rylant, Cynthia. 2004. *The Relatives Came*. Pine Plains, NY: Live Oaks Media.

Smucker, Anna. 1994. *No Star Nights*. New York: Dragonfly Books.

Steig, William. 2009. *Amos & Boris*. New York: Square Fish.

Walton, Rick. 2011. *Just Me and 6,000 Rats: A Tale of Conjunctions*. Layton, UT: Gibbs Smith.

William, Vera B. 1984. *A Chair for My Mother*. New York: Greenwillow Books.

Yolen, Jane. 1987. *Owl Moon*. New York: Philomel.

Organization

Ada, Alma Flor. 1997. *Dear Peter Rabbit*. New York: Aladdin.

———. 2001. *Yours Truly, Goldilocks*. New York: Atheneum Books for Young Readers.

Arnosky, Jim. 2009. *Slither and Crawl: Eye to Eye with Reptiles*. New York: Sterling Publishing Company.

———. 2011. *Thunder Birds: Nature's Flying Predators*. New York: Sterling Publishing Company.

Aylesworth, Jim. 1998. *The Gingerbread Man*. New York: Scholastic Press.

Bolin, Frances S. 2008. *Poetry for Young People: Emily Dickinson*. New York: Sterling Publishing Company.

Brett, Jan. 1996. *Goldilocks and the Three Bears*. New York: Puffin.

Brinckloe, Julie. 1986. *Fireflies*. New York: Aladdin.

Buehner, Caralyn. 2004. *Snowmen at Night*. New York: Scholastic.

Cherry, Lynne. 1990. *The Great Kapok Tree*: A Tale of the Amazon Rain Forest. Boston: Harcourt Children's Books.

Cobb, Vicki. 2003. *I Face the Wind*. New York: HarperCollins.

Creech, Sharon. 2003. *Love That Dog*. New York: HarperCollins.

———. 2008. *Hate That Cat*: A Novel. New York: HarperCollins.

Crews, Donald. 1996. *Shortcut*. New York: Greenwillow Books.

Frazee, Marla. 2003. *Roller Coaster*. Boston: Harcourt Children's Books.

Harley, Avis. 2012. *African Acrostics: A Word in Edgeways*. Somerville, MA: Candlewick.

Henson, Heather. 2008. *That Book Woman*. New York: Simon & Schuster.

James, Simon. 1997. *Dear Mr. Blueberry*. New York: Aladdin.

Jane, Pamela W., Sylvia Lollis, and Joyce Hogan. 2003. *Should We Have Pets?: A Persuasive Text*. New York: Mondo Publishing.

Janeczko, Paul. 2009. *A Kick in the Head: An Everyday Guide to Poetic Forms*. Somerville, MA: Candlewick.

Mentor Text List (cont.)

Organization (cont.)

Jenkins, Steven. 2003. *What Do You Do With a Tail Like This?* Boston: Houghton Mifflin Books for Children.

Keats, Ezra Jack. 2005. *Whistle for Willie*. Pine Plains, NY: Live Oak Media.

Laminack, Lester. 1998. *The Sunsets of Miss Olivia Wiggins*. Atlanta, GA: Peachtree Publishers.

———. 2007. *Snow Day!* Atlanta, GA: Peachtree Publishers.

Lollis, Sylvia. 2002. *Should We Have Pets? A Persuasive Text*. New York: Mondo Publishing.

Marshall, James. 1993. *Red Riding Hood*. New York: Picture Puffins.

Moss, Marissa. 2006. *Amelia's Notebook*. New York: Simon & Schuster.

Nelson, Julie. 2007. *Families Change: A Book for Children Experiencing Termination of Parental Rights*. Minneapolis, MN: Free Spirit Publishing.

Orloff, Karen Kaufman. 2010. *I Wanna New Room*. New York: Putnam Juvenile.

Palatini, Margie. 2003. *Bedhead*. New York: Simon & Schuster Books for Young Readers.

Pallotta, Jerry. 1990. *The Ocean Alphabet Book*. Watertown, MAL Charlesbridge Publishing.

———. 1993. *The Extinct Alphabet Book*. Watertown, MA: Charlesbridge Publishing.

Pilkey, Dav. 1999. *The Paperboy*. New York: Scholastic.

Polacco, Patricia. 2001. *Thank You, Mr. Falker*. New York: Philomel Books.

Prelutsky, Jack. 2008. *Pizza, Pigs, and Poetry: How to Write a Poem*. New York: Greenwillow Books.

Routman, Regie. 1999. *Conversations: Strategies for Teaching, Learning and Evaluating*. Portmouth, NH: Heinemann.

———. *Kid's Poems: Teaching Third & Fourth Graders to Love Writing Poetry*. New York: Scholastic Teaching Resources.

Rylant, Cynthia. 2004. *The Relatives Came*. Pine Plains, NY: Live Oaks Media.

Schmidt, Gary D. 2008. *Poetry for Young People: Robert Frost*. New York: Sterling Publishing Company.

Schnur, Steven. 1997. *Autumn: An Alphabet Acrostic*. New York: Clarion Books.

———. 1997. *Spring: An Alphabet Acrostic*. New York: Clarion Books.

———. 1997. *Summer: An Alphabet Acrostic*. New York: Clarion Books.

———. 1997. *Winter: An Alphabet Acrostic*. New York: Clarion Books.

Silverstein, Shel. 2004. *Where the Sidewalk Ends*. New York: HarperCollins.

Stevens, Janet. 1989. *The Princess and the Pea*. New York: Holiday House.

Stewart, Sarah. 2007. *The Gardner*. New York: Square Fish.

Teague, Mark. 2002. *Dear Mrs. LaRue: Letters from Obedience School*. New York: Scholastic.

Yolen, Jane. 1987. *Owl Moon*. New York: Philomel.

Mentor Text List *(cont.)*

Word Choice

Arnold, Tedd. 2003. *More Parts*. New York: Puffin

———. 2007. *Even More Parts*. New York: Puffin.

Bauer, Marion D. 1996. *When I Go Camping with Grandma*. New York: Troll Communications.

Brennan-Nelson, Denise. 2011. *My Teacher Likes to Say*. Chelsea, MI: Sleeping Bear Press.

Cherry, Lynne. 2003. *How Groundhog's Garden Grew*. New York: Blue Sky Press.

Cleary, Brian. 2001. *Hairy, Scary, Ordinary: What Is an Adjective?* Minneapolis, MN: Carolrhoda Books.

Cook, Julia. 2008. *It's Hard to be a Verb!* Chattanooga, TN: National Center for Youth Issues.

Dahl, Michael. 2007. *If You Were a Synonym*. Mankato, MN: Picture Window Books.

Dahl, Roald. 2007. *The Twits*. New York: Puffin.

———. 2011. *James and the Giant Peach*. New York: Puffin.

DiCamillo, Katie. 2003. *The Tale of Desperaux*. Somerville, MA: Candlewick.

Fox, Mem. 1994. *Tough Boris*. Boston: Harcourt Children's Books.

Haseley, Dennis. 2002. *A Story for Bear*. Boston: Harcourt Children's Books.

Heller Ruth. 1998. *Kites Sail High*. New York: Puffin.

———. 1998. *Many Luscious Lollipops*. New York: Puffin.

———. 1998. *Merry-Go-Round*. New York: Puffin.

———. 1998. *Up, Up and Away: A Book About Adverbs*. New York: Puffin.

Leedy, Loreen. 2003. *There's a Frog in my Throat! 400 Animal Sayings a Little Bird Told Me*. New York: Holiday House.

———. 2009. *Crazy Like a Fox: A Simile Story*. New York: Holiday House.

MacLachlan, Patricia. 1994. *All the Places to Love*. New York: HarperCollins.

———. 1998. *What You Know First*. New York: HarperCollins.

———. 2004. *Sarah, Plain and Tall*. New York: HarperCollins.

Palatini, Margie. 2000. *Zoom Broom*. New York: Hyperion Paperbacks for Children.

———. 2003. *Bedhead*. New York: Simon & Schuster Books for Young Readers.

Parish, Peggy. 2003. *Amelia Bedelia*. New York: Greenwillow Books.

Pulver, Robin. 2007. *Nouns and Verbs Have a Field Day*. New York: Holiday House.

Raschka, Christopher. 1997. *Charlie Parker Played Be Bop*. New York: Scholastic.

Rylant, Cynthia. 2004. *The Relatives Came*. Pine Plains, NY: Live Oaks Media.

Schotter, Roni. 1999. *Nothing Ever Happens on 90th Street*. New York: Scholastic.

Steig, William. 2010. *Shrek!* New York: Farrar, Straus and Giroux.

Mentor Text List (cont.)

Word Choice (cont.)

Terban, Marvin. 2007. *In a Pickle and Other Funny Idioms*. Boston: Sandpiper.

Terban, Marvin. 1993. *It Figures! Fun Figures of Speech*. Boston: Sandpiper.

Walton, Rick. 2011. *Suddenly Alligator: Adventures in Adverbs*. Layton, UT: Gibbs Smith.

———. 2011. *Why the Banana Split*. Layton, UT: Gibbs Smith.

Wood, Audrey. 1996. *Quick as a Cricket*. Swindon, London: Child's Play International.

Yashima, Taro. 1987. *Umbrella*. Pine Plains, NY: Live Oak Media.

Yolen, Jane. 1987. *Owl Moon*. New York: Philomel.

Voice

Bridges, Ruby. 1999. *Through My Eyes: Ruby Bridges*. New York: Scholastic.

Browne, Anthony. 2001. *Voices in the Park*. New York: DK Publishing.

Bunting, Eve. 1992. *The Wall*. Boston: Sandpiper.

———. 1993. *Fly Away Home*. Boston: Sandpiper.

———. 2000. *The Memory String*. New York: Clarion Books.

———. 2000. *Train to Somewhere*. Boston: Sandpiper.

Cain, Janan. 2000. *The Way I Feel*. Seattle, WA: Parenting Press.

Cronin, Doreen. 2003. *Diary of a Worm*. New York: HarperCollins.

Forward, Toby. 2005. *Wolf's Story-What Really Happened to Little Red Riding Hood*. Somerville, MA: Candlewick.

Freymann, Saxton. 2004. *How Are You Peeling! Foods with Moods*. New York: Scholastic.

Gantos, Jack. 2011. *Joey Pigza Swallowed the Key*. New York: Square Fish.

Hall, Donald. 1994. *I Am the Dog I Am the Cat*. New York: Dial.

Heller, Ruth. 2000. *Fantastic! Wow! and Unreal! A Book About Interjections and Conjunctions*. New York: Puffin.

Kirk, Daniel. 2003. *Dogs Rule!* New York: Hyperion.

Loewen, Nancy. 2007. *If You Were An Interjection*. Mankato, MN: Picture Window Books.

Moss, Marissa. 2006. *Amelia's Notebook*. New York: Simon & Schuster.

Nicklin, Flip. 2010. *Face to Face with Whales*. Washington, DC: National Geographic Children's Books.

O'Malley, Kevin. 2006. *Straight to the Pole*. New York: Walker Children's.

O'Neill, Alexis. 2002. *The Recess Queen*. New York: Scholastic.

Palatini, Margie. 2003. *Bedhead*. New York: Simon & Schuster Books for Young Readers.

Mentor Text List (cont.)

Voice (cont.)

Polacco, Patricia. 1994. *Pink and Say*. New York: Philomel.

———. 1998. *My Rotten Redheaded Older Brother*. New York: Aladdin.

———. 2001. *Thank You, Mr. Falker*. New York: Philomel Books.

Polacco, Patricia. 2012. *The Art of Miss Chew*. New York: Putnam Juvenile.

Ryder, Joanne. 1999. *Earthdance*. New York: Henry Holt and Company.

Rylant, Cynthia. 2004. *The Relatives Came*. Pine Plains, NY: Live Oaks Media.

Scieszka, Jon. 1996. *The True Story of The Three Little Pigs!* New York: Puffin.

Seidensticker, Josh. 2008. *Predators*. New York: Simon and Schuster Books for Young Readers.

Shannon, David. 1998. *No, David!* New York: Blue Sky Press.

———. 2006. *Good Boy, Fergus!* New York: Blue Sky Press.

Viorst, Judith. 2009. *Alexander and the Terrible, Horrible, No Good, Very Bad Day*. New York: Atheneum Books for Young Readers.

Ware, Cheryl. 1999. *Flea Circus Summer*. New York: Scholastic.

Conventions

Buzzeo, Toni. 2006. *Our Librarian Won't Tell Us Anything!* Madison, WI: Upstart Books.

Clement, Rod. 1999. *Grandpa's Teeth*. New York: HarperCollins, 1999.

Crews, Donald. 1996. *Shortcut*. New York: Greenwillow Books.

Hall, Pamela. 2009. *Punk-tuation Celebration*. Minneapolis, MN: Magic Wagon.

Leedy, Loreen. 2005. *Look at My Book: How Kids Can Write & Illustrate Terrific Books*. New York: Holiday House.

Moss, Marissa. 2006. *Amelia's Notebook*. New York: Simon & Schuster.

Palatini, Margie. 2003. *Bedhead*. New York: Simon & Schuster Books for Young Readers.

Polacco, Patricia. 2001. *Thank You, Mr. Falker*. New York: Philomel Books.

Pulver, Robin. 2008. *Punctuation Takes a Vacation*. Pine Plains, NY: Live Oak Media.

Raschka, Chris. 2007. *Yo! Yes?* New York: Scholastic.

Shulevitz, Uri. 2003. *One Monday Morning*. New York: Farrar, Straus and Giroux.

Truss, Lynne. 2006. *Eats, Shoots & Leaves: Why, Commas Really Do Make a Difference!* New York: Putnam Juvenile.

———. 2007. *The Girl's Like Spaghetti: Why, You Can't Manage without Apostrophes!* New York: Putnam Juvenile.

———. 2008. *Twenty-Odd Ducks: Why, every punctuation mark counts!* New York: Putnam Juvenile.

Sample Home Connections Letter

Dear Parents,

One of our first writing projects is to decorate our Writer's Notebook. The notebook is a very important part of our writing time together. In the notebook, students will practice the many skills learned during Writer's Workshop. The notebook serves as an ongoing resource as your child becomes a writer.

Over the weekend, students are asked to decorate the cover of their Writer's Notebook in the form of a collage, and return them to school on Monday. The notebook decorations should reflect your child's interests. Here is a list of possible items you might include on the notebook:

- photographs
- magazine clippings
- stickers
- scrapbooking items

- shapes and letters
- printed clipart
- construction paper
- illustrations and drawings

Attached is a copy of the cover of the notebook that I made last year. Some of the items that I have on it are pictures of my close family members and my pet, music notes, a picture of an mp3 player (because I love music), a picture of a book by my favorite author, roses (because that is my middle name), airplanes and sandals (because I like to travel), and credit cards (because I love to shop). I also used some various scrapbooking items to decorate.

Remember these ideas should reflect your child's interests, hobbies, family, favorites, etc. Take the next step! Share stories and memories and record a list of writing ideas to give your child a jump start.

Please contact me if you have any questions or concerns about the notebook project.

Thank you in advance for your support!

Sincerely,

Ms. Olivito

Supporting with Technology

Whether communicating via cell phones, texts, blogs, tweets, Facebook, email or gathering information via Internet, Google, and eBooks, today's students will live in a world increasingly shaped by technology. For this reason, Common Core State Standards highlight the effective use of technology-integrated instruction across the curriculum. Incorporating technology into instruction increases opportunities for students to be active learners, rather than passive receivers of information, and offers new ways of learning and sharing information.

The challenge for most teachers is how to seamlessly integrate technology use so that it does not take time away from writing instruction but enhances that instruction and increases students' interest and involvement. While uses of technology are seemingly limitless and constantly being updated, here are seven important ways teachers are successfully integrating technology into Writer's Workshop:

1. Digital and flip cameras can add excitement to any writing project. Student projects that capture pictures of the life cycle of a chick or a class field trip instantly invite students into a writing project. Digital photos can be used to generate a photo album of writing ideas, organize storyboards, promote language and vocabulary, illustrate student writing, and even be included in slide show presentations.

2. Document cameras are easily integrated in writing lessons and activities by both teachers and students. The benefits of using mentor texts for modeling are sometimes lost on students who may not be close enough to see the specific texts. Whether presenting photographs to gather writing ideas, sharing multiple beginnings from mentor texts, or displaying leaves and fossils to model descriptive language, the document camera offers a myriad of opportunities for modeling writing instruction for all students to see. Using the document camera allows you to zoom in on specific text features and details in illustrations. Students frequently volunteer to display their writing with the document camera and gather feedback from classmates on revising and editing. Teachers and students also enjoy presenting examples of good writing work and highlighting quality features in writing using the document camera.

3. Interactive whiteboards can serve a number of purposes for writing instruction. They provide the opportunity for student engagement and involvement of almost any materials or activity that can be viewed on a computer screen. Consider using the interactive whiteboard to teach whole group keyboarding skills, revising word choice by highlighting verbs or adjectives, using editing marks, building story webs, or reinforcing skills by accessing interactive websites. Of course, whiteboards are an excellent source to demonstrate and model lessons, present presentations and create class books and word banks.

Supporting with Technology *(cont.)*

4. Publishing tools abound in the technology realm. Students may be involved in illustrating their writing with Microsoft® Paint or a software program like KidPix®. Through word processing, students can create letters, essays, brochures, and even class newsletters. Many teachers use Microsoft® PowerPoint for publishing individual, team, or class writing projects, which can easily be printed and bound into classroom books or saved as eBooks. Podcasts are used to record students as they read their writing. This can support the revising and editing process as they listen carefully to their writing and add a special touch to a final published project. Technology enhances the writer's options for publishing their work. For example, parents and students enjoy viewing and listening to final projects on the school website.

5. Research has never been easier. Though writing teachers must be cognizant of Internet safety, misuse, plagiarism, and follow district policies, they know technology allows for new and purposeful ways to gather and synthesize research. Writing teachers demonstrate technology-driven research procedures and help students locate and bookmark trusted websites. Collaborating with colleagues about their student research websites can make research easy and accessible.

6. URLs (Uniform Resource Locator) are great to include in your classroom newsletter. Offer links for students to practice skills, view presentations, or learn about future topics like Arbor Day. And don't forget the authors! With activities like Ralph Fletcher's

Tips for Young Writers, Patricia Pollacco's *Who Am I*, or *Poetry Writing with Jack Prelutsky*, author websites are filled with an assortment of information and activities to engage and motivate student writing. Visit author sites while teaching students how to create their own Author's Page. The possibilities are limitless.

7. Collaborative writing projects like ePals and virtual field trips open classroom boundaries to endless learning opportunities. EPals is a modern pen pal project in which students can collaborate on academic and cultural projects as well as establish everlasting friendships in other districts, states, or countries. Virtual field trips (VFT) offer learning opportunities that might otherwise be limited by distance and funding. Writing projects may be further enhanced by a virtual visit to the San Diego Zoo to learn about animal characteristics and habitats or to the National Aeronautics and Space Administration (NASA) to interview an astronaut.

Terminology Used

In order to adequately implement the lessons included in *Getting to the Core of Writing*, it is necessary to understand the terminology used throughout the resources.

Analytics—In order to be consistent with National Assessment of Educational Progress (NAEP) standards, the following analytics are used when describing writing proficiency:

- **Below Basic/Score 0**—Writing demonstrates an attempt to write, but the result is illegible, insufficient, or otherwise fails to meet the criteria for a score of 1.

- **Basic/Score 1**—Writing demonstrates little or marginal skill in responding to the writing benchmark tasks. Few traits of quality writing are present.

- **Proficient/Score 2**—Writing demonstrates developing skills in responding to the writing benchmark tasks. Most traits of quality writing are evident.

- **Advanced/Score 3**—Writing demonstrates effective skills in responding to the writing benchmark tasks. All traits of quality writing are obvious.

Anchor Charts—Anchor charts are used to track student thinking. In this resource, anchor charts are created cooperatively by the teacher and students. The charts are used to scaffold learning and chart key concepts of writing such as ideas for writing, vocabulary words, and examples of sentence structure. Anchor charts are displayed throughout the room to support a print-rich environment that promotes literacy acquisition.

Anecdotal Observations—Throughout Writer's Workshop, teachers practice the art of becoming astute observers of student writing behaviors. The teacher's Conferring Notebook is an excellent resource to store observations for the entire year of instruction (See Appendix A). As you observe, remember to present a statement of praise and develop a teaching point as this will guide future instructional decisions.

Author's Chair—Students are selected to share their writing with classmates. Usually students sit in a designated chair/stool. Classmates provide feedback to authors in the form of a question or a compliment.

Author's Tea/Author's Luncheon—An author's tea can be held anytime to support student writing efforts. Students invite parents and special loved ones to join them, sometimes with refreshments, to celebrate accomplishments in writing. Each student writes, illustrates, publishes, and presents a favorite piece of writing from the past year. It is important that every student has someone to listen to his or her especially planned presentation. You might invite the principal, cafeteria cook, librarian, or teacher specialists as part of the celebration.

Benchmark Assessments—The beginning-of-the-year benchmark serves as baseline information about a student's writing. Middle-of-the-year and end-of-the-year benchmarks represent a student's progress toward state, district, and/or school benchmark goals.

Terminology Used *(cont.)*

Heads-up, Stand-up, Partner-up—This is an activity in which the teacher gains students' attention, they stand up and quickly move to find partners, and they begin a discussion of focused writing talk. Partners can be assigned based upon the needs of the class or they can be chosen spontaneously. However, it is crucial that students move quickly and in an orderly fashion without any wasted time.

Mentor Texts—A mentor text is a book that offers multiple learning opportunities as both teacher and student develop writing skills. Mentor texts contain explicit and strong examples of the author's craft and are visited repeatedly to explore the traits of quality writing. Your favorite books to share often make the best mentor texts. You may wish to use the recommended mentor text as a read-aloud during your reading block with spirited discussions or quickly review it during Writer's Workshop. During writing block, focus on small samples of text that match the mini-lesson skill. A recommended list of mentor texts is provided as part of each lesson and additional titles are provided in Appendix C.

Notebook Entry—Notebook entries are pages that students will cut out and glue into their Writer's Notebook. They reinforce the lesson with the key points for students to remember. At the bottom of most notebook entries is a *Your Turn* section where students can practice the skill taught in the lesson.

Turn and Talk—*Turn and Talk* is a management tool for giving opportunities to students to have partner conversations. This procedure may take place at the meeting area or at desks. Students make eye contact, lean toward their partner, talk quietly, or listen attentively.

Triads and Quads—These are terms used to quickly divide the class into groups of three or four.

References

Anderson, Carl. 2000. *How's It Going? A Practical Guide to Conferring with Student Writers.* Portsmouth, NH: Heinemann.

Bjorklund, David F. 1999. *Children's Thinking: Developmental Function and Individual Differences.* New York: Brooks/Cole Publishing Company.

Buckner, Aimee. 2005. *Notebook Know How: Strategies for the Writer's Notebook.* Portland, ME: Stenhouse Publishers.

Calkins, Lucy M. 1994. *The Art of Teaching Writing* (New ed.). Portsmouth, NH: Heinemann.

Calkins, Lucy, Amanda Hartman, and Zoe White. 2003. *The Conferring Handbook.* Portmouth, NH: Heinemann.

———. 2005. *One to One: The Art of Conferring with Young Writers.* Portsmouth, NH: Heinemann.

Culham, Ruth. 2003. *6 + 1 Traits of Writing: The Complete Guide (Grades 3 and Up).* New York: Scholastic.

———. 2005. *One to One: The Art of Conferring with Young Writers.* Portsmouth, NH: Heinemann.

———. 2008. *6 + 1 Traits of Writing: The Complete Guide for the Primary Grades.* New York: Scholastic.

———. 2008. *Using Picture Books to Teach Writing With the Traits K–2.* New York: Scholastic.

Cunningham, Patricia M. and James W. Cunningham. 2009. *What Really Matters in Writing: Research-Based Practices Across the Curriculum.* Boston, MA: Allyn & Bacon/Pearson.

Davis, Judy, and Sharon Hill. 2003. *The No-Nonsense Guide to Teaching Writing: Strategies, Structures, Solutions.* Portsmouth, NH: Heinemann.

Dolch, Edward W. 1941. *Teaching Primary Reading.* Champaign: The Garrard Press.

Dorn, Linda J., and Carla Soffos. 2001. *Scaffolding Young Writers: A Writers' Workshop Approach.* Portland, ME: Stenhouse Publishers.

Ehri, Linnea C. 1997. "Learning to Read and Write Are One and the Same, Almost." in *Learning to Spell: Research, Theory, and Practice Across Languages.* Edited by Charles A. Perfetti, Laurence Rieben, and Michael F. Maywah. London: Lawrence Erlbaum Associates.

Erlauer, Laura. 2003. *The Brain-Compatible Classroom: Using What We Know About Learning to Improve Teaching.* Alexandria, VA: Association for Supervison and Curriculum Development.

Fletcher, Ralph. 1996. *A Writer's Notebook: Unlocking the Writer Within You.* New York: HarperCollins.

———. 1999. *Live Writing: Breathing Life Into Your Words.* New York: HarperCollins.

———. 2000. "Craft Lessons to Improve the Quality of Student Writing." Presentation at the 28th Annual Conference of The Maryland International Reading Association. Baltimore, MD.

———. 2002. *Poetry Matters: Writing a Poem From the Inside Out.* New York: HarperCollins.

Fletcher, Ralph, and JoAnn Portalupi. 1998. *Craft Lessons: Teaching Writing K–8.* Portland, ME: Stenhouse Publishers.

Fletcher, Ralph, and JoAnn Portalupi. 2001. *Writing Workshop: The Essential Guide.* Portsmouth, NH: Heinemann.

References (cont.)

Frayer, Dorothy, Wayne Frederick, and Herbert Klausmeier. 1969. *A Schema for Testing the Level of Cognitive Mastery.* Madison, WI: Wisconsin Center for Education Research.

Freeman, Marcia. 1998. *Teaching the Youngest Writers: A Practical Guide.* Gainesville, FL: Maupin House Publishing, Inc.

———. 2001. *Non-Fiction Writing Strategies: Using Science Big Books as Models.* Gainesville, FL: Maupin House Publishing, Inc.

Gentry, J. Richard. 2000. *The Literacy Map: Guiding Children to Where They Need to Be (K–3).* New York: Mondo Publishing.

———. 2002. *The Literacy Map: Guiding Children to Where They Need to Be (4–6).* New York: Mondo Publishing.

———. 2004. *The Science of Spelling: The Explicit Specifics That Make Greater Readers and Writers (and Spellers!).* Portsmouth, NH: Heinemann.

———. 2006. *Breaking the Code: New Science of Beginning Reading and Writing.* Portsmouth, NH: Heinemann.

———. 2007. *Breakthrough in Beginning Reading and Writing.* New York: Scholastic, Inc.

———. 2008. *Step-by-Step: Assessment Guide to Code Breaking.* New York: Scholastic, Inc.

———. 2010. *Raising Confident Readers: How to Teach Your Child to Read and Write—from Baby to Age 7.* Cambridge, MA: Da Capo Lifelong Books.

Gentry, J. Richard, and Jean Gillet. 1993. *Teaching Kids to Spell.* Portsmouth, NH: Heinemann.

Ginott, Hiam G. 1972. *Teacher & Child: A Book for Parents and Teachers.* New York: Macmillan Publishing Company.

Gould, Judith. 1999. *Four Square Writing Method: A Unique Approach to Teach Basic Writing Skills for Grades 1–3.* Carthage, IL: Teaching and Learning Company.

Graham, Steve, and Michael Hebert. 2010. *Writing to Read: Evidence for How Writing Can Improve Reading. A Carnegie Corporation Time to Act Report.* Washington, DC: Alliance for Excellent Education.

Graham, Steve, Virginia Berninger, and Robert Abbott. 2012. "Are Attitudes Toward Writing and Reading Separable Constructs? A Study with Primary Grade Children." *Reading & Writing Quarterly, 28* (1), 51-69.

Graves, Donald H. 1994. *A Fresh Look at Writing.* Portsmouth, NH: Heinemann.

———. 2003. *Writing: Teachers and Children at Work 20th Anniversary Edition.* Portsmouth, NH: Heinemann.

Jensen, Eric. 2009. *Different Brains, Different Learners: How to Reach the Hard to Reach* (Second ed.). Thousand Oaks, CA: Corwin Press.

Mann, Jean. 2002. "Writing in Grades Four, Five, and Six." In *The Literacy Map: Guiding Children to Where They Need to Be (4–6).* New York: Mondo Publishing.

References (cont.)

McKenna, Michael C., and Dennis J. Kear. 1990. "Measuring attitude toward Reading: A new tool for teachers." *The Reading Teacher, 43* (9), 626–639.

McMahon, Carolyn, and Peggy Warrick. 2005. *Wee Can Write: Using 6 + 1 Trait Writing Strategies with Renowned Children's Literature.* Portland, OR: Northwest Regional Educational Laboratory.

Murray, Donald. 2004. *Write to Learn.* Independence, KY: Cengage Learning.

National Governors Association Center for Best Practices and Council of Chief State School Officers. 2011. *Common Core State Standards Initiative: The Standards.* Retrieved June 2011, from Common Core State Standards Initiative: http://www.corestandards.org

Pearson, P. David, and Margaret C. Gallagher. 1983. "The instruction of reading comprehension." *Contemporary Educational Psychology*, 8, 317-344

Ray, Katie W. 2001. *The Writing Workshop: Working Through the Hard Parts (And They're All Hard Parts).* Urbana, IL: National Council Of Teachers of English.

Ray, Katie W., and Lisa Cleaveland. 2004. *About the Authors: Writing Workshop with Our Youngest Writers.* Portsmouth, NH: Heinemann.

Rog, Lori Jamison, and Paul Kropp. 2004. *The Write Genre: Classroom Activities and Mini-Lessons That Promote Writing with Clarity, Style, and Flashes of Brilliance.* Ontario, Canada: Pembroke Publishers.

Routman, Regie. 1999. *Conversations: Strategies for Teaching, Learning and Evaluating.* Portsmouth, NH: Heinemann.

———. 2000. *Kids' poems: Teaching Third & Fourth Graders to Love Writing Poetry.* New York: Scholastic.

———. 2005. *Writing Essentials: Raising Expectations and Results While Simplifying Teaching.* Portsmouth, NH: Heinemann.

Shanahan, T. (In Press). *College and Career Readiness Standards for Reading, Writing, and Speaking and Listening-Draft for Review and Comment.*

Spandel, Vicki. 2001. *Books, Lessons, Ideas for Teaching the Six Traits: Writing in the Elementary and Middle Grades.* Wilmington, MA: Great Source Education Group.

———. 2005. *Seeing with New Eyes: A Guidebook on Teaching and Assessing Beginning Writers Using the Six-Trait Writing Model* (6th Edition.) Portland, OR: Northwest Regional Educational Laboratory.

———. 2008. *Creating Young Writers: Using the Six Traits to Enrich Writing Process in Primary Classrooms* (2nd Edition.). New York: Allyn & Bacon.

Sprenger, Marilee B. 2007. *Becoming a "Wiz" at Brain-Based Teaching: How to Make Every Year Your Best Year.* Thousand Oaks, CA: Corwin Press.

Vygotsky, Lev. 1978. *Mind in Society: The Development of Higher Psychological Processes.* Edited by Michael Cole, Vera John-Steiner, Sylvia Scribner, and Ellen Souberman. Cambridge, MA: Harvard University Press.

Yates, Elizabeth. 1995. *Someday You'll Write.* Greensville, SC: Bob Jones University Press.

Contents of the Teacher Resource CD

Teacher Resources

Page Number	Title	Filename
N/A	The Traits Team	traitsteam.pdf
N/A	Year-at-a-Glance	yearataglance.pdf
12–13	Suggested Pacing Guide	pacingguide.pdf
24–30	Correlation to Standards	standards.pdf
254	Conferring Notebook Cover	cover.pdf
255	Mini-Lesson Log	minilessonlog1.pdf
256	Conference Log	conferencelog.pdf
257	Conference Countdown	conferencecountdown.pdf
263–264	Third Grade Writing Rubric	writingrubric.pdf
265	Third Grade Writing Report	writingreport.pdf
266	Third Grade Writing Grouping Mat	groupingmat.pdf
273–279	Mentor Text List	mentortextlist.pdf
280	Sample Home Connection Letter	samplehomeletter.pdf

Managing Writer's Workshop

Page Number	Title	Filename
37	Components of Writer's Workshop Anchor Chart	writersworkshop.pdf
40	Sample Looks Like, Sounds Like, Feels Like Anchor Chart	lookssoundsfeelschart.pdf
43	Student Mini-Lesson Log	minilessonlog2.pdf
44	Dolch Sight Word List	dolchwordlist.pdf
45	Fry Sight Word List	frywordlist.pdf
46–47	Short and Long Vowel Charts	shortlongvowelcharts.pdf
48–49	Vowel Teams Chart	vowelteamschart.pdf
54	Traits of Writing Notebook Entry	traitswriting.pdf
55–57	Traits Team Mini Posters	traitsteamposters.pdf
60	Sharing Notebook Entry	sharing.pdf
61	Compliment and Comment Cards	complicommentcards.pdf
64	Turn and Talk Notebook Entry	turntalk.pdf
67	Guidelines for Writer's Workshop Notebook Entry	guidelineswritersws.pdf
70	Peer Conference Notebook Entry	peerconference.pdf
73	The Five-Step Writing Process Notebook Entry	fivestepprocess.pdf

Contents of the Teacher Resource CD *(cont.)*

Ideas

Page Number	Title	Filename
76	Ida, Idea Creator	ida.pdf
79	My Expert List Notebook Entry	myexpertlist.pdf
82	I Can Write Like That! Notebook Entry	canwritelikethat.pdf
85	Collection Pocket Label Template	collectionpocket.pdf
88	People I Love Notebook Entry	peopleilove.pdf
91	Fabulous Faunae Notebook Entry	fabulousfaunae.pdf
94	Story Seeds Notebook Entry	storyseeds.pdf
95	Story Seeds Model Chart	storyseedschart.pdf
98	Famous People I Admire Notebook Entry	famouspeopleadmire.pdf
101	What Should I Write? Notebook Entry	whatshouldwrite.pdf

Sentence Fluency

Page Number	Title	Filename
104	Simon, Sentence Builder	simon.pdf
107	Popcorn Sentences Notebook Entry	popcornsentences.pdf
110	A Simple Sentence Notebook Entry	simplesentence.pdf
113	The Compound Subject Notebook Entry	compoundsubject.pdf
116	Types of Sentences Notebook Entry	typessentences.pdf
119	The Compound Verb Notebook Entry	compoundverb.pdf
122	The Compound Sentence Notebook Entry	compoundsentence.pdf
125	Rubber Band Sentences Notebook Entry	rubbandsentences.pdf
126	Question Word Cards	questionwordcards.pdf
129	A Complex Sentence Notebook Entry	complexsentence.pdf

Organization

Page Number	Title	Filename
132	Owen, Organization Conductor	owen.pdf
135	Name Poetry Notebook Entry	namepoetry.pdf
138	123 Paragraphs: Opinion Notebook Entry	123opinion.pdf
141	123 Paragraphs: Story Notebook Entry	123story.pdf
144	123 Paragraphs: Informing Notebook Entry	123informing.pdf
147	Building a Story Mountain Notebook Entry	buildingstory.pdf
148	The Princess and the Pea Story Cards	princesspeacards.pdf

Contents of the Teacher Resource CD

Organization *(cont.)*

Page Number	Title	Filename
149	Little Red Riding Hood Story Cards	redridinghoodcards.pdf
150–151	Suggested Story Mountain Texts	mountaintexts.pdf
154	Telling a Story Notebook Entry	tellingstory.pdf
157	The Gingerbread Man Hook Cards	gingerbreadmancards.pdf
158	More Than "Once Upon a Time" Notebook Entry	moreonceuponatime.pdf
161	Circular Endings Notebook Entry	circularendings.pdf
164	Writing a Friendly Letter Notebook Entry	writingfriendlyletter.pdf
165	Writing a Business Letter Notebook Entry	writingbusinessletter.pdf
168	It's My Opinion! Notebook Entry	itsmyopinion.pdf
169	It's My Opinion! Organizer	itsmyopinionorganizer.pdf
172	Just Stating the Facts Notebook Entry	juststatingfacts.pdf
173	Just Stating the Facts Organizer	statingfactsorganizer.pdf
176	Poetry Fun Notebook Entry	poetryfun.pdf

Word Choice

Page Number	Title	Filename
178	Wally, Word Choice Detective	wally.pdf
181	Be Specific! Notebook Entry	bespecific.pdf
184	Vivid Verbs Notebook Entry	vividverbs.pdf
187	Amazing Adjectives Notebook Entry	amazingadjectives.pdf
190	Banished, Boring Words Notebook Entry	banishedboringwords.pdf
191–192	Banished Word Cards	banishedwordcards.pdf
195	Transition Words Notebook Entry	transitionwords.pdf
196–197	Transition Word Cards	transitionwordcards.pdf
200	Super Similes Notebook Entry	supersimiles.pdf
203	Awesome Adverbs Notebook Entry	awesomeadverbs.pdf
204	Adverb Picture Cards	adverbpicturecards.pdf
205	Adverb Word Cards	adverbwordcards.pdf
208	Interesting Idioms Notebook Entry	interestingidioms.pdf

Contents of the Teacher Resource CD (cont.)

Voice

Page Number	Title	Filename
210	Val and Van, Voice	valvan.pdf
213	How Do You Feel? Notebook Entry	howfeel.pdf
214–215	Voice Cards	voicecards.pdf
218	Looking and Listening for Voice Notebook Entry	lookinglisteningvoice.pdf
221	Informing Interjections Notebook Entry	informinginterjections.pdf
224	Know Your Audience Notebook Entry	knowaudience.pdf

Conventions

Page Number	Title	Filename
226	Callie, Super Conventions Checker	callie.pdf
229	The Capital Rap Notebook Entry	capitalrap.pdf
232	Punctuation Takes a Holiday Notebook Entry	punctuationholiday.pdf
235	See It! Spell It! Write It! Check It! Notebook Entry	seespellwritecheckit.pdf
238	Editing with CUPS Notebook Entry	editingcups.pdf
239	CUPS Writing Sample	cupswritingsample.pdf
242	Quotation Marks: "Who Said That?" Notebook Entry	quotationmarks.pdf
245	Caution Comma Chant Notebook Entry	cautioncommachant.pdf
248	Using Editing Marks Notebook Entry	editingmarks.pdf
249	Using Editing Marks Writing Sample	editingmarkssample.pdf
252	Writing Traits Checklist Notebook Entry	writingtraitschecklist.pdf

Notes

Notes

#50917—Getting to the Core of Writing—Level 3 © Shell Education